DIRECTING FOR ANIMATION

DIRECTING FOR ANIMATION

EVERYTHING YOU DIDN'T LEARN IN ART SCHOOL

TONY BANCROFT

Routledge
Taylor & Francis Group

LONDON AND NEW YORK

First published 2014
by Focal Press

Published 2019 by Routledge
2 Park Square, Milton Park, Abingdon, Oxon OX14 4RN
52 Vanderbilt Avenue, New York, NY 10017

Routledge is an imprint of the Taylor & Francis Group, an informa business

Library of Congress Cataloging in Publication Data
    Directing for animation : everything you didn't learn in art school /
    Tony Bancroft. — 1 [edition].
        pages cm.
    ISBN 978-0-240-81802-3 (pbk.)
    1. Animated films. 2. Motion pictures--Production and direction. I. Title.
    NC1765.B35 2013
    791.43'34—dc23   2012044472

ISBN 13: 978-0-240-81802-3 (pbk)

Typeset in Utopia

By Keystroke, Station Road, Codsall, Wolverhampton

To my loving and supportive wife René – Thanks for supporting me through the missed vacations, late nights and worked weekends in this life of animation. You signed up for this journey not knowing that you would often be an "animation widow" and yet have given me the gift of a wonderful life.

To my beautiful girls – You have been the animated characters that have inspired the animated characters enjoyed all over the world. I love you my princesses.

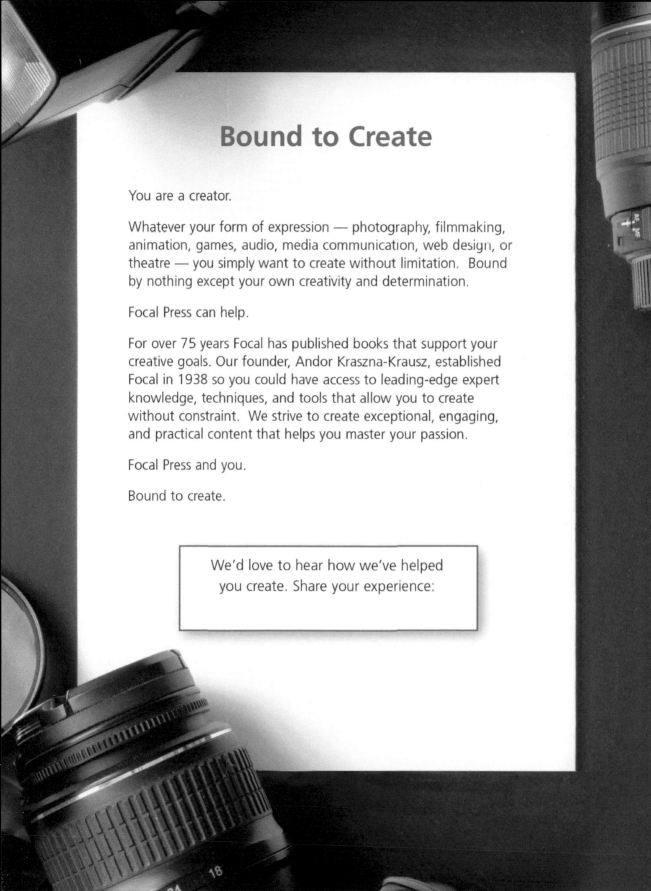

Bound to Create

You are a creator.

Whatever your form of expression — photography, filmmaking, animation, games, audio, media communication, web design, or theatre — you simply want to create without limitation. Bound by nothing except your own creativity and determination.

Focal Press can help.

For over 75 years Focal has published books that support your creative goals. Our founder, Andor Kraszna-Krausz, established Focal in 1938 so you could have access to leading-edge expert knowledge, techniques, and tools that allow you to create without constraint. We strive to create exceptional, engaging, and practical content that helps you master your passion.

Focal Press and you.

Bound to create.

We'd love to hear how we've helped you create. Share your experience:

CONTENTS

ACKNOWLEDGMENTS

I would like to acknowledge the support of all my friends and family, without whom this book would not exist:

To my brother **Tom Bancroft**, who threw down the gauntlet when he produced two books before me! Thanks for your encouragement and inspiration. To my mother and father **Cori and Jim Crismon** for their unconditional love and support. My sister, **Cami Avery**, my buddy **Ben Chambers** and **Tracey Miller-Zarneke** who helped with editing suggestions and writing help. My friend **Eric Stirpe** who came in at the eleventh hour to help edit down some massive interview text for me. For the beautiful work by the guys at **Creature Box** who did the final layout of the cover for this tome. I did not want to produce a book of just my opinions on directing in the world of animation and so called upon a special group of friends and talent. A very special thank you to all of the directors I interviewed for this book, **Dean DeBlois, Pete Docter, Eric Goldberg, Tim Miller, John Musker, Jennifer Yuh Nelson, Nick Park and Chris Wedge**. Last but not least, the folks at **Focal Press** who went on this journey with me, believing that I would:

1. Get the talent I promised to contribute interviews and 2. Actually finish the book. I finally did and they supported me the whole way. Thank you to my two editors; **Anais Wheeler** who started this journey with me and the guy who made it real, **David Bevans**.

FOREWORD BY ROB MINKOFF

"But what I really want to do is direct." A phrase you're likely to hear in any Starbucks or Coffee Bean & Tea Leaf within the greater Los Angeles area.

And why not? Directing movies is a pretty good gig.

Alfred Hitchcock, Billy Wilder and Steven Spielberg, to name a few, have had their illustrious careers analyzed and profiled in dozens of books, but the directors of animated features and their craft have escaped the spotlight, until now.

Sure, you've heard of Walt Disney, and maybe even Chuck Jones or John Lassetter, but the vast majorities of animation directors work in the shadows and are relatively unknown to the general public. But that is all beginning to change.

Over the last several decades, animated films have risen in popularity and importance in the motion picture industry. On any given Monday, you're likely to see an animated feature has climbed to the top of the box office charts winning their opening weekend. And with that popular acceptance, so has the public's interest grown in how these films are made.

But directing for animation is often misunderstood. Not only by the fans who wait eagerly for each new release, but the very men and women who work within the industry. In a live action film we're used to seeing the director shouting, "Action!" and "Cut!" But how do animation directors ply their trade?

It's safe to say that all filmmakers start from the same place, with an ambition to tell a story. But it's the combined efforts of legions of artists that form the bulwark of any filmed entertainment. And this is nowhere truer than in animated films. Hundreds of creative individuals work tirelessly to create each new animated entertainment. But how do all these diverse artists join together to bring a unified vision to the screen?

Enter the Director

It's his/her job to lead an army of artists to create a film one frame at a time. Every speck of dust every beam of light is created for the screen. There are no happy accidents. But that's what makes the job so challenging and rewarding. And there is nothing quite as satisfying as seeing your dreams become reality on the big screen.

So whether you're a student wondering how to make the transition to gainful employment, an animator or story artist already at work in the animation industry, or a fan who loves sitting in the dark with a tub of popcorn hoping to get a glimpse behind the scenes to see the wizards at work, this book is for you.

And if you have a story to tell and a yearning to see it realized in animation, then keep dreaming and perhaps one day your dream will become the next great animated motion picture.

Rob Minkoff
Director – *The Lion King, Stuart Little,*
and *Mr. Peabody and Sherman*

Introduction

Why this Book?

My head hurts sometimes. It hurts because, in my career, I have hit it against the proverbial wall so many times. Having worked in the animation industry for over 22 years, my head has found many walls to hit. There is just so much to know and communicate, both to your fellow artists and to your audience. As a young animation student, I read all of the animation books hoping to develop my artistic talents but nothing prepared me for directing an entire crew on an animated film. My hope is that this book enlightens the reader so that he or she may recognize the walls in his career and maybe . . . just maybe, hit his head against a few less.

> "Once you have heard a strange audience burst into laughter at a film you directed, you realize what the word joy is all about."
>
> Chuck Jones

My Journey to the Big Chair

Like many young animation enthusiasts, I grew accustomed to the skepticism of friends and family when I expressed my interest in cartoons. To make things worse, there were two of us. My identical twin brother, Tom, and I would spend hours in our room drawing while other kids were outside playing sports. To us *football* was for nerds! That's how out of touch we were. Tom and I loved to create our own characters and spent hours copying our favorite newspaper comic strips such as *Peanuts*, *Calvin and Hobbes* and *B.C.* I naively assumed that a person had to be some sort of math genius to

The author in his youth pursuing his dream. Nerd alert: notice the *Star Wars* bedspread and curtains in the background.

pursue a career in animation. There was just something about creating a performance from a series of drawings that had no movement by themselves that stumped me. So, I was content to think of myself as a future comic strip artist who would develop the next *Peanuts*. It wasn't until Tom and I were in college that we met a guy who was animating inventive little films and music videos out of clay. That's when I initially discovered the potential of animation as a pursuit in my life. My brother and I joined our new friend in producing a short film that summer. The thrilling experience of seeing our little, clay characters come to life on Super 8mm film got me hooked! I thought if I could make characters come to life in clay, then surely I could do the same with my beloved still drawings. In spite of the fact that so many before me had already broken this "new ground," from that day forward a 2D animator was born! By the end of that summer, my brother and I decided to pursue animation as a career and went about figuring out how to do it.

We both loved Disney animated films, so naturally (and naively) we thought that's where we belonged. We read Frank and Ollie's *The Illusion of Life* and Preston Blair's *Animation* and felt like we were ready to earn our "ears" by joining Disney Studios on their next animated feature. First, we required a far greater education than simply digesting a couple of books on animation. We discovered that, at the time, Disney hired primarily from the talented pool of students who emerged from California Institute of the Arts (CalArts) located in the hills just northeast of Los Angeles. It didn't hurt that CalArts was founded by Walt Disney himself and the instructors in the Character Animation department were all past and present employees of Disney Animation – the icons of our industry. During this time, in the early 1990's, Disney and Don Bluth were the only two studios in town that were

Me at my first desk as a freshman at CalArts. Inspiration was all around.

The late Joe Ranft, my beloved story teacher.

The energetic Chris Buck who taught me animation fundamentals.

Design teacher and program head, Bob Winquist trying to bring order to my freshman class at CalArts. That is my brother Tom in the foreground and Pixar director Pete Docter waving in the background.

doing traditional feature animation. Computer animation was nothing more than an experimental hobby reserved for flying logos and motion graphics, so 2D animation was king! Tom and I thrived at CalArts having the benefit of such a rich, creative learning environment that boasted the likes of the late Joe Ranft, Dan Hansen, Michael Giamo, Chris Buck and our wonderful design teacher and head of the department, Bob Winquist – animation legends all. Those were fun times, but also intense learning that often felt like drinking water from a fire hose! It was there that I first experienced the thrill of making a film from start to finish. Each student had to complete a short film on their own each year of the four-year program. You were the writer, storyboard artist, character designer, layout artist, camera operator and editor. At the end of the year, all of the student films were screened in the school's theatre to the applause of friends, family, and our instructors. What a great way to learn a snapshot of the entire animation

Tom and I at CalArts. Tom holds up his pan background from his freshman film while I celebrate with a snack.

My graduation photo from my nine-week Disney internship. We got a diploma and everything! From left to right: Paul Curasi, Marty Korth, Matt O'Callaghan, Peter Schneider, me, Bill Dennis, Bill Matthews and Max Howard.

process! Forget still comic strips. Forget illustration. People were laughing at a character that I had brought to life! It was all about animation from then on – I was a film maker!

Like a major league baseball team scouting talent from the minor leagues, we heard that Disney Studios was heading to CalArts to review artists' portfolios. They were staffing for a special internship that would employ and train young animators for the opening of a brand new animation studio. Fortunately, Tom and I were two of four students brought on board by Disney that day and we felt like astronauts being shot into space! My brother and I had finally earned our "ears" and officially began our professional careers as assistant animators at the new animation studio at Disney/MGM Studios Theme Park in Orlando, Florida. My brother and I immediately relocated to Florida upon Disney's promise that the team would be working on a series of original *Roger Rabbit* shorts. However, the best-laid plans had to change

The opening day photo for the Disney Florida Animation studio. Tom and I are in the middle with glasses.

after the Florida studio produced only three shorts. Our very young, still wet-behind-the-ears crew (about 75 percent were fresh out of school) quickly proved ourselves worthy enough to assist as a secondary animation unit to the California feature crew. The main Burbank crew was behind schedule and their films needed to get done. It was like playing backup support to the star players, but we didn't care. We were working on animated *features* . . . and not just any features. We all had a creative hand in animating Disney classics!

After about a year and a half on the Florida team, I was halfway through my first feature, *Rescuers Down Under*. I decided to apply for and secured a beginning animator position back at Disney's main studio in Burbank. Upon returning to California, I was placed with a supremely talented and generous animator named Will Finn who taught me many of the basics of working with dialogue and comedic timing.

I went on to work in Finn's animation unit on such characters as Frank the Frilled-Neck Lizard in *Rescuers Down Under*, Cogsworth the Clock in *Beauty and the Beast* and Iago the Parrot in *Aladdin*. Then came *The Lion King* or, as I like to call it, the "game changer." Upon completing animation on Iago, I was hoping to get the opportunity to supervise *The Lion King's* Zazu. It seemed, to me, to be the most obvious transition – from bird to bird. Things were not quite so easy, because all of us junior animators were asked to submit a video of our best animated scenes for consideration for a character lead. When I got a call from the directors I was surprised to

My fine animation mentor and supervisor Will Finn.

learn that they not only wanted me to take the lead on a character, but were putting the now-famous warthog in my hands. Being cast to supervise on Pumbaa was one of the happiest days of my life – a dream come true! To add to the good news, my best friend and office mate, Mike

Mike Surrey and I clowning around on *The Lion King*. Just a normal day in the office for us.

An animation drawing of mine of Pumbaa.

Surrey, was cast to supervise on Timon. Like us, Pumbaa and Timon were the purveyors of comic hi-jinks.

Contrary to its unbelievable success, *The Lion King* was originally thought by the studio to be the lesser "B" project to *Pocahontas*. Disney executives were sure that *Pocahontas* was a "homerun" and that *The Lion King* was a "ground ball single" at best. In addition, then studio head, Jeffery Katzenberg, had a new mandate for the animation department to produce one animated feature per year; an aggressive schedule that had not been achieved by any studio at that time. So, one half of the animation crew would go onto *Pocahontas* – while the other half stayed on *The Lion King*. The most experienced animators, heads of departments and directors were assigned to the "A" project – *Pocahontas*, while *The Lion King* was assigned to the studios' fresh-faced, up-and-comers like me, with limited experience. The film was challenging work with many surprises, but the greatest of which was the opening weekend box office numbers that cemented *The Lion King* as the biggest smash hit of all time for an animated feature. More satisfying was the fact that it was produced by first time directors, department heads, and the "greenest" crew of animators in the history of Disney Feature Animation.

It was a short seven months later that opportunity knocked again. I was supervising the three characters of the Gargoyles for Disney's *Hunchback of Notre Dame* when I got a phone call. I was asked up to the Vice-President (V.P.) of Development's office for a Friday meeting. Being that Fridays were notorious layoff days and that I had never, ever met with that executive before, my mind raced with thoughts of receiving my pink slip that day. Boy, was I wrong. The executive asked me if I would join the team of a movie in early development that needed a second

Me at my desk on *The Lion King.*

Barry Cook and I directing on Disney's *Mulan.*

director. A director with character animation experience to contrast the first director that had mostly a special effects background. That movie turned out to be Disney's *Mulan*. Upon accepting the position of co-director with Barry Cook at the age of 27, I had become the youngest director at the time in Disney's long history. Here I was in just my fifth year at Disney and I was living out my dream! However, I must admit that there was much fear and trembling over the thought of heading a crew with far more experience than I had at that point. After all, I was directing some of the same artists who had previously been my bosses and mentors only a few short years before.

My initial preconceptions about directing an animated feature at a major studio were shattered within my first month on the job. I learned a very important lesson on my introductory meeting with the crew of the film. It's a simple one that has stayed with me all of these years. "Respect does not come by title but by actions." I may have been given the authority over this amazingly creative crew at Disney's Florida Animation Studio but that did not mean they would listen to what I had to say. And so it went. Mulan was a director's course in itself and certainly a trial by fire for me. But because of the talented Florida animation folks it was the rollercoaster ride of a lifetime. The most important thing I took away from my first directing experience? One very important rule and the theme of this book: The director should serve his crew and the crew will serve his vision.

In the years since Mulan and my time at Disney, I have developed independent features, run my own animation studio, served as a director and animation supervisor on various projects ranging from DVDs, corporate IDs, commercials, live action/animated combo features and everything in-between. I have had the privilege of managing large teams of over 400 and teams of less than 10. No matter what the project, the one thing that has fascinated me the most is witnessing multiple creative minds coming together under one vision in order to create art. After all, at its core, that's what animation is – shared art.

And So...

How do you lead a crew? What are the skills needed? How do you get the best out of your crew, while focusing on a singular goal? These are the things you rarely learn in film school, which I will explore in the following chapters with the help of some of the industry's top directors from across the landscape of animation. These world famous directors include such luminaries as Dean DeBlois, Pete Docter, Eric Goldberg, Tim Miller, John Musker, Jennifer Yuh Nelson, Nick Park and Chris Wedge. Each shares his or her anecdotes and words of wisdom on directing for animation, whether in features, television, shorts or commercials.

My definition of a director is a person working with, guiding and inspiring a team of artists in a corporate environment to create a film, television show, commercial, visual effect or video game. This book is for those directors and future directors who share the belief that animation is a "team sport." Lastly, by writing this book and interviewing some of my idols and mentors my hope was to better my own directing skills as well. It has been an invaluable experience for me. By reading this I hope that you will find your own potential in animation as well.

C.C.V. – CHIEF CREATIVE VISIONARY

What is an *Animation* Director?

At family gatherings, church activities or at a party the dreaded question arises after I tell a stranger what I do for a living. "An *Animation* Director? How do you direct a *cartoon*?" The alchemy of how animation is made is such a mystery to people outside the entertainment industry that they cannot fathom why an animated project would even require direction. After all, presumably there are no "real actors." My trite answer: "Well, you know how a live action director oversees the creative process of a film – from script, casting, production design and costumes to developing the scenes, editing, and score? Well, I do all of that, except I do it **one frame at a time**!" Usually that leaves them with an even more confused look on their faces. In a nutshell, that is one of the reasons I decided to write this book. To help others understand what a director or supervisor in charge of a creative team does to make the magic happen.

A director must be a policeman, a midwife, a psychoanalyst, a sycophant and a bastard.

– Billy Wilder

The Love Affair Begins . . .

"In a galaxy far, far, away . . ." that's where it all started for me. We all have those defining moments in our lives where we realize what we want to do in life. I was 10 years old in 1977 when my brother and I rode our bikes to the local theatre and bought our tickets for *Star Wars*. My mother had seen it already and told us it was too scary for us to see. After a week of hearing gushing reviews from every 10 year old in the neighborhood, we begged our mom on bended knee and she finally conceded to let us go see

The stars and filmmakers of our first Super 8 movie, *Blind Date*: Tom and Tony Bancroft. Surprisingly, Tom agreed to wear the dress.

the movie. By the time the lights came up in the theatre my life was changed. My brother and I talked about *Star Wars* all the time and created our own stories and characters to help Lucas expand upon the legend (as if he needed our help). That summer we became film buffs and went to the theatre as much as our allowance would allow. The Academy Awards became a staple on our family TV every year and we collected all manner of toys, bed sheets and apparel from whatever new film character craze we were into. I was mesmerized by the magic of movies.

Names like Spielberg and Lucas were regulars in our house. They weren't actually at our dinner table but they certainly were talked about around it. The 1980s were when directors like Coppola, Spielberg, Lucas and Scorsese became household names. I didn't fully understand what a director did back then but I knew I wanted to be one. My brother and I dreamed of directing our own movies and by the time we were in college we were shooting our own Super 8mm film productions. We crafted fine cinematic master-pieces such as "Fly Boy" about a boy who wished he could fly like Superman and then does (not a lot of plot development on that one) and "Blind Date" about a boy who has everything go wrong as he is excitedly preparing for his big date to the point that when he shows up at the girl's door he is a bruised and battered mess with green hair (for some reason that I can't remember). Of course to his happy surprise, the door swings open to reveal a girl (my brother dressed in drag) who looks exactly like him having gone through all of the same experiences preparing for the evening out. And the list cinematic genius went on from there. But, while the Bancroft Brother's film library was not long in story development there was no denying – we were making films! My brother and I were the writers, actors, make-up, costumes, special effects department and editors all wrapped up in two scrawny twin teens but more than that we were **directors**!

It was soon after that my brother and I discovered our talent for drawing comic strips could be combined with our love of movies in the form of animation. After some time at California Institute of the Arts (CalArts) studying character animation, Tom and I were asked to join the Walt Disney Studios in their Feature Animation division. It was here at Disney that I learned the difference between a live action director and a director on an animated movie. What's the difference? In short, not much. The live action director is in charge of the story, writers, actors, set designers, costumers, lighting, cinematography, sound effects, music, visual effects, and final color of the film. Basically, all creative elements involved with a movie. The director of an animated feature is involved with all of those elements also but has control of them at 24 frames a second. It's like directing in slow motion.

At my college, CalArts, there were no courses in directing in the animation department and no discussion about how to become one either. Everything I learned about directing came after working as an animator at Disney on classics such as *Aladdin, Beauty and the Beast,* and *The Lion King* working under some of the best animation directors in the industry. Ron Clements and John Musker, Gary Trousdale and Kirk Wise, and Roger Allers and Rob Minkoff (respectively) became my teachers. It was by their example, that I discovered what they don't teach in art school about directing or supervising a crew could fill a book. This book in fact. Case in point: I was a young first-time supervising animator on *The Lion King* when my production manager told me that I had to write a review on each animator that I supervised on my team on the character Pumbaa. My review of their work did not stop at my opinion of their artistic merits (did they squash when they were supposed to stretch?) but also their professional behavior, how well they took direction, their time management skills and so on. My review would help determine if my colleagues got considered for promotion, salary raises or worse case, fired. These were managerial pressures I didn't read about in the animation bible *The Illusion of Life*. This was real life!

Disney directing team: John Musker and Ron Clements.

Disney directing team: Gary Trousdale and Kirk Wise.

Disney directing team: Roger Allers and Rob Minkoff.

From *The Lion King.* © 1994
Disney.

While much of my focus on the job of directing will be from the perspective of an animated feature film director, the elements I discuss through the course of this book will also be helpful to the visual effects supervisor, director of animation on a commercial or video game, a director of a television series, or director of a short film. They all have one important thing in common; they all have to share and enforce their vision to a crew of not-so-like-minded artists. The thing that makes directing difficult and wonderful at the same time is working with all of the unique personalities in your creative team **AND** getting them focused in one direction. There are numerous skill sets that will come into play while directing that go well beyond the obvious artistic principals on cinema taught in school. At some point or another you will be a: coach, cheerleader, politician, negotiator, diplomat, parent, salesman, executive, and servant to your crew. That's a lot of hats to wear! This directing thing is not for the faint of heart.

In the next several chapters I will explore what it means to be an animation director and helpful hints on playing well with others while creating great art.

Terms and Titles Defined

In the entertainment industry you will come across a lot of different titles for the role you play on a project. When I first started at Disney as a matter of fact, I was an *assistant animator* but I didn't assist an animator at all. I was a glorified clean-up artist in a crew of clean-up artists doing the final line drawing on a 2D animated film. Then I was promoted to a beginning animator who worked closely with a senior animator. My new title: *animating assistant.* Confusing? You bet. Two very similar titles could be two totally different jobs.

In supervising and directing for animation it can be confusing too. I would say that titles don't matter but that would be a lie. Even if it's not a big deal to you, it will be to studio executives, producers, unions and your attorney negotiating your deal. Contracts are fought over, offices are changed and salaries increased because of them. And yes, blame is pointed and respect is given based on your title. Titles change from studio to studio for the same job. One studio may call you an *animation supervisor* while another, the *animation director*. Both jobs could have the exact same responsibilities.

When I was negotiating my title credit with Sony Pictures for *Stuart Little 2,* I was told that the title promised me of "animation director" was not possible because of the DGA contract. The DGA is the Director's Guild of America – the negotiating union working on behalf of live action directors. Basically, they had negotiated with all the studios a bylaw of their contract that said that there could only be one "director" title on a live action film and *Stuart Little 2* was considered "a live action movie with post production visual effects." That is, the animation of the title character that I oversaw and represented 70 percent of the film was considered a visual effect in the live action world. The film's overall director was Robert Minkoff and since I was hired

As the Animation Supervisor on *Stuart Little 2*, I also over saw the story team shown here.

by Rob to oversee all aspects of the character animation I certainly didn't want to take anything away from him so I settled on my credited title of *Animation Supervisor*. But, come to find out, Sony Pictures Imageworks already had their own *Animation Supervisor* title for someone working on the film so he had to become "*Animation Supervisor – Sony Pictures Imageworks*" in the final credits. It's all so crazy. I was just happy to have worked on the film and would have taken *Animation Dude* if I thought it would make life simpler.

Below I will define some of the more common titles in the world of animation and visual effects.

Supervising Animator

A senior or lead animator who has proven himself experienced enough in his or her work to shepherd a crew of animators under his or her supervision. This is the title I had at Disney Feature Animation on films such as *The Lion King* and *The Emperor's New Groove* where I supervised the characters of Pumbaa and Kronk respectively. Of course the characters didn't need any supervising but it meant that I had 3–4 other animators who worked under me on those characters. I was in charge of making sure those characters where consistent in look and performance throughout the entire film – not only in my work but my crew's also.

Tony Bancroft Animation Supervisor of Kronk, Disney's *Emperor's New Groove*.

Animation Supervisor

This tends to be a senior animator that is in charge of all aspects of animation on a project, not just a character or a sequence. Oftentimes this is the title a person may have on a special effects project that is an animation/live action hybrid film. The Animation Supervisor would oversee the character animation crew working under the film's overall live action director. This can be a difficult role as it can be an uncomfortable position being between the animators you supervise and the director who is your boss.

Animation Director

This term is used more in Japanese animation these days and refers to a senior animator who is in charge of entire sequences of the film. There would be multiple *animation directors* on one production with an overall director as their creative boss.

It has been used sparingly in the US because of the Director's Guild of America agreement that I mentioned above.

From *The Emperor's New Groove.* © 2000 Disney.

Director of an Animated Film

This is really the same as just plain old director. The rest of the title is how live action executives delineate for themselves who they are talking about when they speak of the director of an completely animated feature. Historically, most animated features have had more than one director. Mostly two directors (and in some cases four – whew!) that split the work load. For example, on *Mulan* I directed the film with my partner Barry Cook. In our case we split the directorial responsibilities by departments. Since Barry came from a background of effects animation and painting, it naturally fell to him to be in charge of layout, backgrounds and effects animation. While I came from a clean-up and character animation background so I was in charge of the clean-up and computer animation (used in the "Hun Charge" sequence mostly) departments. Then we shared the all important departments of story, character animation, editorial, ink and paint and all of postproduction. Making these responsibility splits helped the project become easier to control through the demanding and time-consuming phase of production.

Auteur Directing vs. Corporate "Brain Trust" Directing

Since a director is often times hired by a studio to direct an animated feature, it is important to understand the two totally different styles of directing that are coming out of the studios these days. There is the **auteur style** of directing and the **corporate style** of directing.

Auteur style means the film reflects the director's personal creative vision, as if they were the primary "auteur" (the French word for "author"). In spite of the production of the film being part of an industrial process, the author's creative voice is distinct enough to shine through all kinds of studio interference and through the collective process. In recent years the best example of auteur-style animation directors are Hayao Miyazaki, Henry Selick, Nick Park, and even Chris Sanders. I say "even" Chris Sanders because unlike the other three mentioned he

From *Coraline*. Courtesy of Laika, Inc. Henry Selick is an example of a director who uses auteur style direction.

has developed his films in the highly corporate realm of a major studio which is unique for an auteur style of directing to exist. In the films directed by all of these individuals the viewer can clearly see the artist's specific touch when it comes to the styling of the film, storytelling style, humor and quirky tone. The auteur-style director is afforded more control over his or her choices without interference for reasons unknown or as common as the producer's faith in his or her direction. This style of directing is usually the luxury of an independent film company that is on the fringe of the major studios and therefore can take more chances with the content of their film canon.

The opposite is the **corporate style** of directing which has been popularized more recently by many studios' mandate that none of their films will be developed outside of their own corporate "brain trust" group. The brain trust is made up of the company's top directors and story people that give constant input into all features and shorts produced at the studio. This corporate style is often called *directing by committee* for the obvious reason that all substantial story decisions are reached through consensus of a group. Many major animation studios work under the committee system. They are the commercial films that don't particularly feel personal but do connect with the widest possible audience. Why? Because they are pure entertainment! And that is why most movie watchers go to theatres – to be entertained. But with so many outside inputs from throughout the studio, negotiating these political waters can be very difficult for the film's director(s). Since I have had most of my own personal experience in this corporate style of working, much of my philosophy on directing that I preach in this book is in working with and against the joys and pitfalls of this system of working.

Get Your Head Straight First!

Whether it is at a big studio or small independent, one thing is for sure, animation is big business. There are millions and millions of dollars on the line. Jobs are at stake. Shareholders' stocks could plummet. The pressure on the animation director can be tremendous. How do we cope with these outside pressures?

I was in my second year of CalArts college when my animation teacher shared with me his secret to relieve stress in the animation business. I was working very late one night at my animation desk trying to finish my "epic" student film when my instructor came by and must have seen the worry on my face (either that or the huge pile of discarded drawings in my trash can). He simply said, **"Don't worry – it's just a cartoon!"**

This little golden rule has helped me release myself of stress over the years, but also helped to improve my perspective on my job. It has a two-fold meaning to me. First, "we aren't saving lives here so calm down" and second, "where making entertainment it should be fun!" I truly believe there is no greater honor than to be called a *cartoonist* and to *make cartoons*. Oh, I know, these days animation has grown up. We are to refer to the projects we produce as "animated films." That's all well and good for the marketing and PR departments, but between us creative artists, we make cartoons. Cartoons entertain. Cartoons make you laugh. Cartoons make you feel. But most of all, cartoons make you forget your troubles and escape (if even for a couple of minutes). That is why "animated films" are popular with young and old for now and forever; we bring people's imaginations to life.

From *The Emperor's New Groove.* © 2000 Disney.

A member of the legendary CalArts class of '76 and one of the directors of the "Disney Renaissance" of the 1980s and 1990s, John Musker, along with his directing partner Ron Clements, has undoubtedly made his mark as one of the animation industry's most prolific and successful directors. Originally from Chicago before he moved to California, John started at Disney Studios as a character animator on *The Fox and the Hound* before quickly working his way up the ranks and making his directorial debut in 1986 on *The Great Mouse Detective*. Next, he and Ron wrote and directed the smash hit *The Little Mermaid* in 1989, heralded by many as the return of critical and commercial success for feature animation, followed shortly after by *Aladdin* in 1992. For the next 20 years, John and Ron would continue to write and direct some of Disney's biggest films including *Hercules, Treasure Planet* and, most recently, *The Princess and the Frog* in 2009. John continues to work today as one of Disney's most famous writers and directors. I met with John over lunch, in his office at Disney Animation Studios, where he and Clements are developing a new, yet to be announced, animated feature for Disney.

Tony: John, how did you get into the animation industry?

John: Weirdly enough, when I was a little kid I was interested in animation, and I read the Bob Thomas book *The Art of Animation*, which was sort of the rewrite of the Don Graham book, and it was centered on *Sleeping Beauty*. I checked it out of my local library a couple of times. I read the biography of Walt Disney, so actually, as a seven year old, when someone would ask, "What do you wanna be when you grow up, Johnny?" I'd reply with "Be an animator." I actually knew what it was, but then as I got older my interest drifted a little bit. Even though I was a huge fan of the Disney films that I saw as a kid, and the Warner Bros. films that I saw on television, I sort of drifted away from that. But I always did drawing, always did cartooning, was always patted on the head for my drawing stuff and encouraged. I went to Catholic schools where they had very little actual, formal art training, because it's like an elective, and they had no money for it, and even through high school I became the cartoonist on my various school papers, but they had no art programs, or anything like that, so I wound up going to college as an English major, actually. I went to Northwestern University, back in Chicago, and I did that probably because this Jesuit priest that was sort of a mentor at my high school encouraged us to have a broad-based Humanities background, and not get too vocational too quickly in school. I took that to heart, and so, even though

I could have majored in Art at Northwestern, I majored in English so that I would force myself to read the great books that I might otherwise not read. So I did that, but then I was like, "What am I gonna do for a living? I gotta make a living," and all that, and, and in the meantime I was making live action films with my friends. I did Super 8 with the sound strip on it, and all that and I actually did a feature at Northwestern. As much as I may remember my college career, I remember spending three years making a feature-length Super 8 film with my friends called *Long Summer's Dream*, and, Tim Burton did eventually see it here. It influenced

From *Hercules*. © 1997 Disney.

him heavily in the bad moviemaking school, and I kind of wrote, and directed it with a friend of mine. Anyway, but, as I was nearing the end of my Northwestern career I said to myself "OK, what am I going to do for real now?" and three key things happened to me that pushed me back toward animation. One was I saw a retrospective of Richard Williams' work at the Chicago Film Festival. It was right when he had done *Christmas Carol* that he did in the style of the

original illustrations, and he came and spoke at the film festival. So I heard him talk, and he talked about animation, and he was so excited about animation. He talked about Disney, and he didn't mention Milt Kahl's name, but he said, "They got this guy that did this tiger" And someone else was talking too and that guy said, "Oh yeah. Well, it was all rotoscope," and Richard said, "No. No. It wasn't rotoscoped. No, he did the whole thing, and these guys, they're geniuses." He made it seem really enticing, and then Chuck Jones, independently of that, who actually had produced that film, came and spoke at Northwestern like a year after that. There was a big animation festival at Northwestern, and he was doing the college circuit then, so he showed about eight of his cartoons, including *Bully for Bugs*, and *What's Opera, Doc?* He talked about 'em, was very entertaining, and made animation seem like a career that you could actually get to be an older person in, and it seemed like he projected a feeling of he was still learning, even though he was an older guy, and I thought, "Wow. That seems kinda fun." The Christopher Finch book on the Disney art of animation came out at the same time, and the author talked about a training program at the Disney studio. So, I heard about that, and I just thought, "That seems cool," so I put together a portfolio for Disney . . . and it was rejected. It was funny because when I put together my portfolio they said they wanted drawings of animals, so I went out in the winter to draw the animals that were shivering out at the Lincoln Park Zoo in Chicago, and it was just so cold. I thought, "This is just too cold. I can't do this," so I went to the Natural History Museum in Chicago, and I did drawings of the animals in the dioramas and I was nice and warm. It worked out much better, except that then when Disney rejected my portfolio, they

> **I put together a portfolio for Disney . . . and it was rejected.**

said my drawings of animals were too stiff. I said "Stiff? They were stuffed! I drew them exactly as I saw them." What the heck? So, I was like "Gee. Now what do I do?" and so I put together a portfolio for Marvel Comics. So, I did a sample page of Spider-Man, and Daredevil, and a mystery thing, and I was a big fan of comic books, sent that off to Marvel. They rejected me too. I think it was John Romita Sr., "Do not ever darken our door again. You don't draw well." "What happened to my plan?" I said to myself, "It's backfiring on me." But then, Disney sent me a follow-up letter, and they said, "Maybe you meant to send your portfolio to CalArts . . ." I had never heard of CalArts, didn't know what they were talking about. I had sworn I would never go to graduate school because I was afraid of becoming a professional student and delaying my entry into the real world and being a grown-up. But I wrote to CalArts, got their information. I said, "What the heck. If I'm interested in animation, this is still a way of possibly pursuing it." The Marvel thing had fallen through. So, I sent CalArts a portfolio, and I got accepted there. So, I wound up being in the first year of the animation program there, with Henry Selick, Brad Bird, John Lasseter, and Tim Burton was a year behind us was Chris Buck, Mike Giaimo, Mike Peraza . . . Those were all the following year, but our year was Nancy Beiman, and all those folks, and Doug Lefler, Bruce Morris, Darrell Van Citters . . . so I wound up there not really knowing much about animation, but I was in a class with people, like Brad, and like Jerry Rees, and Darrell Van Citters, all of whom knew a lot more about animation than I did, so it became a learning environment where we had our class, and we had some wonderful instructors. We had Elmore Plummer, Ken O'Connor, T. Hee, and Bill Moore, the design teacher, but even more than that we had this collegiate atmosphere of students who were very willing to share information, so I really learned a lot in this very supportive atmosphere. It was just fun, so I wound up going there for two years. Actually, after my first year, Disney came out, and it was the first producer's show at CalArts, although they just suddenly said, "Hey we're gonna have the Disney review board come by, and look at your work," and so we threw drawings up on the wall, and the people that actually finished a little bit of animation strung it together. We had no idea why we were doing it, that anyone would ever see anything that we had done, and so I did a few different tests. I did a terribly drawn version of Tony, from *Lady and the Tramp*, which was pantomime, and not so good, and then I did a longer test based on a Will Eisner-y thing, a little bit, but it was based on a caricature of Lauren Bacall, and I had her walking, with a slinky walk, into a bar. She sat down on a stool and took a drag on a cigarette, and just, kind of, puffed out the smoke and gave a little look at the camera. They really liked that test, and they invited me to come to work at the Disney Studio. At that time, "Woolie" Reitherman was there, Eric Larson, Don Bluth, and Frank, and Ollie, and all that, and out of that they invited me to come to work at the Disney studio for the summer, but I was thrown, because I wasn't expecting that to happen . . . So I spent six weeks working with Eric Larson that summer, and it was fantastic, and he taught me so many things, and a lot that I felt like, yeah, I never learned any of this stuff, about clarity, and staging, and arcs, and timing, and all this stuff, and strong graphic statements, and phrasing, and, and so I went back to CalArts that second year, armed with all that. I tried to apply that to my test. I wound up doing, like, a six-minute film my second year at CalArts, which was, sort of, a short, actually, based on some of the experiences I had in Chicago, but the characters were greasers. It was a couple of greasers vying over the affections of a girl, who was a caricature of a girl I had met at Disney that summer before . . .

Tony: You won't say who?

John: No, Betsy Betos was her name. She was a quirky, eccentric girl. She was a clean-up artist, but her real interest was dancing. She was a dancer, and she was interested in vaudeville. She was like a throwback to the 1920s. She'd play ukulele and do these eccentric dance steps and all this stuff, and she was very much a character. I was very smitten, in a way, and so the girl they were vying for in my film was a caricature of Betsy. Anyway, I did that test, and at the end of the year it was going to be shown again, but as we got closer to the test I called up Disney. I thought the deal was "Go back to school for a year, and then come back here," so, I called up and I talked to Ed Hansen, the head of the department then, and I said, "OK, it's the end of the year, and here I am, and, ready to go," you know, "I'm finishing up," And they were like, "Well, what are you talking about?" I said, "Well, remember the whole thing, and you offered me the job?" and they replied "We didn't make any promises to you, we don't know if we're gonna take you . . ." and I'm like, "Oh my goodness. I just made the blunder of all time. I turned down a job there, and now here I am, and I'm not going to school anymore. This is it for me. I'm done, but, I might not have a job. I thought I had a job locked up." So the review board came again, second year, and they saw my work. Fortunately they liked my test so, out of that year, four of us were invited to come. We were the first expatriates of the CalArts animation program to come to work at the Disney studio. It was me, Jerry Rees, Doug Lefler, Brad Bird, and actually

Henry Selick, so five of us. We all started at the studio at the same time, and ironically that was the same week that Bill Kroyer and Dan Haskett, and another guy started at the studio so we were all trainees together and we became known as "The Rat's Nest," which was the pejorative name

> **we became known as "The Rat's Nest,"**

that Don Bluth gave to us when we were working on this Christmas featurette. We were the CalArts rebels . . . We were coming in at an interesting time, with a lot of chaos. Still a lot of the great artists and legends were there, but they weren't playing at their best position. They were too involved and, when they were less involved, the films were better. I mean, you know, the films of the 1940s, and the 1950s, they were better, and I don't know if Frank and Ollie would ever admit that, or I think they sometimes left-handedly did, but they weren't playing to their own strengths, and, so, ironically the system I was coming into at Disney, in the 1970s was still, kind of, that system. They were looking for new blood to get into the directing ranks when I came in, just as an accident of timing, in a way, because "Woolie" Reitherman was sort of retiring, and Art Stevens, who had been the director working with "Woolie" on *Fox and the Hound*, wasn't being allowed to do anything. "Woolie" was such a dictator, I mean, you know, a hands-on guy. Art didn't get to do anything, and, so even though he was in his sixties, he was completely frustrated by "Woolie" and upset, and finally it got to a point where Art said, "You gotta let me direct this movie. I'm the director. I'm not directing." They said, "'Woolie' I think you should retire," so, he, finally, you know,

> **We were the CalArts rebels . . .**

somewhat kicking and screaming retired, and, so, Art moved into those ranks of being a proper director. But then there was a feeling that Art wasn't listening to the younger people enough, so they were looking to get a younger voice into the directing ranks, and by "they," I mean, particularly Tom Wilhite, who was an executive. He was a live action executive who was maybe a year older than I was. He was the guy who got Tim Burton his gig doing *Vincent*, and he really saw the younger CalArts people's talent and helped them find opportunities. And so, during all of this chaos on *Black Cauldron*, there was an opening and so he appointed me a director and that's how I became an additional director on *Black Cauldron*, because of Tom.

Tony: Oh, I didn't know that you were a director on *Cauldron*?

John: Yeah, it was sort of imposed on them. They didn't want me there, so, it was a crazy situation, 'cause I was definitely the odd man out. They didn't even want me on the movie, but Tom put me on the movie, and he put Joe Hale as the producer of the movie over those things. Now, Joe was a friend of the other established directors, and that was fine, but me, it was like, "What is this guy doing here?" Now, ironically, I was given that job partly because I would be no great loss to the animator's ranks at the time. I had done animation. My animation was OK. It was decent-ish, and I did a fair amount on *The Fox and the Hound*, but I think at that time it was the directing animator who was the king, and it was key to keep those people and so it was like, "Yeah. You go off and be a director, 'cause it's no great loss," but, I think, part of the reason some of the people that Wilhite canvassed supported me being a director was that I was open to people's ideas. It wasn't so much "This guy's got a lot of ideas that he should get to the screen." No. It was "This guy listens to us, and he will help us

get our ideas to the screen," which was true, which was absolutely true.

Tony: It sounds like the studio was pretty split back then from a managerial standpoint . . .

John: Yeah, there was us CalArts kids, then Bluth's guys. And then there were the sort of odd floaters who were like Ron Clements, and Glen Keane . . . And there was an attempt to try and pull them together but it remained fragmented, even as I went on to *Black Cauldron*. One of the first things that was suggested to me when I came onto *Black Cauldron* was from John Lasseter, John, who by now had graduated CalArts and started at Disney. He said "You know who you should get to do some stuff on this? Tim Burton. Have you seen his stuff?" and I said, "Well, I know Tim's animation," and he goes "Yeah, but have you seen his sketch books?" and I went, "No, actually, I haven't seen his sketch books," and he told me "Look at Tim's sketch books," so, Tim had these great sketch books that he had done of people he saw and just oddball, one-shot ideas he had . . . They were Ronald Searle influenced, and Dan Wilson, and Edward Gory, and Chuck Jones and all that . . . All that mix that turned into Tim . . . So I showed them to Joe Hale, the producer and said "We should get Tim to do drawings on this," and he said, "Yeah, definitely. Let's do it," So, Tim did a whole set of drawings. They were very Tim, and Joe Hale initially, is, like, "Yeah, let's do *Black Cauldron* like this. Let's just use these Tim designs. There's no reason why it always has to look the same. Let's use Tim designs." But the other directors were horrified. They were, like, "This isn't Disney. This is something weird. What are you doing?" And so, ultimately Joe didn't know which way to go. He went to Ron Miller, the executive producer, who was Walt Disney's son-in-law, and he said, "I'm being pulled in these different directions." The story guys wanted to do

Black Cauldron more like the books, and wanted a younger protagonist, and the other directors just saw it differently, and they were like, "Let's make it more like *Star Wars*." So finally, Joe presented to Ron as "Now, on one hand you could do something really different. You could do this UPA kind of crazy Tim Burton, avant-garde new thing, or you could do the classic thing. You know, the classic Disney thing." and Ron said "Well I want to do the classic Disney thing." He said, "*Lady and the Tramp* was just re-released in France, and it's doing great. Why would we want to change that? No. I want to do classic Disney." I tried to argue it and said that the question wasn't framed fairly but I got nowhere. It's funny, if you look back at that time I storyboarded a number of sequences but they didn't like my boards. I never got to the point of actually directing anything. I was there when we auditioned actors, and we recorded some of the actors. I never got to direct the actors, but I was at various auditions and things like that and so I did watch the other directors and so I learned about directing that way. Burny Mattinson had his style of directing where he would stand in the studio with the voice actors, and be over their shoulders, and, kind of, coach them through it, right there in the room, and he would give them line readings too, which I learned fairly quickly, "No, no, actors do not want line readings."

Tony: What do you like most about working in animation?

John: Well, I like to draw, so I get to keep drawing. And when I started, I wasn't sure if I would go into comics or what. I wanted to be an editorial cartoonist at one point. I like graphic design. I like poster-y things. I'm a caricaturist, and, and I still get to do all that by being in animation, but I also did live action films. I like

being a storyteller, and, it sounds goofy, but I don't think of myself as an artist – I think of myself as an entertainer. Despite my verbosity now, I grew up a fairly introverted guy. I was part of a big, Irish-Catholic family. I had five sisters. I never needed to talk 'cause they were always talking. But I saw plays when I was in high school. I saw *Guys and Dolls* at my local high school and I just thought that there was something so cool about seeing guys I know being on stage and communicating to an audience. And then I could do it through my drawings as well. I would do these drawings, I'd do caricatures of teachers in my school, and next day, after the paper came out, there'd be a buzz in the school, "Oh, did you see this, and that?," and it was like communicating with people I didn't know. I did these little, live action Super 8 films, and they were shown at my high school, and people I didn't know saw them, and laughed at my jokes, and things like that, and I got a rush out of that. I just felt like, "I'm connecting with people," I mean, it's that connection with people, and storytelling, and entertaining that I'm addicted to.

> but I don't think of myself as an artist – I think of myself as an entertainer.

Tony: Maybe you get this question a lot: What does a director in animation do? What are some of your day-to-day responsibilities at Disney?

John: I always do this joke, because people always ask about being an animation director: "How's that different from a live action director?," and I say, "Well, in, in live action you get to yell 'Action!', and the actors do their thing, and then you say 'Cut!' when they're done. But what we do when we deal with the animators is we say 'Draw!,' and then we wait. And then we say, 'Erase!'" [laughter] But day-to-day responsibilities, that's the other thing, people feel, of course. You tell them about animation, "It's tedious. You're doing one-million drawings" and "Oh my God." I think Bill Kroyer's father once said something, I think it was about animation. He said "That'd drive me outta my box!" and I think that a lot of people have that feeling. The irony, of course, is that with animation directing, actually every day is different. The production process is such that, over the course of the years that you're working on a film your responsibilities vary hugely. Now Ron and I, traditionally, have written our films, so an initial period is spent coming up with the story, and outlining that story, and developing the characters, and then we co-write the script, and our writing system is such that I kind of do improve on paper, and Ron's more of a structure guy, and he helps pull it all together. I'd say even though I think of myself as having a fair amount of ideas, and being a fairly creative guy, we are also very collaborative guys, and we encourage input. Not every director does that, nor is it a job requisite. You don't have to do that to be a good director, but I think we have found that the films are enriched and the film becomes more than it would be if it was confined to what we do. Every film becomes different depending on the team of people that's connected to it. So because of all that, as directors, our day-to-day things vary. We are looking at color. We're looking at animation. We're dealing with voice actors. We're dealing with the marketing of the films. One of the good things about the Disney system is that we try and keep the film as fluid as possible for as long as possible to accommodate new ideas that may not necessarily change the whole film, but perhaps new ways to tell the story that we're trying to tell. Being able to incorporate those things and do it efficiently becomes more and

more important the smaller your budget is. "Why can't we just write a script, storyboard exactly that script, animate that script, put it on the screen . . ." However, that doesn't take into account, first, and foremost, the fact that in live action you shoot coverage. You shoot the scene from many different angles, and so you have opportunities to re-fashion the film in the editing room. Animation is more akin to theatre, where you try something out on the road, and you re-write on the fly . . . Because it takes longer, you have more time to make mid-course corrections, and that, I think, is part of the reason why the Pixar films and the best Disney films have been so good, because you can make things work better while you're doing it and find things that work, and tailor things to some of the things that work, and things that aren't working . . . That's one of the pluses of working in feature animation, where there is enough time built into the system to fix things, and money, obviously. It's time, and money.

Tony: That is one thing that live-action has going for it. They have the gift of spontaneity as a resource.

John: And that's one of the challenges in animation: to produce a film that has a feeling of spontaneity, because it is the least spontaneous medium imaginable. You have to work hard to get that spontaneity, but the best animated films, whether, or not it's, you know, *Pinocchio* or *The Incredibles*, or *Toy Story*, have an improv-y feel to them. Yeah. Even in the straighter scenes, it feels like it's playing out in front of your eyes spontaneously.

Tony: What would you say is the most important tool in your director's toolbox?

John: If I could only say one, I would say that I do think it helps that I can draw. I'm able

> One of the good things about the Disney system is that we try and keep the film as fluid as possible for as long as possible

to draw, so I can express my ideas. If I'm directing animation, I could literally do a little drawing, and the fact that I have animated, I have a vocabulary with which to address animation critique. There's a common question, "Can you be a good director who does not draw, in animation?" Most directors were animators, or they were story artists. There are some though, that do neither, and I think it is possible, but I think it's harder.

Tony: Absolutely, because it's such a visual language. Now, regarding story and character: Where do you start when you're developing a story for a project in the very beginning?

John: I think that story is character – they're really interwoven. You can't have one without the other, and characters motivate the story. One book that I think is really valuable is *The Art Of Dramatic Writing* by Lajos Egri. I still think that is one of the best books that really talks about character as the basis of all drama, and he gets into themes as well. These films are really about locking into unique, appealing characters . . . "Appeal" is one of those words that you always heard around here [at Disney], and it is one of those buzzwords, but it's essential. It doesn't necessarily mean pretty, or handsome, or cute. It goes deeper than that. You need to create a character that makes you want to watch them and that you can invest yourself in emotionally. It can be the villain, as well as the hero, and it can be the supporting characters as well, and I think

From *Aladdin*. © 1992 Disney.

that idea of appeal permeates the best films, both Disney and non-Disney.

Tony: Now, you and Ron Clements have been screenwriters for most of your films but from time-to-time you've also worked with a scriptwriter. How do you work with a scriptwriter to develop your vision for the project?

John: We're getting more into that now. On just about every project we've done we've written, if not the first draft, then one of the earliest drafts of these films, and that's been a helpful tool for the two of us to get on the same page. When we were doing *Aladdin*, one of the executives had a meltdown when he didn't like what we were doing at all, and he said, "Start over," and we interviewed writers, and the pair of writers that we interviewed that we really liked were Ted Elliott and Terry Rossio, who, later did this little film called *Pirates of the Caribbean*. They're now kajillionaires, I think, based on that. They were funny, they knew story, and they had a sense of animation, the possibilities of animation, and they pitched us ideas about the story that we liked. And they were inventing whole new things and sometimes new structural elements – often they would then write a scene and we would perform it: Ron and I and whoever our head of story is, and the writers usually. We read the scene aloud and do a little performance of it, just to hear the lines spoken and get a sense of how it plays. Then we give notes. They go off, and they would re-work it, and they'd come back a time or two, and then that material gets pitched, sequence by sequence, much as you would pitch a scene of animation to be issued to an animator. We then issue it to a story artist who's going to do that sequence and then they do a first pass, and sometimes

they're collaborating with the writer while we're doing that. Usually these writers are people that stay with the project. They're not people who've just written a script, and go away. They're on the staff, and it's a very fun, collaborative process.

Tony: Can you talk about storyboards a little bit? Nowadays animatics are a valuable tool. How important is the animatic to you, in your process?

John: At a certain point the script becomes immaterial and the boards become the next thing, but more important, even than the boards, are the reels. The reels are the working draft of the movie, and they're the most malleable clay. They are the blueprint of the movie, but they are an organic, fluid, dynamic, ever-changing writing instrument for the movie, and so they're really a crucial step. We're exploring different ways of staging things, and cutting things and putting over story ideas, and putting over jokes, and getting emotion . . . And now with the new technology, you can work out performance in even more detail, and staging ideas, effects animation ideas, color – you name it. It's become a very useful tool, I think, that we didn't used to have in terms of exploring ideas, developing them, and communicating ideas to people in the various departments down the road who can more look at that, and know, "Oh, this is what's going to be coming for my department," whether that's the effects department, or background department, or whatever, you know. It's just extremely helpful.

Tony: So between writing and storyboarding and all the other parts of the story process, is there one that's more important to you than another?

> You need to create a character that makes you want to watch them and that you can invest yourself in emotionally.

From *The Great Mouse Detective*. © 1986 Disney.

John: No. It's a process, I would say, and there are different steps along the way. I don't think great animation can save a bad story and so I think that the story is crucial. I also think a great story, poorly executed or poorly directed doesn't work so well either, but the story is the foundation that you're building this house on and so if you have structural issues your film will invariably only get to a certain point, because of the weaknesses in those areas.

Tony: How about working with animators? What is the process like for you "issuing" or "launching" a scene to an animator?

John: Well, I'm a director who has always collaborated with Ron Clements as my co-director,

and we both grew up in a system of sequence directors. So we divide the movie into sequences and we each take a sequence, because we like to have some autonomy. As much as we've collaborated, it's more satisfying to have some things where we have more autonomy. So in theory we each have the final say on any of our particular sequences. We try to have a mix of sequences, so I do some action scenes but I also try and do some personality scenes. And certainly with the songs in these films, we divvy those up. We'll have a meeting as we get into a sequence and assemble the people that are going to be animating on that sequence. Certainly the supervising animators who really are the key players in terms of the performance, because we rely on them to maintain the unity of performance through several animators, both in terms of drawing, and the way the characters move, react, and think. We usually like to issue a scene to the directing animator or supervising animator with an animator so that we can talk about the performance. Now, occasionally I've storyboarded sequences that people animate, and that's obviously been helpful for me, in a way, because I've done poses in there, which really is a little bit more like the Chuck Jones system of directing, where he's drawing poses, and the animators use those poses.

Tony: What do you look for in a creative team when you're staffing up a film: an art director, an editor, storyboard artist, an animator . . . What do you look for in an artist?

John: For those roles, we look for people, obviously, who are very talented. People who are very skilled and who are gonna bring something to it that we didn't think of. I don't think we try and look for mini versions of ourselves, but, actually, people that have skill sets that are unlike our own, or that bring another point-of-view. On our last film, *Princess and the Frog*, Jeff Draheim was our editor, and he really was a fairly active voice in making suggestions about how the story was told. He really brought his own point-of-view, and certainly we discussed things with him, and sometimes we said, "We hear what you're saying, but we think something differently," but it really plussed the film to have him on it. When it comes to building teams, every director has their own strengths or things that they're more comfortable with. In Ron and my case, because both of us were animators we were always comfortable with that phase. Even Peter Schneider [past President of Disney Animation] used to hassle us, because he's like "You should have a head of

animation," and, we're, like "Peter, we *are* the head of animation." It's always different, but for the most part we're our own animation supervisor, which still seemed right to me because we are more versed in that. As we get outside of that into, let's say art direction, I feel, like, we really rely on an art director, or a production designer, because we're not as oriented that way. Likewise, there's other directors who are very skilled in that area and maybe not so much in animation and so you shape a team around you partly to support the areas that you need the most help in. If you can do that well in the first place, everything gets easier. Sometimes you have to work with someone new, and you have to hope that it works out. We've worked with people for the first time on a number of films just because the person we wanted wasn't available and we just try and make

From *Aladdin*. © 1992 Disney.

our best guess. It's always encouraging when that pans out well because you get to develop this sort of relationship and they bring something to it that you wouldn't expect, and that you know you could never have supplied yourself, and really that makes it more fun.

Tony: Yeah. That's great. Well, this kinda leads into the next question, which you somewhat answered, but how much responsibility are your creative department heads given on one of your films?

John: I'd say that Ron and I tend to give them a pretty fair amount of responsibility. I do think we remain as editors, almost, with the idea of keeping the overall film in mind. We do try and empower the department heads to really shape the film and help them bring their own talents. There are people who we work with repeatedly, like Rasoul Azadani, who's done layout on a bunch of our films and who we really think has got a strong eye in terms of composition, filmmaking, cutting, staging, and contrast . . . He's empowered. Now, that can be tricky for people in that department, because he's such a dominant personality, and the people that he's working with might not be as collaborative as we are. And yet we really love his work, so we do try and empower people like that. And that can be good news, and bad news, I guess, for some of the people in those areas that work with the person that we've empowered.

Tony: How do you combat the "Us against Them," attitude that arises on a production between management and creative artist?

John: We've done enough of these films that it is an ongoing thing, and it's a shame that there are those lines because I have come, through the course of the many years I've been doing this, to really respect the people on the production side of things. Me being so disorganized, if I was totally left to my own devices, maybe we could get the movie done . . . But it would be very difficult. And the other thing is, Ron and I are not good cheerleader-types, and we've been harassed about that at various times. We're low-key. I mean, we don't scream at people. I've heard of some directors who really are screamers, or who get

angry at people and can kind of tell 'em off and we don't do that. We're low-key guys so we can be really ecstatic and enthusiastic, but we are just not bubbly extroverts, so sometimes it's hard for us to show it. Some people sometimes interpret it as a lack of enthusiasm, or something, and that's not the case. So, sometimes it's good in the overall production if we have production people who are higher-key, who can offset some of our low-key-ness. Our ongoing thing with production is to try and get people who are in production to look at the real world, and not the pieces of paper in front of them, because many times they're managing a budget, there's a schedule, and it can be deceiving. On charts, scenes can all look completely equal, but some are far more difficult than others. Even if there's a thirty-foot scene, but it's practically a moving camera shot it's not gonna be that bad, whereas you might have a two-foot scene, but it's got a thousand characters in it. Some producers try to be more sensitive to that, but, sometimes we have to remind people a little bit, you know, that not everything is equal. We like the producer to be our advocate in this studio system, where there are competing productions, and there are people over our film in a way that are watching the money, and the resources, and we want that producer to be our advocate. We worked with Peter Del Vecho on *The Princess and the Frog*, and he really was a wonderful producer to work with, and had this tricky role being between the studio end, the people that are worried if we're behind schedule, and then us on the creative end who are trying to get as much up on the screen as we can. I think the best producers are the ones that can somehow keep both groups happy, and I think Peter did that, and I think that's a real skill, 'cause sometimes they can tend to go one way or the other but the best producers try to favor both equally.

Tony: Do you find it difficult to be true to your original vision for the project as time goes by? If so, how do you keep it on track?

John: Most of the movies we've directed, Ron and I have written, at least, the first draft, so we have that document to go back to. I think the challenge is to try and be open to ideas that can improve the film and be objective about it enough that you can see where areas aren't working. That's where screenings come in, and I do think working with John Lasseter has been really fun for us. John has a really good story sense, and he's a filmmaker, so it helps to have someone sort of outside and not as intimately involved as you

> **Animation is tricky; it takes so long;**

are. They can help bring some objectivity to it. Animation is tricky; it takes so long; you can lose the freshness of it; and you can forget why, for example, something was funny in the first place. So that's where screenings are helpful, because you can get input from people seeing it fresh, and you can be reminded about things that are funny or what characters are working.

Tony: We know that budgets and schedules are part of life for the filmmaker . . . How do you look at them personally, friend, or foe?

John: I do think they're mostly friend if the original budget and schedule are reasonable. I don't think it's unreasonable for the company that's producing these films to feel that they wanna make a profit on these movies. They're in a business. If you get it done, and it's way, way, way expensive, then your chances of making a profit, obviously, are less, and, therefore, the people that make those decisions may say,

> **you can forget why, for example, something was funny in the first place.**

"We're not gonna make another one," and that's not a good thing. So I think that fiscal prudence in making these movies is good. Part of what has defined Disney's films and made them stand out is "the Disney system" and, on paper, it's definitely a lot less efficient. Looking at it logically, the most efficient system would be you write a script, you get that right, you storyboard that script, you buy off on that, you animate exactly what's in that, you release it, and there it is. But what that doesn't allow for is any improvisation or mid-course corrections. That's one of the benefits of animation taking such a long time – You can fix problems mid-course. It lets you bring the film toward what's working, and to fix what's not working, and, I think, the best Disney films have obviously benefited from having the time, and money. That's not the only solution. I mean, you could spend a lot of money, and spend a lot of time, and not get something. It may not be improving, but time and money with a system where you've got good critiques of a film, and fairly objective critiques from good people giving notes then that's a pretty good, healthy system. With that, in theory, your film will progress from screening to screening, and it will be getting better each time as you fix problems.

Tony: At Disney, do meetings help make the film, or do they distract from the creative process?

John: I feel that a film with no meetings would be hard to just get everybody on the same page, but meetings can go on too long. There can be too many. Sometimes, as a director, you can have so many meetings in your day that you need to *schedule* your five-minute bathroom breaks. I do think, at times, that the meetings can seem more important, and sometimes that comes from the production end – they forget that it's more important for the

From *The Great Mouse Detective.* © 1986 Disney.

artists to be drawing than it is for them to be in a meeting. But there certainly is a time, and a place, for getting people together. It is a collaborative art form, after all.

Tony: Do you have to interact with a producer and/or a studio executive on a continual basis, and, if so, what is that relationship like for you?

John: We [Ron and I] do work very closely with the producer. Sometimes we've been the

producer, but the producer is your key partner in this team, so you want someone that really has your back. The best producers do that, and they add something. And the producer is there in helping to book the voice talent, and also to be our advocate in this world of where we're trying to get certain resources from the studio that may be allocated to other productions. We need X, Y, or Z person and they go in and do battle to try and get those resources directed over to our film. That's a full-time job in itself. And they do run interference with the studio, with the people who are just concerned about the money being spent and the time it's taking and all that sort of stuff. We do interact with studio executives, but less frequently. The producer does much more of that than we do. They have weekly meetings with those people. We see those people more periodically and, I think, that's the better way.

in terms of efficiency, new technologies can be an aid to you.

Tony: As a director, how important is it to you to keep up with current technology – The latest software and hardware?

John: Technology's a funny thing, because back when I was studying animation, Chuck Jones came and spoke about animation at CalArts and he made the joke: "When you talk about technical stuff with me, I am someone who has never understood past the infinite mysteries of the screwdriver." [laughter] I'm not that technically savvy either, but you surround yourself with people who are. I think in a broad sense it is good to have some sense of what technology can do, and to evolve with the technology, or to learn about new tools. I think that is good. If you're really stuck, if you really haven't embraced that . . . I know some directors even, who came out of story, and they wouldn't use a Cintiq. They're like, "I really think it should be drawn on paper," and, to me that was a little bit crazy. I would say "Wait. If you're boarding then a Cintiq is an ideal tool for storyboarding!" But, just in terms of efficiency, new technologies can be an aid to you. The other thing I think, when you talk about keeping current, is that it's good to see contemporary live action films, and contemporary theatre, and contemporary animation. You need to see the

animation of other studios, see what they're doing. The other thing that we have nowadays that I think is a fun thing is how much content there is out there on the Internet. Different people have their blogs, and there's just a lot of interesting people around the world. Artists whose work I look at and I just enjoy seeing that. And that's all work that I would have never seen without the Internet. And then you see student projects, you know, with Vimeo or YouTube and things like that, where you can see work from studios and artists from around the world. And student work from around the world even. That's a whole world that didn't exist when I was in school. I think it is a resource, and I don't know if it will develop into a system that people can make money from or make a living doing it . . . But the Internet can be the platform that people see these things on. I think it's changing. It's evolving. I don't know where it's going to wind up, but there's an aspect of it that I think is exciting. It's kind of decentralizing animation and artwork and there's such a huge appetite, I think, for stories and visual stimuli. I don't think there's any less of an appetite for that than there was thirty years ago, yet somehow I think the Internet is going to play a huge role in that, or whatever the Internet evolves into.

Tony: Well, I know you're a modest guy, but, just so you know, you're highly regarded in this animation industry. You and Ron, the films that you guys have put forth and the work that you've done . . . You've probably directed more animated features than any other directors in animation history.

John: [Laughs] Yeah, well, we're older, I think.

Tony: Well I think you guys definitely have the record. But all that is to lead up to this: with all of your experience, any last words for young artists that want to get into directing themselves?

John: I would encourage anyone who's interested in it to pursue it. The irony, for me, is that when I got into animation, I didn't even know that much about the different roles. I had directed, in effect, little live action films when I was in high school with friends of mine. I did a whole feature and it took us, like, three years to make. It was a prelude to getting into animation, I guess, but, I would encourage anyone who's interested to follow their passion. You need to really see the world around you, the people that you know, what is it about them that excites you and what stories do you have that you want to tell. Stories that either: you create, that you want to share with people, or that you've found and you want to interpret and share with an audience. I think my advice on most of these things, always, for anybody doing this is to be your own worst critic, and that you'll only improve to the extent that you're hard on yourself. You've really gotta be willing to put your work out there and take criticism. You need to learn from that and evolve. I do think that, for any young person now, there's such a wealth of material so the challenge could be to find your own voice in the midst of so much great work that's preceded you. Now, in our case, we looked at the great Disney features and all that and there was a question: Can you ever make a movie that can compete with those animated classics? But that was a stimulus too, and the interest, as it should be for any young director, is you wanna carve out your own space. You don't wanna reiterate something that's come before, and yet you want to learn from what's preceded you. I think there are things to learn and you'd be a fool not to study

things that have worked, and to dissect them. You need to reverse engineer films that you like, go back and storyboard something based on a film. Break it back down into boards. How did they construct that? How is it staged? Why did the director put the camera there? Here's the acting choices, the arc of the scene, where it begins, and where it ends, and both from a filming point-of-view, and from an acting point-of-view you need to try and dissect those things. Be critical of your own work. Be a sponge. Try and soak up knowledge from every resource possible and all of that you funnel into yourself. The idea is that you synthesize all these different influences, and what emerges is something that's uniquely yours, hopefully, that is influenced by your own character, and your own upbringing, your own tastes, your own sensibilities, the things you've been exposed to, and the stories that excite you . . . And hopefully out of all those influences what will emerge will be you giving some point-of-view about stories to an audience. If you're lucky, and you get the opportunity to do that, share your stories with an audience, it's very stimulating and it's fun just to communicate with people outside yourself. That's what so much of this medium is about, making a connection with an audience, and having done it a number of times I can say that it really doesn't get old. It doesn't lose its allure and it's also fun to be a member of an audience, as much fun as it is to be a director and take in an artist that you haven't seen before . . . Or have a director show you something that you didn't know, or didn't think of and it opens your eyes. It just makes you glad to be alive. What can I say?

Tony: That's a great ending to a very special interview. Thank you John.

> **you'll only improve to the extent that you're hard on yourself.**

THE CREATIVE PROCESS

The Secret Sauce

Just like a car is made on an assembly line, a film, video game or television show is made through a process of many specialized artists all adding their parts to the overall project until it is finished. And just like the proverbial automobile assembly line, to back up the production line because you realize that the steering wheel was put on wrong, after the fact, is an expensive dilemma. One of the most important things a director must know is *when* to make a change in the process and be able to weigh the repercussions – if any. Knowing the process of how an animated production is made is crucial to creating a flow for all of the artists to create comfortably and for you, as the director, to get your vision on the screen. Furthermore, knowing what each artist contributes in the process will not only help you get the most out of each contributor but also help you to *plus* their work down the production line. What do I mean by *plusing*? It is the true "secret sauce" behind the success of many of the early Disney films and practiced by all studios that do great work. It is the general rule that an artist must *plus* or **improve** upon a design, scene, drawing, layout, idea, or painting that comes across their desk from the previous department. In that way, each artist is responsible for not only doing their part in the production but for adding to it, building something that is so much more than what came to them. It was not enough for the artists of Disney past to just make a film *good*; they had to make it *great*. And so should you.

No matter what type of animated project you are directing, you will, more or less, go through these basic process steps in this order:

> **"** I feel like I'm the manager of an animation cinema factory. I am not an executive. I'm rather like a foreman, like the boss of a team of craftsmen. That is the spirit of how I work. **"**
>
> – Hayao Miyazaki

1 The Concept

a) What is it?
b) Why do we care?

2 The Business

a) Determining the right budget
b) Creating a schedule to serve the budget and the project
c) Building the right team

3 Preproduction

a) The script
b) Character design
c) Location design
d) Voice recording
e) Establishing a visual style
f) Storyboards and animatic

4 Production

a) Editing (happens throughout film)
b) Modeling/rigging (CGI)
c) Layout
d) Animation
e) Visual effects
f) Texturing/lighting (CGI)
g) Final rendering and compositing (CGI)

5 Postproduction

a) Color timing
b) Sound effects
c) Score
d) Final mix

The Concept

This is where it all starts unless you are directing a visual effects work, commercial, or video game. If that is you, then most likely the concept was given to you by a client that hired you to direct or supervise their animation for their product. If you are directing a film or TV series than the concept is in your ball park. This is the crucial beginning of the project where anything goes. Because of this fact, it can be the most difficult, too. What is my story about? Who is the main character? Why will anyone care? There are so many options at this stage that it can be creatively stunting. The most important thing to do is just make a decision. "The story is about a girl who, to save her elderly father's life, dresses as a man and takes his place to fight for China." That is, in fact, the basic logline for Disney's *Mulan* an animated feature which I co-directed with Barry Cook. For us, the concept was already there, found in a 2,000-year-old Chinese poem. But the characters, tone, setting and various story details needed to be explored. Make a

From Disney's *Mulan*. © 1998 Disney.

decision and then another. The building of these choices will lead in a direction that is either pleasing to you or not. If not, then back up and start over. This is one of the only times in the process of creating your animated project that it will not cost you a fortune to back up and start over. So do it as often as you need and make sure it's right! Your biggest concern at this point should be: Is this a movie or show that I would like to see? Or at the very least, is it appealing to the audience I want to enjoy it? If success and profitability are anywhere in your sights, then one or both of these questions needs to be answered in the positive. And so the process begins . . .

The Business

Soon after you know *what* it is that needs to be made you have to answer the question of *how* it is going to be made. Producers and accountants may drive this part of the process but as director of the project you no doubt will be involved in the next steps of the process: budgets, schedules and hiring the creative team. This is where the creative and the business come together. If done properly (and with your help) the project will successfully find life outside your head.

Determining the budget can be a very difficult part of the process. It is dependent on as many known elements as it is unknown elements. One rule of thumb is that the budget will change as fast as a car depreciates when you drive it off the lot, but it is necessary to be in the ball park and be as prepared as possible for the surprises that arise in the process. Since time is money, the schedule is one of the first things to help determine the budget. How long do you have to create your project? If not dependent on a release date or client expectation then how long should it take to produce? Determining your schedule will also help in answering the next question of how many artists, technicians, and production people will I need? "Head count" as it's called is based on your schedule and funds. If your project has a tight schedule then you will most likely need a higher budget to afford more artists and tighter overlap in your departments. A longer schedule should mean fewer personnel and therefore, more consistency in the animation. A longer schedule on an animated project is usually always preferred for a higher quality of work but rarely seems to happen in Hollywood. The famous visual effects director John Dykstra sums it up nicely when he said, "There are three ways to do any shot. There's fast, there's good and there's cheap. But you can only work in combinations of two. You can have it cheap and you can have it fast, but can't have it good; you can have it fast and you can have it good, but you can't have it cheap; you can have it good and you can have it cheap, but you can't have it fast."

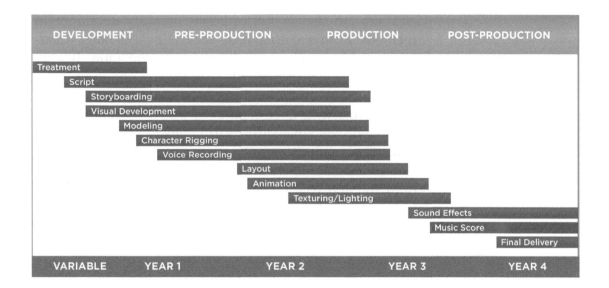

Here is an example of an average animated (CG) feature production schedule broken down by departments:

The overlap of the departments is important to have a proper flow from one department to the next. You never want a department to be *waiting* for work to come to their desk.

Pre-production

This is the most important step in the process. Development is where the concept becomes a story and the story a film. All of the elements in this step are crucial to the success of your project and should not be rushed to get to production. There have been large handfuls of studios that have allowed the pressure of stock holders, investors and producers to rush them into production before the story was solid. Then changes and compromises are made at the most expensive part of the process when you have the most people on the project and money is flying out the door at a rapid rate. This is why when a director from Pixar is asked what are the three most important elements of a Pixar film they all respond with, "story, story, story." And it shows.

There are shelves full of books on story development methods from creating beat sheets, beat boards, treatments, loglines, character biographies and more but no matter what your process they all lead to one thing – the script. I mention some of my favorite books on the subject of story in a later chapter of this book, but for now know that they are all just instruments to provoke thought and inform you on proper story structure. No book will give you a good story or characters. That will only come from you and your team. Try to be as unique and original as possible with how you tell your story. It is OK to say "It's like *Star Wars* meets *Bambi*" to paint a broad picture of your concept, but if it really feels like *Star Wars* and *Bambi* put together, then you're in trouble. Whether you work with writers or you brave the writing process yourself, the script is the true blue-print for your project. It's the thing that will be judged by producer, studio executive, investor, voice actor, and you're entire crew to see if you have a potentially successful film. I say "potentially" because even with a good script, there are so many moving parts to juggle as it moves into production that change can take the story in many unwanted directions. I don't mean to be pessimistic, but the reality is that many studio executives are "risk adverse" and therefore something new and original will be scary to them. It is, after all, human nature to destroy what we don't understand. And it is difficult to get others to fully understand your original creation, like you do, until it is complete.

A production assistant placing visual development art on the boards for the production *Mulan*.

As you are developing the script you no doubt already know who your cast is and what your stories' locations are so it is a good time to start the visual development process. Vis dev (slang in the industry) is the process in which you as the director work with character designers, location designers and painters to develop the visual side of your film. Whether you are developing a film, TV series, short, video game, or commercial you will need to visualize what the world of your story looks like. Try to create a "look" or "style" that suits your story and your potential audience. If you are making a children's television series aimed at the kindergarten demographic than a realistic style may not be the best choice. Children seem to respond more to the cartoonier, or more caricatured approach to design and color. Although with video games, especially first-person play games, where the game play is meant to be as immersive as possible, realism tends to be preferred. The style of your project should be a matter of your own personal taste, your vision for the material and what you feel will help it to be the most marketable for your chosen audience.

In my earlier days working at Disney, we used to find an artist we liked and use their work as a sort of "style guide" for the feature. For *The Hunchback of Notre Dame* it was Ronald Searle, *Aladdin* it was Al Hirschfeld, *Hercules* it was Gerald Scarfe, and *Pocahontas* it was N.C. Wyeth. Some of those artists' influence on the film are obvious and others not so much, but the idea was to try and fashion the design in a direction to make each film as unique as possible while utilizing pretty much the same artistic staff. Even on other Disney films, we tried to find an in-house artist that became the production pesigner or guide for the style. On *Mulan* we had two – Hans Bacher was hired as the overall production designer who created the look of the locations and color styling, and Chen Yi Chang was the talented young designer that became our character design lead. It was the combination of these two strong artistic visions that made Disney's *Mulan* "look" unique and consistent. The animated films from the past that did not have an overall designer to use as a guide have usually suffered for it. It becomes fairly obvious to even the most unsophisticated viewer when a film marries characters that are realistically rendered against characters rendered in a more cartoony style on the same stage. That stands out as being inconsistent and pulls the viewer from the film.

Style should be about creating a believable world that the viewer feels comfortable in and excited to explore. Consistency of design style is what holds the viewer in that world.

The other element that needs to be considered in your project's style is the location design. You want to have designers that understand the look you are envisioning for your locations and what the characters look like in front of their "stage." Ultimately, that is what you are designing, a stage for your characters to perform in. We have all seen examples of films where the characters just don't seem to "sit" into the back ground well. It just feels "uncomfortable." But what about films like Disney's *Sleeping Beauty* or *One Hundred and One Dalmatians*? Or, on the more modern side of CG animation, *The Incredibles* or *Kung Fu Panda*? All are great studies of locations and characters working together to make a fantastic world for the story to be told. Choosing carefully your art director or production designer is important to bring these elements together.

At the point that you have the script written and now some preliminary rough designs of characters and backgrounds, it is time to explore the project through storyboarding. Since the job of the board artist is to visualize the script through shot selection, cutting, and character performance, it is important to start each board artist off with a design packet consisting of rough character designs and all interior and exterior location designs for that particular sequence. Don't expect the board artist to invent designs themselves. Good board artists can and will but it is a waste of their time. The board artist should be set free to explore the script from the characters out. I have always tried to hire the very best board artists as what they do inspires the rest of production to come. Their job is to find the entertainment value of each scene, to find the core of the conflict and resolve it. As the boards are finished as drawings and approved by the director, then it is time to cut them together in editorial to create the animatic. The animatic is a key tool for story development of paramount importance on the level of the script. The animatic (sometime called *story reels*) are the individual storyboards cut together in sequence and timed out with appropriate

sound effects and dialogue in sync to them. Editorial is the department that brings all of these individual elements together in the computer to match the director's pacing ideas. I have always thought that the storyboard animatic is the animation director's best friend, for it is here that he or she gets to make the film once entirely (at least in storyboards) before production starts. This is still a relatively inexpensive process so I like to fully board the film,

The storyboard phase is key to success on an animated production.

record scratch dialogue (temporary voice recordings by non-professional actors) and add sound effects and even temporary music tracks to fill it out. Now, the project starts to show life! Working with the editor and the storyboard artists you can see the script come to life with pacing and emotion that is not possible on the written page. Your storyboard animatic becomes your blueprint for the film.

Besides the script, the animatic is also the strongest element to show to a client, investor, or executive if you need their buy-off to go into production. Beware, though! Many right-brained thinkers have a difficult time understanding how to "read" an animation storyboard or animatic. The tell-tale signs of this are comments like, "I thought it would *move* more. "or, " *That's* what you guys have been doing for three months?" or my favorite, "Very nice, but when will we see their *mouths* move?" If approvals of your animatic screening are what you need, then here are a few suggestions:

- **Add more drawings.** It's more work for your storyboard staff and your editorial team but by adding more poses of the characters you will make it look more animated with performance and acting.
- **Color your drawings.** Probably not for a whole feature (too laborious) but for important sequences that should have a feeling of added production value (an action scene or a song) you may want to add color to the drawings. This will help it look more finished. Also, adding color to drawings can help a lot if you have characters that are very similar designs in scenes together. Like multiple rats in Pixar's *Ratatouille*.
- **Record some (or all) of your final voices.** Nothing is more impressive to executives than hearing the recognizable voices of star talent. If you don't have star names, pro voice over actors are just as good. They will help boost the acting in the project.
- **Add sound effects and music.** These simple elements will add punch (literally sometimes) and emotion to bring clarity to a moment.
- **Pace the animatic a little faster than normal.** Talk to your editor about cutting the storyboards a little faster

than what you would need for animation. It may take a character four-and-a-half seconds to cross a room but that is deadly dull in an animatic so cut the travel time out for the "executive screening" and added it back in later before animation starts.

Production

Assuming you received the proper approvals on your animatic or even most of the animatic, you are now ready for production. This is the phase in the process where things start to move very quickly – and for good reason because this is the most expensive part of the production. Your team usually doubles or triples as you now employ the talents of (for CG animation) modelers, riggers, layout artists, animators, technicians, texture painters, effects animators, lighting artists, compositors and many more. These are the talented folks who will take the project from an "interesting concept" to a fully realized film.

When it comes to production, there are several options that can be chosen based on budget needs. All are valid for their own reasons and none makes the process much easier really.

First, is the *hybrid production method.* This means that the development and preproduction phases of the project are done in the States (usually) and the heavy lifting of production is done at an overseas (or at least out-of-country) production studio that is budgetarily less expensive. If you are working with an overseas production studio, then make sure your "preproduction design package" is full of all the necessary details that artists not familiar with your project would need to know to carry out your wishes. This would include, but is not limited to: storyboards, character and prop model sheets, color models of all characters, props and background keys, timing sheets (more for TV animation), and layout workbooks. Even then, plan on taking as many trips to the production studio as possible. Nothing helps the creative process more than working face to face. These days, many animated projects are being done at overseas (other than the US) studios because it's easier on the budget. There are quite a few that are strong and some that are even able to do quality feature productions. For a feature the director should plan on packing his or her bags and being on location with the crew for the 12–18 months that production is going on. If that is not possible for whatever reason, perhaps you can hire a trustworthy overseas supervisor to carry out your vision through production with the foreign studio. Still communicating constantly with that individual will be crucial. There are just too many moment-to-moment decisions to be made on the grander scale of the feature.

As of this writing, there have been some strides made for doing your animation production through the *virtual studio system*. What is a "virtual studio"? It is a studio with no real brick and mortar home office. Everything and everyone is online. From your modelers to your animators and beyond, all of your creative talent is in different states, countries or even continents. And your producer, production manager and director can log on to check dailies on his or her personal computer at home and then they can give notes and feedback either on video conference systems or written in on group forums and the like. The positive element to this is that you can find the best talent around the world to work on your project. The downfalls are numerous though: no face-to-face communication, time zone problems, no way to maintain a person's work schedule and so on. It's an odd way to make an animated project but it can work because of the technology but managing a group that is never together and in multiple time zones is a special form of madness!

To me, nothing beats the old fashioned "everyone under one roof" studio approach to animation. Whether the studio is in the States or abroad the idea of all of the creative energy being formed and contained at one location from start to finish is preferable. While the studio carries the highest overhead in this production model, it is hard to argue with the quality and creative output that this tried-and-true system of working yields. This way the director has the most control over his vision and the crew is as unified as possible.

No matter which method of production you produce your project under one thing remains the same: the stress is high during the production stage. There will be hundreds of big and little decisions to make on a daily basis for the director. It will sometimes seem that, as the director, you are just a glorified foreman on the factory floor of animation. The constant demand of the schedule and the need to get work out will be a constant pressure in your head and *compromise* will seem like the easy elixir. Resist I say, resist! There will be times in production where compromise will be the creative way to make something better but never compromise quality to just get it done. That will be the beginning of the end of your career as a director.

Postproduction

Postproduction on a fully animated film, commercial, television show, or short is limited to the final few weeks (for a short or commercial) or months (for a feature) in your project's schedule. This is often the fun part for the director. By this point, you should be done with most all

Matthew Wilder hams it up in the recording studio. He brought a great musical sense to Disney's *Mulan.*

of the scenes in your film and in postproduction you are concentrating on "sweetening" your project. If there are minor dialogue changes to make a scene funnier you can re-record it over the animation in *ADR*. If the impact in the animation doesn't quite *feel* hard enough in the visuals, then you can give it more psychological boost in the *sound effect* you choose. If the emotional mood isn't as strong as you need in a scene, you have the magic of the *score* composition to stimulate the moment. If the dialogue is not coming through over the sound effects, you have the final *sound mix* to tweak for audio clarity. If the colors are not what you approved in color models, then you have the final *color timing* to bring more contrast or saturation to your team's beautiful work. If all has gone well in production then postproduction is all about adding the icing on the cake.

In the world of a live-action visual effects film, the **entire** animation process is considered part of the postproduction.

I discovered this oddity on *Stuart Little 2* when I was told by a pompous live-action producer that the three months spent on the live action set shooting the *real* actors was considered *production* and the 10 months of hard work that I was supervising was the back-end of the film or postproduction. The attitude was that the "effect" of adding Stuart Little and the other CG characters were on the same scale as adding the sound effects. This on a film where the **main character** was animated!

Stuart Little 2 © 2002 Columbia Pictures Industries, Inc. All Rights Reserved. Courtesy of Columbia Pictures

Entire books have been written about the process of making an animated film that I just breezed through above. My intention is to outline the major steps in the process so that as you grow into the role of director it will not be a surprise. Know the process. Love the process. Work within the process or it will be your doom. Knowing when you have to make a change within the production process will help you in your decisions. Why get upset about a temporary sound effect in your reel when you have months to make it perfect in postproduction? Worry about perfecting the production stage that is in front of you. Understand the process to anticipate the next stage and prepare for it. If you know animation is gearing up soon, then you should be sure you are happy with the props that will be in those forthcoming scenes. If you are moving into scoring, then make sure you have thought through where you want your cues to begin and end. Success is a matter of preparation and planning. Make the schedule and the process your friend!

interview: nick park

Nick Park is one of the true pioneers and leaders of stop-motion animation working today. His signature characters, Wallace and Gromit, are known and beloved around the world. Born in Preston in Lancashire, England, Nick Park started making his own movies from a very young age, eventually attending Sheffield Polytechnic to study Communication Arts and then National Film and Television School where he started making his first Wallace and Gromit film, *A Grand Day Out*. It was while still working on that film that he was hired to work at Aardman Animations in 1985, where he continued to work on the film, finishing it in 1989 the same year that he created another film, *Creature Comforts*, which would give him his first Oscar. Two more Academy Awards would follow, for his next two Wallace and Gromit shorts in 1993 and 1995, and then he and Peter Lord directed Aardman's first feature

Wallace & Gromit – A Grand Day Out
© NFTS 1989

film, *Chicken Run*, in 2000. Since then, Nick Park has directed, written and produced Wallace and Gromit's first feature, *The Curse of the Were-Rabbit*, as I was fortunate to connect with Nick via phone on a day where he was working from home and enjoying the quiet.

Tony: Nick, thank you for this time. Let's start at the beginning, how did you get your start in the animation industry?

Nick: Well, I was a young animator, as a teenager. I made my own movies at home on an 8mm camera and I always loved drawing, cartoons, and making models out of clay. I discovered that my parents had a movie camera that could do single frames, so I got going on that, and I did a few small projects. I went to art school, did a BA, honors fine arts program in filmmaking and communication arts in Sheffield, England, in the north of England, and got a degree.

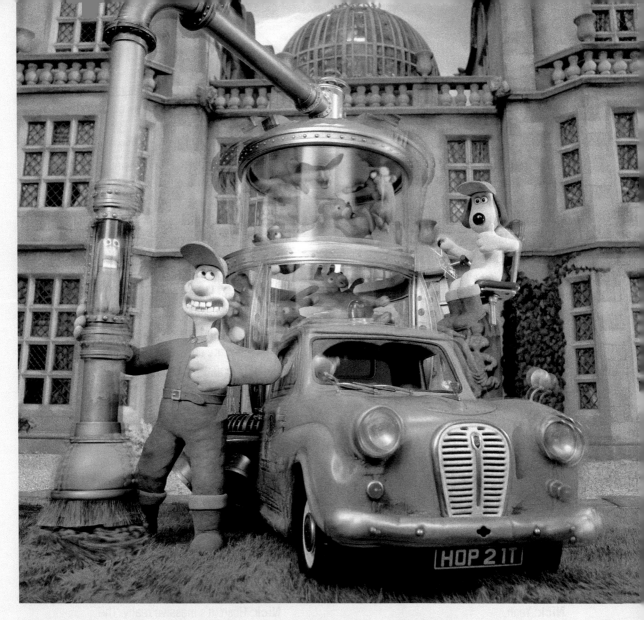

Wallace & Gromit – The Curse of the Were-Rabbit © Aaardman Animation / DreamWorks 2005

I did a series of puppet animation films, and drawn animation, using chalk on a chalkboard. Simple stuff really, playing around with sound effects, puppet animation, and clay, and then went on to the postgrad course at the National Film and Television School near London. That was a three-year course and I created the characters of Wallace and Gromit there. That was the first Wallace and Gromit movie, *A Grand Day Out*. I started it there and then I met Peter Lord and

David Sproxton, who had already started Aardman Animations a few years beforehand, and they were looking for new animators. I happened to meet them and they invited me to come and work for them at Aardman. Because I wanted to finish my film, I kept refusing, and they kept getting me as someone who worked in the summer as a student, helping out on stuff: commercials and things and kids' TV stuff they were doing. I was running out of money and time at college, so eventually they said, "Why don't you work for us part time, and we'll help you finish your college film?"

Tony: Perfect, right?

Nick: Yeah, worked out really well, but because I was working part time it took me another four years to finish the film. It took seven years altogether to do *A Grand Day Out* because they just gave me a corner of the studio where I worked on it in between commercials and things – Peter Gabriel's *Sledgehammer* video and *Pee-wee's Playhouse* and stuff like that.

Tony: And nobody else helped you with *Grand Day Out*? You just did it all yourself in the corner of the studio?

Nick: I got bits of help, but pretty much. I did probably 90 percent of it myself. Making the models, filming it . . . I had to learn from people, because I couldn't tie anyone down for very long, because it was all phases of different people, so I had to learn the camera, loading the camera, and lighting . . . I knew how to make models anyway and designed the whole thing myself. There were little sequences and bits of animation that I got friends to do.

Tony: You've worked with a lot of different materials, it sounds like, before you kind of settled on doing a lot of clay animation for your career.

Nick: Yeah.

Tony: What was it about clay that made you prefer it?

Nick: Well, I didn't really know I would settle with clay. Even at film school I was open to all kinds: from Disney right through Chuck Jones, all the Hanna-Barbera cartoons, to all kinds of Eastern European puppet animation. I was, in fact, just dabbling and doing drawn stuff till film school and then I just happened upon clay again. I did some

tests, I remember, and I just remember seeing people's response to it. It was so amazing that I could get that kind of expression out of a piece of clay, and I always remember my dad reacting to my home movies as well, and saying what pathos there was in it. So I thought that's where I could express myself better, that's all.

Tony: What do you like most about working in animation?

Nick: Most? I think I just love the whole thing of being able to think up ideas, and then the satisfaction of seeing them on screen and seeing the audience's pleasure at seeing them, and making people laugh I guess. Telling stories, hopefully that are compelling, and making people laugh, and, yeah, the satisfaction of them seeing that. It's the in-between bit that's the difficult thing.

Tony: So it sounds like you're an entertainer, deep down.

Nick: Yeah. I think I do love entertaining, and I feel so grateful that I've found a way, a channel, through which to do that.

Tony: That's great. I know a lot of people ask me, as an animation director, "What does an animation director do? How do you direct animation?" So, what are your day-to-day responsibilities as a director there at Aardman?

Nick: Gosh. It's massive really. The responsibilities are big, and I'm not really that good at delegating. I do work with a great team of people, but in the puppet clay-animation world, because of time and budget restraints you're often filming many scenes at the same time, and so you have different animators on different scenes, and each has a set ranging in size from a dining room table to a whole living room or something, so we have to

> It was so amazing that I could get that kind of expression out of a piece of clay

have all these different units all cordoned off so the light doesn't spill from one unit to another. So because of that we need to have a studio the size of a couple of football fields and we have almost a village, or a town of different sets. It's like a metropolis, or a labyrinth, really, of different sets . . . Each animator will be shooting two or three seconds a day, and we'll have like 25 animators; when we're at maximum speed, we'll have about twenty-five animators each doing two or three seconds a day on different units, and so you see the dailies from the day before, and now with digital you can see the shots as they come in. As they're finished we have a pipeline that takes all the shots up to the edit suite and so you spend your day looking at people's shots, and deciding if you like it, and if you don't like it you re-brief them to do that kind of thing, to adjust something, or you have to set up a new shot. And getting around, since the floor is massive, I probably walk miles every day.

Tony: That's good. That's good exercise for an animator.

Nick: I did actually buy one of those little pedometers one day, and I think I clocked up about a mile or two in one day [laughter]. It was from just walking around, talking to people, and spending time with each animator. I've heard of other directors who don't spend so much time on the floor; they just spend their time in the edit room looking at the shots and then talking to the animators, and directing from there. I like to get down on the floor because I like to look through the camera and manipulate the camera and find the best angle. I find that I get it done quicker myself, finding the right lens, and all that kind of thing . . . And then you need time with the animator just talking through what the action is,

> That's one of my favorite bits: seeing the shots when they work and cutting them into the film.

and then we have this video suite where we go in, and video ourselves, we act through the shot. I find that it's a really good way of conveying to the animator what I'm looking for and I don't mind. I ended up on the last film doing every shot myself.

Tony: What would you say is the best and worst part of your job as the director?

Nick: The best and the worst part . . . I think just the amount of work is the worst part. The best part though, is it's great to be in control of such a big, big thing and having worked on the script, and the storyboard, coming up with so much stuff and just seeing it come to fruition. I love working with all the different people as well: the different animators, and model makers, lighting, camera people . . . And it's the creativity. I love being in the editing room as well, just as the shots come in. That's one of my favorite bits: seeing the shots when they work and cutting them into the film.

Tony: Yeah. It's exciting, isn't it?

Nick: Yeah. I love all that, and the difficult bit is if a shot doesn't come out the way you want it there's no time to re-shoot. Because the problem with this kind of animation is that if a shot isn't really what you want, you have to start again, and sometimes it can be my fault. It's not always the animator's. Sometimes something just isn't working about the shot, and it's trying to pin down what it is, and that's why I like to, as the shots come in, work with the editor to try and make the shot work, or, maybe it works in a different place in the film. I find there's always a lot of leeway, even though you've got a locked-down story reel. I don't know if it's the same in drawn animation, but I find that there's a lot of leeway still in the edit, and you can swap shots around.

Tony: What was that transition like for you as a director, who started out doing *A Grand Day Out* all by yourself, now being in charge of a crew, and working with others?

Nick: Well, it's been gradual, really, over a number of films. After *A Grand Day Out*, I made *Creature Comforts*. I guess that was my first short with, you know, a crew, but I did do the animation myself. I had lighting and camera people, probably about eight people working on that film, and then there was me, and another animator, Steve Box, who was mainly doing the penguin. So, yeah, a crew of about 12, including all the model makers, so, it wasn't that big, but it was a learning process, really, and then the next film was 40 people.

Tony: And then *Chicken Run* must have been one of the bigger ones for you?

Nick: I think what happened, I remember on *A Close Shave*, [which was the third of the short films], things became exponentially much,

Chicken Run © DreamWorks LLC. Aardman Features/ Pathe Image 2000

much bigger, like 40 people suddenly. I had to learn to respond honestly, and tactfully, and learn that people actually wanted to help me. I had to learn that because I come from a culture where animation isn't much of an industry really, you know. It's always been a cottage industry in Britain, and especially puppet animation is always a cottage industry everywhere it seems, and so we've tried to industrialize the process, at the same time as keeping the auteur, you know, the individuality as if it's made by one person, and sometimes I've felt that it's becoming out of control, and that's been less satisfying. I've worked with some great artists, but I've just learned over the years that you've gotta work hard at keeping the sense of individuality, and style to a piece, and it's hard, when you're at the top of the pyramid it just makes it a lot of work, but slowly, the people that I work with have kind of learned this culture, and so I feel that things have been reined back in in a good way. I think *Chicken Run* was a big learning process for that, and then, *Curse of the Were-Rabbit*, things were becoming much more handmade again, and with a kind of fingerprint. It had chunky texture again, which we just kind of find more attractive.

Tony: Yeah. I think so too. I love that about your work, you know, that it has that hands-on, handmade feel, very singularly-crafted, which is a really cool thing.

Nick: Ah, thanks. It's hard to maintain it, you know. It doesn't always happen naturally.

Tony: What do you consider to be the most important tool in your director's toolbox?

Nick: Oh gosh, that's interesting. One thing I found really useful, especially on the last film, was that thing of acting stuff through, acting each shot through on video. That's been a useful tool, just practically-speaking in communicating with the animators. One of the biggest difficulties I find

Wallace & Gromit – A Grand Day Out © NFTS 1989

as a director is communicating what's in my head, and I work with a great team who want to know what that is and know how to interpret that. So the video is great way to go about that. I really

> **sometimes, as a director, you've gotta say, "That doesn't matter. This is what matters."**

wouldn't want people to copy what they see, but it's something I can talk about and say "That little look. That's what I want. It's important to hit that beat." It's a helpful tool for me to talk through what's important here in the story, because

animators love moving things in small amounts, and are perfectionist about what they do, so sometimes, as a director, you've gotta say, "That doesn't matter. This is what matters."

Tony: What do you start with in developing the story for one of your projects? One of the shorts, or a feature; what do you start with, in the very beginning?

Nick: Well, in the beginning, obviously having a good idea is the most important thing, and I love just doodling and keeping sketch books and I just doodle like crazy. I often come across ideas that way. I've always, apart from *A Grand Day Out* and *Creature Comforts*, worked with a writing partner on board. So many times, I'll have an idea which I've pitched a few times to people and, like many artists, I find it very useful to have someone come in who's good at structure, like story structure. I find that's very useful; having someone to bounce off, who responds well to my ideas. I'm working with Mark Burton at the moment — I worked with him on *Chicken Run*, and on *Curse of the Were-Rabbit*, and he's very responsive, and he's got a much better head for story structure than I have. I'll come up with lots of the ideas, but he'll constantly tell me honestly if it's good, and how we can fit it together and explore how we can make this the best story. But we don't write anything at first. We may write the odd treatment every now and again, but we work just pinning post cards up on the wall, just writing all the different story beats up on the wall and just jiggling them around. Mark has this phrase, "Test it to destruction," which I think is great, and the process can be very tiring but you just keep going through the story, time and time again. Mark will say, "OK, that's good. Now let's tell the story from the bad guy's point-of-view," then "Now let's tell it from this guy's point-of-view," just to see if there are any glitches . . . You know, "Why would he do that? Why would he say that?"

Tony: Now, I'm sure that you've read all the books on story structure. Do you have a preference and is there a certain book that makes you say "Oh. This one really speaks to me, and how I think about story"?

Nick: Yeah, I'm a bit of a sucker for these things. When I take the four-hour drive north to visit my folks, I listen to Robert McKee's audio books. I have his audio books and I've listened to them probably 20 times now.

Tony: Are you familiar with the book, *Save the Cat!* by Blake Snyder? That's a favorite of mine.

Nick: Yeah. I'm reading that right now and it's very accessible. It's a good checklist, it's all good stuff. I think all these things are useful tools, really, but I do kind of believe that you have to have a good idea to start with, and it has to be intuitive. But it's great to have these books to help you get thinking when your story's feeling a bit flat, or when it runs out of steam somewhere. It's great to be able to look up what might be going wrong.

Tony: Yeah, and kind of re-check it with the structure. Exactly.

Nick: Yeah, because I think that all these problems all come down to structure. I also like Laurie Hutzler, as well. Have you come across her?

> I listen to Robert McKee's audio books. I have his audio books and I've listened to them probably 20 times now.

Tony: No, what books has she written?

Nick: I'm not sure if she has any books out. She does talks. She's from California and she goes around lecturing. She goes around Europe as well. She doesn't so much talk about structure, but just character, and how stories have to come from character. [Author's note: More information about Laurie Hutzler and her seminars can be found at her website: http://www.etbscreenwriting.com].

Tony: Speaking of which, how do you develop engaging characters?

Nick: Yeah. I wish I knew.

Tony: Well, you've done it so many times, I mean, Wallace, and Gromit are prime examples of engaging characters.

Nick: Ah, thanks. I mean, it's just one of those things. It's nice that things have worked but I always kind of think, "Gosh. What did I do? What did we do? How did we do it?" It's like starting afresh each time. In a way, I'm kind of learning the theory about story structure and character and all that after the fact. I've been working with writers, working by intuition, really, and, and then you realize afterwards, "Oh, yeah. I've done exactly what it says in the book."

Tony: You have good common-sense instincts then.

Nick: Yeah. It probably just comes from copying people, ripping people off. Wallace and Gromit just seemed to kind of evolve, really, and it is, like you say, it's just gut instinct, isn't it? It's been a process of having a feel for something, and thinking, "Oh, yeah. I like this dynamic," and how,

with Wallace and Gromit for example, I remember at one point, Gromit was gonna be a very extroverted dog that was always leaping around. And Wallace was saying, "Roll over. Play dead," and Gromit had a voice as well . . . But it was on the very first day of animating Gromit, I did a shot where Gromit was looking a bit, well, pissed off, that he was having to support Wallace, and he was underneath a plank acting like a trestle, you know, holding up a plank while Wallace sawed through it, and I couldn't really access him very well [physically], and so I just moved his eyebrow instead of his mouth. And just like that I found, it was like magic, really, that suddenly that was

Wallace & Gromit – The Curse of the Were-Rabbit © Aaardman Animation / DreamWorks 2005

his character. He expressed exactly what I wanted just by moving his eyebrow, you know, looking a bit peeved. And suddenly he was introverted, intelligent, and full of feeling, and he was much more human than Wallace actually. Everyone I showed it to related to him. So suddenly I found he became more the human than Wallace, if you know what I mean. It was like a role reversal.

Tony: They're just a classic comedic duo. I fell in love with Wallace and Gromit early on. I've always been a huge fan.

Nick: Oh, well thank you. That's very nice.

Tony: It's rare that a director, an artist, an animator, will have the opportunity, through time, to develop two characters as fully as you have with Wallace and Gromit. Has that been enjoyable for you to revisit them so many times over the years?

Nick: Yes, it's nice to have characters, actually, that are already established, and, in fact, I could just keep doing them, really. I could keep making Wallace and Gromit films till the cows come home.

Tony: You certainly have an audience for them, and I think we'd all love to keep seeing them.

Nick: Yeah. The problem is that I have other ideas. But, I mean, I have another movie idea for them, which unfortunately has to wait, but I do expect to come back to them. It's nice to have that kind of dynamic — it's like an old married couple, really. There's like a love/hate relationship, more love, I think, than hate, but, yeah.

Tony: Well, going back to the story process a little bit . . . How important is the animatic to you?

Nick: Yeah, really useful, actually. I just used to do storyboards, until we worked with DreamWorks, and we learned all about doing the story reel. We used to do animatics for commercials, but that was more to show clients and stuff so, when we came to do feature length films, that was a really great way of seeing the shape of it all before you start filming. That obviously saves a lot of time and money in terms of re-shooting, so you can see how it works, or doesn't work. The animatic is great for that. I think it can have a downside to it as well though, in that you work so hard on making the animatic work, the story reel work, and you have to show it to the studio, or to the executives, and so you color it all in, and you've got more and more sound, and more and more music, and it almost becomes a finished film . . . But it's nothing like the finished film, and almost can be misleading, so I think it has to stay useful for the director, and for the team. Another useful thing in the toolbox, I think, is having a good storyboard. That's always been useful as well. I love to storyboard because it shows everybody everything that you're intending. It shows, not just the edit, but the sets, and what's needed, what the look is gonna be, what the feel of its gonna be, what the

> **I see the story reel as a part of the writing, really.**

comedy is gonna be . . . It shows you what props to make, what characters are gonna wear. It's a good guide for everybody. I see the story reel as a part of the writing, really. The writing continues way into the story reel, and even while filming we're kind of re-cutting scenes and re-writing the script and re-recording dialogue and stuff, because it's like a template, really, for the movie.

Tony: Working with animators is one of the next steps in the process, how do you issue or hand-off a scene to an animator?

Nick: Well, it kind of overlaps as well with character development, and designing characters, and building into the character . . . What it's going to be made of, how does that character have to behave, what's going to be demanded of that character, how much does their clothing have to stretch and what are they going to be made out of? We get animators working very early on, testing, how do their mouths move? How extreme do we have to make replacement mouths? We start testing early-on, and so it gets the animators kind of owning the characters, really, and getting used to them and seeing who's best at what. A lot of that is you can tell if an animator likes a character, and I think that speaks volumes in terms of who should be doing what. If an animator has a love of that character, they'll have this burning ambition to make that really fly.

Tony: This must be where videotaping yourself for performance comes in handy to share with the animator, is that right?

Nick: Yeah, it does – absolutely. Sometimes in the past, we've had acting coaches come in, and talk about acting to the animators, and there's a guy, he's a mime artist. He's come in a couple of times, and he talks about mime, and we all have to do all kinds of acting exercises like actors do at school, kind of thing, and that's always great fun. We act through various scenes, we talk about, whether a character is pushed, or pulled, or what motivates them. How they walk, whether they walk being pulled by the hips, or by the shoulders, or whatever. There's all sorts of stuff. Then when it comes to the actual shot, I think you wanna help the animator understand the scene, and the, the whole movie really. We watch the reel and talk through it, just so that everybody gets on the same page and up-to-speed until you're thinking and breathing that character. But because of scheduling, people have to swap from one character to another as well. You can't just have one. It never works out practically just to have one animator on one character, and there are some animators that won't take certain characters.

Tony: What do you look for in a creative team? When you're, just starting on the film, and you're picking an art director, or an editor, a storyboard artist, an animator, what do you look for in those key hires?

Nick: Well, a lot of the team I've worked with from the early days, and they know what I like. For example, if it's a Wallace and Gromit film we've kind of developed the whole look together. On the art direction team, for example, there are certain people I've worked with and animators too: people who get the humor, which is important, and people who kind of understand the style and the level of cartoony-ness; the level of reality that we're working with. The level of realism versus level of cartoony-ness. So we would kind of look at people's work, and audition people, almost. A lot of people have grown up with the style, so they know it already and that takes a lot of the work out of it – teaching the style, how chunky stuff should be, all the furniture and props, etc. It's great to have those people on the team – you don't have to say much to them because they just know.

Tony: Do you have different department heads, people who lead different teams? If so, how much responsibility do you give them on one of your films?

Nick: I'm guilty of not being very good at delegating, because I like to be very hands-on. I don't do the animation myself, but, I micro-manage things. I care for exactly how a character moves, and how everything looks. But there are big areas where people, from having worked with me on other films, they already get what I want. I have to make a few comments, but they kind of run with it. I do a lot of sketching to show people what I want. But if there's, say, a whole room full of props to build, we may look at books and reference material, but they'll kind of run with it, really, knowing how much chunkiness they have to give everything or whatever else. I like to work on storyboards too and I have a very good team for that. Peter Lord always used to say "It's best to work with people who are better than you are at things."

Tony: I like that motto. That's a motto I follow too. I was always trying to find people that would do a better job than I would at things. It makes life easier.

Nick: Yeah. Absolutely.

Tony: Now, you're kind of on the management side in a lot of ways at Aardman, right? So how do you combat the, "Us vs. Them," attitude that can arise between production, management and your creative crew?

Nick: I try to stay out of the managing, really. Well, I do stay out. I'm not really a manager of the company. I'm a director of the company and the managers have a management team that run the company.

Tony: But even as a director you must have some responsibilities to the production side, getting the film done, staying on budget, right?

Nick: Yeah, I do, but again, I just try to stay on the creative side, and you've always got to pay attention to budget. You always seem to be trying to cut corners no matter what you do, no matter how much of a budget there is, you're always fighting to cut corners, and get things done more quickly, and more economically. I work with good producers. I think it's important to work with a producer who's sympathetic, that you're not at odds with. Who has respect for what you need creatively, and to make a great film.

Tony: Speaking of the producer role, as a director, do you have to interact with a producer, or studio executive on a daily, or continual basis, and what is that relationship like for you?

Nick: We worked with DreamWorks for a few years, and now we're working with Sony, and it's always been very respectful I would say. The relationship has always had a kind of mutual respect, and all of our objectives have been the same: To create something that we are all proud of. So I haven't really had any clashes like that, creatively speaking.

> **Peter Lord always used to say "It's best to work with people who are better than you are at things."**

Tony: Well, that's good to hear that it's been a positive relationship. You said you work with good producers; have you worked consistently with a particular producer over the years?

Nick: Well, no, different ones who have changed from film to film. There have been ones that have stayed on a couple of films, but I'm not tied to one. It's all about them accommodating what I need, and understanding that we're trying to make is a great film. So the work comes first, really.

Tony: Do you find it difficult, especially with animation being such a slow laborious process, to be true to your original vision for the project as time goes by?

Nick: I think being true to your vision is very important. What motivates me, really, is having a vision for a film that demands to be made. I find it quite difficult to work on something if it doesn't kind of grab me by the scruff of the neck and demand to be made. I couldn't do something that I had a passing interest in, or mild interest. It's always an obsession.

Tony: Well, is there anything that you do to keep that original flame of the idea burning so it doesn't burn out?

Nick: Yeah. I think I have to find it funny and I think working with people is important for me. What's great about working at Aardman, is that I've got colleagues and I've got people to keep me on track. Like a producer or a co-director who can be a sounding board. Someone who can share the laughter but also help carry the burden of it, really. That's been important so far. I think also someone to question you in a healthy way when you are losing the vision, or when you're kind of going off track a bit and losing the plot, so to speak.

Tony: On the subject of budgets, and schedules. We all know that they're part of the life of a filmmaker. Do you see them as friend, or foe?

Nick: Well, when I took seven years to make *A Grand Day Out*, that was torture, in way, because I would have loved to have someone come in, and say, "No, you're taking too much time. You should have help, you know." I think there's nothing wrong with discipline or being held accountable: Can you afford this? Does this help with the story? Do you need this scene? That's all important stuff, and it's a discipline that comes not just from the budget and the schedule but it's the making

> **What motivates me, really, is having a vision for a film that demands to be made.**

> **I couldn't do something that I had a passing interest in, or mild interest. It's always an obsession.**

a great story, as well. The discipline of telling a story, and I think there's nothing wrong with restrictions. That's been a big lesson for me, over the years, and as I described earlier, just moving Gromit's eyebrow brought about his character. It was an economic decision that brought about his character, because creative things come out of economy, I think.

Tony: When I directed at Disney, meetings were a big part of our day. It felt like, "Are we really making a movie or are we just having a meeting about a meeting?" In your experience, do you find that meetings help make the film, or do they distract from the creative process?

Nick: Yeah. I try to stay out of as many meetings as I can, generally, at Aardman. If you can send somebody else to the meeting, to report back, I like that best. It depends what the meeting is, obviously. There are vital ones where you, the director *has* to be there to express himself and to guide things, but you can get too much into meetings and, as you said, "We'll have to have a meeting to discuss the next meeting." It can get ridiculous . . .

Tony: How important is it to you to keep up with current technology, new software, new tools, as a filmmaker?

Nick: I think we've just always been moving with the technology, really. We're not known for CG stuff, but we've been doing it for years on commercials and we're putting out our second CG feature film soon [author's note: This interview was recorded before the release of Aardman's *Arthur Christmas*]. But even in our clay films, we use and embrace the digital technology very much. It's like any movie: We'll add effects, we shoot a lot against green screen because it saves studio space, as we may not have the room . . . That's one of our biggest problems with model animation, is studio space. With the amount of sets we're filming, you'll often try to force perspective and stuff, but sometimes it's just better to shoot the background separately. And now it's so easy to match everything up afterwards in postproduction. Plus, theres lots of practical reasons, like we'll try to hide wires, and that's so much easier now: we used to spend ages trying to hide wires. Now we can just, you know, concentrate on the animation, and hide all the rigging afterwards . . . I remember *Wrong Trousers* had like seven effects shots in it, whereas the last short, *A Matter of Loaf and Death* had almost every shot, five-hundred shots or something, had some effects: flour dust, fire, or some other effect . . .

Tony: Are there other animation directors out there in the industry that you admire, that has affected your work?

Nick: Yeah, there are. I think because puppet animation has similar lighting problems, but I've always been as much a fan of live action movies as animation, really, so, that's why I've gone a kind of *film noir* route sometimes. That Hitchcock kind of feel, because I've always loved Hitchcock. I watch everything, really. Anything and everything. I love what Pixar is doing, with different directors there, and I know a few of the guys there . . . I've always loved their work. And others like Henry Selick. And, of course, I've always been a fan of Ray Harryhausen.

Tony: Any last words for young artists that want to direct animation?

Nick: Gosh. Yeah I think that if you've got a burning desire and a hunger, that's the main thing: A hunger to direct, and to see your vision out there on the screen. It's a horribly vulnerable thing to do but if you have the desire and the hunger to do it, that will overcome the fear. I think that's half of it: if you've got this burning need to do that, well that's half the problem over, really.

Tony: Well, I really appreciate all of the time you've given me, Nick. You've been very generous. Thank you.

3

STORY, STORY, STORY!

Warren Remedy started out his young life with great potential but far from the champion that he would later become. He was the offspring of parents that gave him great genes, an athlete's physic but he was also small. In fact, he was the runt in his family. Remedy grew up in the early 1900s when being a "little guy" made things difficult in life. Everyone thought that he would never be anything in life. What would be the disciplined regiment that would take him from an average contestant to the three-time winner of one of the most prestigious competitions in the world? Well, certainly long hours of training, a proper diet and good instruction, but most importantly, a milk bone twice daily. You see, Warren Remedy was a Smooth-Coated Fox Terrier and the only three-times winner of the Best In Show award at the prestigious **Westminster Kennel Club Dog Show**. Like Warren Remedy our story concepts may start out as "runt dogs" but can be groomed into big winners if you can see the potential in them and work hard. Yes, you have to have a good initial idea to build on but many films, commercials, video games, and shorts have had more than that and still failed. So, what if you had a good concept and a lot of cool visuals and special effects? Surely, that is the key to financial success these days. No, we have all seen films that have had those two ingredients and still failed miserably. The key, the one and only thing that matters is . . . story. Great visuals can enhance a good story but no amount of visual wizardry can save a bad story.

One of the great things about being a director as a life choice is that it can never be mastered. Every story is its own kind of expedition, with its own set of challenges.

– Ron Howard

The Director as Storyteller

Many animation directors of features and shorts started their careers as animators or storyboard artists. While the

My partner in all things *Mulan,* Barry Cook.

storyboard artist has the clear advantage of many years training in the art of storytelling, the animator, often times, is lacking in the time put into the study of story. Yet both paths have proven themselves successful in becoming a promising director. Having started my career as an animator myself, story was like climbing a mountain to me. I knew how to think about my character and what he needed to do in any given scene but thinking about the overarching story was something I hadn't trained in much. Then came Disney's *Mulan.* When I was taped to direct (along side of Barry Cook) on Disney's 36th animated feature I was a young animator who had never directed. I was scared to death of the opportunity but nothing scared me more than the thought of seating in a storyboard pitch session while artists waited for my spark of brilliance that would come out in the form of my helpful critiques of their work. How could I be additive to story process when I knew so little about story structure? What I soon learned is that we all have opinions on storytelling. We all have some core understanding of story that is a part of us. It is a universal truth that goes back to the beginning of time. Stories are part of every known culture around the world. We as a people connect through stories. We relate to stories about characters that are like us or someone we know. Our story opinions are based on how we were raised morally (right and wrong), our life experiences, the people we have met and the stories we have heard in our youth – the whole of our life journey. We are all good judges of story because no one knows better than us what is appealing to us. That's why I can look at a storyboarded sequence from a project and have an opinion on whether it moves me, propels the story I want to hear or has a desired emotional impact. These are all subjective things based on good common sense and life experience. The simple truth is a blue-collar familyman off the street probably has a more valid opinion on an animated feature than a highly paid studio executive.

He probably would connect with what is funny, dynamic, emotional and appealing to a mass audience more than an highly educated, overly privileged executive. Why? His simply stated comments on the story would be a product of his life experiences and, because he represents "the common man," much more related to those opinions shared by the universal audience most commercial movies are made for.

Now, that is not to say that I am saying studio executives don't have good and worthy comments and help to improve the stories we tell as directors. Many do. My example is to illustrate the basic fact that we all have some core understanding of story that is a part of us and therefore our opinions matter. This is the simple rule of directing that I had to not only accept but grab a hold of with two hands: **my opinions matter**! Not only do they matter but they are the opinions and judgments driving the product your crew is working on. Claim it and accept it!

What comes next as you journey down the corridors of story knowledge is a richer understanding of character, story structure, and emotional pay-off. This growth is essential to success as a director. You don't have to be so strong in story structure and dialogue writing that you write your own scripts (although that is a good thing to aspire to). In fact, many directors from live action and animation don't write one word of the script for films they direct. But a good director still needs to understand story structure entirely so that they can communicate their story in endless detail to those that will write the script (or executives wondering what it is they are spending money on). That means the director must judge for himself if the script has the elements needed and written in an appealing and emotional way with visually dynamic scenes to resound with an audience as a successful film. That's all. Sounds simple right?

What is Story Structure and Where Do I Get Me Some?

Story *structure, form or pattern,* whatever you prefer to call it, the way a story is put together is the basics of

The recipe for story structure

creating a strong story. It is also given the negative label by many critics as *formula*. In the mid-1990s when I was coming up at Disney, they had what was widely regarded as a "house formula" for crafting an animated film. It was something like this:

Take one "fish out of water" hero (preferably a princess)
Place the hero in an exotic location (China, Middle East, European village, under water, etc.)
Add one love interest (attractive and opposite to the hero)
Add one dastardly villain (hell bent on stopping the hero)
Stir in a myriad of songs (the "I want song," the "big production number song," the "love song," the "villain's song," etc.)
Top with a "lesson-learned" theme ("Don't judge a book by its cover," "Love conquers all," "Be true to yourself," etc.)

And repeat and repeat and repeat until the audience moves
on.

At least, that is what many critics feel is the downfall of
the animated features from their heyday until more recent
days. A recipe for story structure is not a bad thing to follow but when the formula starts to show through because
of perpetuating it constantly and in less and less original
ways, than the audience starts to become bored. It's not a
matter of 2D versus 3D. If the audience can predict the outcome of the story by the songs being sung, then the "tried
and true" becomes cinematic poison.

Story formulas aside, true story structure dates back
to the earliest times of the three-act stage play. Quite
simply there was an Act one, Act two, and Act three (or
beginning, middle and end) to the story. This is still the
basic story structure that the screenplay writer uses in
creating a feature film. For a short time I worked with a
director that did not believe in a three-act story structure and insisted that "who is to say that there can't be
one act or 20 acts?" To me, he was just demonstrating his
lack of understanding of what the three-act structure is
and how it contains in those acts the basic elements of all
stories. Before I continue, I should point out that everything I know about story structure was learned on the
shoulders of some of the best screenwriting books in
the industry. While most of them have never created
a successful screenplay themselves, they are great
teachers of the craft. Whether it be the foundational
classics such as Robert McKee's *Story*, Syd Field's
Screenplay, Christopher Vogler's *The Writer's Journey*
or the newer no-nonsense favorites such as Brian
McDonald's *Invisible Ink* and Blake Snyder's *Save the
Cat* series, they all have their own story structure
theories that are basically the same structure para-
digm. My own simplified version of the structure is
as follows:

One way to learn how to create a strong
story. . .

Act 1

Introduction of the hero.
Set up his normal world and understand who he is in it.
Catalyst (the problem arises or the call to adventure)
Refusal (or the hero debates the logic of the call)
Hero decides to go (or do whatever he/she needs to do)

Act 2

Trials and new discoveries along the way (could include
    new allies or enemies)
The hero approaches the place (or the thing or the deed)
The ordeal (the middle of Act 2 when the hero goes through
    his ordeal, good or bad, with some negative or positive
    outcome)
The hero gets the thing (but there are repercussions . . .)
All is lost (the hero at his lowest point)

Act 3

Recovery (the hero bounces back)
Success! (the hero wins against the ordeal also known as
    "the climax")
Resolution (the hero has changed his ordinary world for the
    better or himself in some unforeseen way)

Yes, the screenplay book authors may have different wording but this is basically what all of the story structure books will tell you are the key stages in creating a successful story structure. You're welcome – I just saved you $77.53! Seriously, these tried-and-true, passed-the-test-of-time, story stages are how man tells stories. I'm not just saying that either. This is how cavemen told each other stories of beating up dinosaurs; this is how Shakespeare wrote a classic stage drama and how Lucas brought the story of *Star Wars* to the big screen. Go ahead and fight it all you want but this is how audiences are used to their stories being served up. As a director it is essential that you know these story paradigms well so you can either apply them successfully to your project or confidently change them at will. Yes, some stories have started with the **all is lost** moment in the very beginning and then rewound the story to tell how the hero got there. That can work. Some stories have started not by **introducing the hero** but the **catalyst** or the bigger problem that becomes the drive for the hero's actions. That can work too. However you create your story burrito, it is important to know the ingredients first. Story structure is the spine of your film.

A Theme that Resonates

"What's it about?" That's the common question around the water cooler on Monday morning when you say you went to see a particular movie over the weekend. The answer is usually part-plot and part-theme. "It's about a beautiful girl who discovers an ugly beast living in an enchanted castle. After learning to see past his ugliness, she falls in love with him. This breaks the magic curse on him and he changes back into a handsome prince." OK, you might not make such a concise synopsis of the movie on a moment's notice but that is the basic story of Disney's *Beauty and the Beast*, right? It's a pretty dry version without mention of the songs, the funny talking objects or villain but they don't really come into play in the simple answer of "what is it"? That's because the basic description of the story is usually just what the hero does and learns. What he "does" is the plot and what he "learns" is the theme. The theme is the "lesson learned" by the hero of the story and the audience. It gives the story a greater value to the movie-going experience and helps the audience connect with the hero. Theme is the thing that gives the story importance and universal appeal.

Recently, I was asked by Disney to do some publicity interviews for a new version of *The Lion King in 3D*, 17 years after the movie originally released. Without a doubt, the one question asked of me by almost every interviewer was, "what is it about *The Lion King* that has made it so popular all over the world for so many years?" It's not the great Elton John songs, fine animation, or beautifully painted Serengeti vistas (although those things certainly do help). It's the story. And more specifically the universal theme of the story that transcends time and language barriers. *The Lion King* is about a young cub prince coming into an understanding that he will become the next great king of the Serengeti. When his father dies unexpectedly (and thinking it's his fault) he runs away from the pride lands and joins two ragamuffins in their "Hakuna Matata" bachelor lifestyle. That is, until a girl from the kingdom discovers the now adult lion and urges him back to save his kingdom from his villainous uncle. He defeats his uncle who framed him for his father's death and resumes balance in the land by taking his rightful place as king. That's the story but it's the theme that makes people say, "I connect with that movie." People connect with a movie about a lion cub that is framed for murder? No, they connect with a story that tells us "we all have our unique purpose in life whether we like it or not." That is the theme of *The Lion King* as revealed to the audience in the first five minutes of the film in the opening song "The Circle of Life." The theme or "life lesson" is what makes the film resonate all over the world and makes it timeless. It's a universal lesson we all know and yet need to hear again and again.

From *The Lion King.* © 1994 Disney.

Be True to Your Story and It Will be True to You

There are so many moving parts in the construction of a story that it is easy to lose your way. I have worked with directors that have forgotten that a gag in the storyboards, that now seemed flat, was actually funny once. It's a good thing there are others on the team to remind you that you once liked an idea even though now it seems contrived. I myself remember my head spinning at a certain point on the film *Mulan* when we had made so many changes to the script that I could not remember if we had chosen to take the story in direction A or direction B. Thank goodness for my co-director Barry Cook whose mind remembers all those details.

There comes a point in the early days of a film's story development that things seem to lose their way. I have seen it time and time again. The key is to stop and remember what it was that you originally loved about your story. Don't lose track of this. This is the element that your audience will fall in love with also. Learn to channel your character and see the journey through their eyes. **Don't have the characters do what you, yourself would do in a given situation, but instead what is best for them and their story.** Soon the solution will present itself. The path will become clear again.

This will sound farfetched but when my partner and I were directing *Mulan* there came a point when we realized the story was "telling" us what it needed. Of course this was a visceral feeling that would occur when we were imposing our own desires upon it but it was real none the less. For example, there is a scene in the film when Mushu first introduces himself to Mulan. Mushu needs to sell himself to Mulan that he is her magical and powerful family guardian and without his help she would no doubt dishonor her ancestors, disgrace her father and get herself killed. Since the movie was designed to be a musical we, logically, thought this would be the perfect point for a Mushu song. And of course, not just any song, but a big production number that was part *Aladdin's* "Friend Like Me" and

a rhythm and blues James Brown number. And why not? Since Mushu was designed to be a dramatic (and humorous) contrast to Mulan's more reverential Chinese world, Barry and I felt justified in bringing this big number to life. It'll be fun, right? Were we wrong! The very first time we screened the film with the fully storyboarded Mushu song in place we felt it. The moment the song came on the screen it was like fingernails being scratched on a chalk board; it was so piercingly obvious that it did not belong. It wasn't the right tone for the film and it was too big a moment for the scene.

Be a Funnel for Good Ideas and a Filter for the Bad Ones

The bigger the project the more people on it and, therefore, the more inputs you have to deal with. Even the best good-intentioned comments from the crew could spin the story in the wrong direction if taken as given. At any one time all of the creative team (from producer to directors to story team) if left to their own devices would have killed what made *Mulan* special. Not on purpose mind you, but nonetheless the result would have been the same. No one has the right idea at the right time all the time. The director's job is to listen and take in all of the creative inputs from his or her team and then sift through them with his or her own story filter firmly in place. What comes out should be sharpened by the team's inputs but still true to what his or her vision is for the story. This process can be a daunting one for any first-time director and I know it was for me. Early on in my directing on *Mulan,* I heard a quote by Frank Capra that helped me a lot. His golden rule for success as a director was, "Hire the best people possible and then get out of their way and let them do their jobs." I don't think Capra was saying for the director to give over the creative reins to the group and camp out in his office playing Tetris all day. No, the troops still need a captain or chaos would ensue. What I think Capra was instructing was to let people excel at what they are good at within your vision of the film. Don't micro-manage the team.

Mulan's directors (me and Barry Cook) flank our producer, Pam Coats.

Change It and Change It Again

As I mentioned in a previous chapter, it is far less expensive and time consuming to make changes in the story development phase than later in production. So, change it all you want. Change it regularly to make sure you have a good idea. Test the concept out on friends or strangers at the mall then change it some more. They say change is good; well it's also really tough too. Our natural inclination is to try and lock down the story quickly and just work hard on polishing it. But polishing a stinky brown turd isn't going to make it any less of a turd. Make sure that the concept, the character arcs, the theme and all of the story structure elements are worked out before moving on-even to the script stage. This is a bit old-school, but the best thing to do is to get a stack of index cards and scribble out ideas for your story structure and characters. If you don't like a scene or idea you can just toss it in the trash and get a new index card. They can be pinned up on a wall and reordered at will. Once your elements are solid then proceed to the script phase.

There is No Such Thing as a Crystal Ball

One of the toughest things about developing your story is being able to predict if it's going to resonate with your audience. Will anyone like it? Will it be successful? No one knows for sure. I think I'm as good as anyone at making weekend box office forecasts but I have had a few bone-headed predictions too. I remember seeing advertisements for a new Pixar film called *Finding Nemo* thinking, "a film about a lost fish? Who's going to relate to a fish? It's going to bomb!" I was way off! My own rule of thumb for judging if something will become successful has developed over the years. Now I generally think, "if I like it but it is way too different then anything out there" than it has a chance to be something special. That's how it was for *The Lion King*. Disney had little faith in this story about a lion cub trying to fill his father's kingly shoes. After all, it had a parent dying in the first 20 minutes. As if that weren't taboo enough, it had elements of Shakespeare wrapped up with the Three Stooges. Oh yeah, and the guy who wrote "Bennie and the Jets"

Will my story bomb?

was doing the music. Even as I was working on animating Pumbaa I wondered the same thing. I knew I liked the story and the character I was working on but who could have predicted what would come next? Our "little film that could" broke every box office record the year it released in 1994 and is still considered to be the biggest success in animation history when considering the Broadway show, numerous video releases (including VHS, DVD, Blu-Ray, 3D and video sequels), licensing products and so on.

What is the secret to story success? No one truly knows. One suggestion: start with something that resonates with you and groom it into something unique. Warren Remedy would be proud.

From *The Lion King.* © 1998 Disney.

interview: dean deBlois

Canadian born animation director Dean DeBlois is best known for co-writing and co-directing (with Chris Sanders) Disney's *Lilo and Stitch* and DreamWorks Animation's *How to Train Your Dragon*. Both highly acclaimed films earning nominations for Best Animated Feature from the Academy of Arts and Sciences. Before, his work in directing and writing, DeBlois started his career as a layout artist and then storyboard artist at Disney Feature Animation. It was at Disney that I was fortunate enough that our paths crossed while I was directing *Mulan*. When the production first hired DeBlois it was as a junior layout artist but because of scheduling and creative changes we needed more help in the story department. Knowing that DeBlois wanted an opportunity to move into storyboarding, the producer of the film, Pam Coats asked DeBlois if he wanted to make the temporary change into the story department. DeBlois happily agreed. His storyboard work was so impactful that, not only did he remain in story, but Coats awarded DeBlois the title of co-head of story by the end of the film. In all my experience in the animation industry I have never witnessed another storyboard artist with such a grasp on layout, character and story structure. I had the opportunity to sit down with Dean DeBlois and record the following interview at DreamWorks Animation while he was in the middle of writing the script for his solo-directing premiere, *How to Train Your Dragon 2*.

Tony: Dean, how did you get into the animation industry?

Dean: I actually wanted to be a comic book artist. I learned to draw by looking at comic books and following them all through my childhood and adolescence. I loved to write and was very much

nurtured to develop that ability by my high school teachers. Writing short stories and I also loved to draw and it came very easily to me. I learned about anatomy, and staging . . . it all came from comic books, and in particular the *Savage Stone of Conan* and Ernie Chan was one of my favorite illustrators. If I could have pictured my dream career at 16 or 17, heading toward the end of high school, it was to work for Marvel or DC.

From *Lilo and Stitch*. © 2002 Disney.

How to Train Your Dragon © 2010 DreamWorks Animation LLC, used with permission of DreamWorks Animation LLC.

The other thing is that when I graduated from high school, in my small town in Quebec, there was no clear avenue to that goal. So, I started looking around at what I could do with drawing ability and the desire to write and create worlds. All I could turn up was architecture or graphic design. I was poking around and pulled up this animation course with Sheridan College which is right outside of Toronto. But Hollywood was just such a lofty dream and it was such a far away prospect that I never entertained it as a goal, even though I loved movies growing up. *Star Wars* was a huge impact on me and the way movies ignite your imagination. So, now here in animation I have the opportunity to create worlds, draw characters. I could lay them out in stories as I saw fit, with interesting staging. Animation had all of those things — but, unlike comic books I could breathe life into it as well. So I stuck with it. Then I got hired out of Sheridan my third year by Don Bluth Studios. It worked out

great so that I never had any loans. I grew up kind of poor so there was no college money to be had. I was either going to figure it out or not go.

Tony: What do you like most about working in animation?

Dean: I love that animation can ignite your imagination. Like with *How to Train Your Dragon* I keep hearing from kids firsthand how much they love the movie and they play act it while they are watching the movie. They're climbing out of the back of the sofa and pretending to ride it like a dragon. That right there is going to impact them and inspire them and those who have that creative gene are going to want to follow that inspiration and create their own things. So it really is a chain effect and I love being a part of that. The great irony in all of this, or the circular nature of

> **I love that animation can ignite your imagination.**

this, is that a relatively poor kid from a tiny town in Quebec, Canada, playing with this figures from George Lucas' Star Wars, inspired me as an eight year old to be a part of that world. Cut to all this time later and I had a meeting with George Lucas. There he was, sitting across from me, saying that he wanted me to be a part of a project that he was embarking on. I was sitting in the office where Star Wars was built. It's amazing how daunting and far away that goal can seem when you're young but when you start to identify it and focus on it, it becomes reality – slowly.

Tony: What were some of the steps you took to become a director?

Dean: Well, everyone always has a different answer for this, which is always interesting and kind of frustrating to me when I was starting out. But I think that you need to look at what's available to you and create your strategy. Because I could draw and because I had an aptitude for animation, I saw that as an avenue toward film-making and creating worlds and stories. But I wasn't getting there as an Assistant Animator. So I had to change a little bit. No one would hire a storyboard artist without any kind of training or internship, so I got a little closer because I started doing layouts and would find myself working with the story department a little bit more. Eventually I was given a shot on your movie [Disney's Mulan] to storyboard, when I hadn't really been given that opportunity before. I was hired as a layout artist for Mulan but when I arrived at the studio there were only about 20 people on the crew and they were nowhere near ready to start layout. So Pam Coats said, "Well, you want to do story so why don't you just give it a shot since

> So Pam Coats said, "Well, you want to do story so why don't you just give it a shot since you're here. What have you got to lose?"

you're here. What have you got to lose?" And that is honestly how I got on the story crew for Mulan. In fact, a couple weeks into it after I'd done my first scene, and everybody liked that sequence, Pam pulled me aside and said, "Pocahontas needs more layout guys and they've asked if they can take you on while Mulan is getting ready for you. I know that you love doing this and I know that we like your work so far, so I'm going to give you the opportunity to make that decision." I said, "Well, if you're asking me, I want to stay in story!" So that's what led to eventually taking over the story department and being co-Head of Story with Chris Sanders and that led to my being considered for directing. It's certainly not like, "Here's what you want to do step by step." A certain amount of it is luck but you need to be prepared as well, and be opportunistic when it happens-in the best sense. When the opportunity comes you need to show your stuff to those people who will listen and let it be known what you want to do.

Tony: How do you answer the common question, "what does a director do on an animated film?"

Dean: Yeah, I get that all the time, especially when the parents ask. My answer is now that it's pretty much the same as what a live-action Director does. We do all the tasks of a live-action Director except, in some ways, in reverse and in other ways really expanded. For example, because we storyboard the script so heavily, we end up with a working model of the movie that is edited together first. Whereas in a live action movie you would go out and shoot your script as blocked through a camera and then all those shots would be filtered by the editor for a first rough cut. We do our first cut [of the film] up front because all of the money is spent on animating all those individual shots, so we want to time it right down to the frame so not to waste time or money. It gives us confidence that knowing the piece of the movie that we're working on works. It also allows everybody to be on board and say, "OK, this three-minute sequence is good to go so we can spend the millions and millions of dollars it's going to cost to create it." So, beyond that you still work with actors, you still try to get the best performance you can out of them. You then sit down with your animators who are the other half of the actor and talk about the interpretation of that line and how it fits with the overall scene and how that scene fits with the overall movie. Beyond even that it's kind of working with the artists and technicians on the movie to make sure that their work is contributing to the individual shot and that that shot is made well and that it makes sense with the other shots; that there's a through line of emotion and logic. That is really the director's job. You need to know the story so well that you know what everyone is doing and you can walk into any department and carry through that focus and clarity, and say "Yes, that's a beautiful watercolor painting except that it's not really getting across the emotion needed for this shot, for this theme." I'm not the kind of guy who's going to sit down and pull out a water color brush and show them how to paint it. Chris [Sanders] and I knew that we were going to be going into departments where we had no authority whatsoever and dealing with things that we didn't know how to do. I mean, they were the pros and we were amateurs at best.

> **This is a collaborative process, and unless you're funding your own indie feature, you have to eventually make some concessions along the way.**

Tony: What is the most difficult part of your job?

Dean: It's probably compromise. This is a collaborative process, and unless you're funding your own indie feature, you have to eventually make some concessions along the way. It's cliché to say, but you have to pick your battles. What's really important to you vs. what you can live with. Whether you're directing with someone else or not, you're always faced with "everybody wants to have some kind of ownership on the project" and there's 300–500 people working on these projects and you're being inundated with ideas and sometimes road blocks over things you feel passionately about. So it becomes a choice of how you articulate or entertain the idea that might not be the one you had in mind but also be mature enough to consider it for real. Would it help? Could I be wrong? Be big enough to step outside of yourself to see someone else's point of view. That can be tough, because sometimes you can fall in love with ideas and not everyone is in love with them.

Tony: What is the best part of your job?

Dean: At the end of the day, if you can manage to weather all that stuff and keep your crew motivated and inspired, and bring it to a finish so that all of those weekends and nights, postponed vacations and time lost from family – if it feels at the end of the day worthwhile, and you can sit down with the crew at the wrap party screening and you feel a swell of pride then you know it was worth it. You should feel proud, that you did something amazing that's going to impact people . . . it's going to "live" out there. That, for me, is the amazing part.

How to Train Your Dragon © 2010 DreamWorks Animation LLC, used with permission of DreamWorks Animation LLC.

Tony: What is the most important tool in your director's tool box?

Dean: Well, I think the most universal tool is story aptitude. I'd say if I was going to encourage any director out there beyond learning camera techniques and camera angles and the language of film, which is important, but right above that is always story. You should read books about it, you should attend seminars about it and learn as much as you can about the techniques, the craft and the art of story. That is first and foremost. Some directors just show no interest in story because they are more interested in another aspect of the filmmaking process. But, in my opinion, it's story

> **it's story first and filmmaking craft second.**

first and filmmaking craft second. Beyond that you also need to be good "in the room." Knowing how to diffuse conflicts when they arise and riding the

storm is a good quality because there can be a lot of chaos on a film set or even on any animated film production. There are inevitably blow-ups and upsets, politics, etc. The director needs to be the solid guy who people can come to and know that they'll get a straight answer and feel supported by.

Tony: What do you start with in developing the story for your project?

Dean: I start with a conversation with myself about "what do I want to see" – what's one of the most exciting thoughts come to mind that would be most entertaining? A thought kind of comes to me, whether in the shower or in a dream or going about my daily activities. Oftentimes it's just an image and I think "that's cool . . . what story could that image be a part of?" and everything extrapolates from there. When we came on to *How to Train Your Dragon*, they'd already been through three years of variations of the movie. A lot of them were based on the original book by Cressida Cowell, *How to Train Your Dragon*. That book is very whimsically written and it's got a great readership out there but it's a very simple story. When Chris Sanders first came onto it, we talked about it on the phone. He wanted to know if I was interested in joining forces on this movie. The first conversation was "Well, it's a dragon movie. There's a lot of dragon movies out there already. How do we lose that stigma?" I read the book as well and thought, you really can't have a dragon movie if you're not going to have characters crawl onto the back of one of the dragons and fly – that's the cinematic thrill of it. But we've seen that in *Aragon* and *Dragon Heart* and we had to think about what we would do differently. The first thing that came to mind was that it was a dragon that was rebuilt. It was damaged and now it's like this cobbled together fusion of organic shapes and DaVinci-like mechanisms and maybe a replaced wing or a tail and on top of that is some kid whose built it.

He's got pedals and pulleys and flying the thing. I mean, that's exciting! That sort of touched upon something Miyazaki-like for me and so going forward, now who does that character become? He needs to have those skills – maybe he's an apprentice to a blacksmith so he has access to those kinds of tools and he knows the skills. Maybe he's going to be the one to cross over the big divide in the story. The big story is that there are two warring clans and one member from each takes a chance to win but they end up forming a bond that together they can change the world. You look at it from its most simple level and try to find the big story. That's really step two. Step

> **Step one is find a cool image, something where you think, "Yeah, I'd pay to see that!"**

How to Train Your Dragon © 2010 DreamWorks Animation LLC, used with permission of DreamWorks Animation LLC

one is find a cool image, something where you think, "Yeah, I'd pay to see that!" and then go to step two, which is "what's the big universal story behind the image?" Then it comes down to something I learned from one of my teachers at Sheridan College, "if it reads as a postage stamp then it will read as a billboard." It reminds me to take a step back and ask "am I making something too complicated?" Any animator could sit down and look at a scene and say, "Yeah it's got flourishes and movements, but what's the big statement." It has to be that clear to communicate the overall story. It's the same with writing a story or acting in a movie, everything is about taking that step back and seeing if it has that punch.

Tony: How do you develop engaging characters?

Dean: My philosophy of making characters, which came from working on [Disney's] *Mulan* with you [and Barry Cook], really was this idea that there should be no purely good or purely bad characters. I think the most relatable character has flaws that we all have. That's mission number one: once you've figured out who is going to be your main players of your story, try to imbue them with lots of moments of heroism and vulnerability. Give them mistakes and make them flawed. Have them not be "right" all the time. The more they can exhibit human behavior, and stuff that we all do [cutting corners, cheating, lying] on top of wanting to do the right thing – then I think you have a winning character. The one thing that I've carried on from *Mulan* is the idea that nobody really roots for the character who puts down their environment or puts down their world

or complains about their lot in life. Everybody roots for the character who's trying; they might not have the goods to deliver but the character who's trying is always a winning character. Their effort is there even though the deck is stacked against them. When we were working on *Mulan* there was a time in the beginning when she was complaining about her lot in life; she really wasn't very likeable but the girl who we developed later, who was really trying and couldn't stand to watch someone else going to fight for her because she was afraid he wouldn't come back, that is a girl that you could get behind. In the case of *How to Train Your Dragon*, the kid who wants to be a big burly Viking, but will never be that, and just wants acceptance and will do whatever it takes to get that acceptance is a character that you can root for. He becomes the bane of the community because of it because he won't stay indoors and he's in the way and he's trying to prove himself and that's what begins the process of how he begins to transform his world.

Tony: How soon do you get into storyboarding? Is the script "locked"?

Dean: This is one of those situations where everybody works in different ways. Some directors like to have a lot of different visuals surrounding them with lots of exploratory work done because it helps them form the writing. In my case, having been a storyboard artist, and knowing what it's like to get crappy pages and then having to refresh them or re-envision them; I see the merit in really knowing what I want in the script first. I think you inspire a crew to do better work if you've done a lot of the work upfront. I push back as much as I can. I don't want a story crew until I am ready with

> **once you've figured out who is going to be your main players of your story, try to imbue them with lots of moments of heroism and vulnerability.**

How to Train Your Dragon © 2010 DreamWorks Animation LLC, used with permission of DreamWorks Animation LLC

a solid script to give them. Because then after that, everything is an embellishment and nothing is an aimless exploration of "I don't know what you want . . . is this working? . . ." How do you answer that? I don't know — because I don't know what the story is.

Tony: How important is the animatic stage to you?

Dean: I think it's very important. Having working story reels tells you everything you need to know about the movie. By that point it should feel like that's your first cut. As you go forward and step into a room with animators, you have a sense of the pace of the film already. So when they ask, "I wish I had another foot." or "can I have 18 frames on the tail of the scene?"; you can say, in the overall moment, that extra footage would ruin the energy of the scene. I think it's important to have a well-timed working story reel with the facts, type of music and everything else.

Tony: How do you "hand off" a scene to an animator?

Dean: They call it a "launch" here [at DreamWorks]. The first thing we do is gather all the animators that will be working in that sequence; we play the storyboard version and then we play the previs [previsualized] version [used for rough layout and camera movement]. Oftentimes, there is a lot of expression that is in

> **Having working story reels tells you everything you need to know about the movie.**

the storyboard version that doesn't get transferred over in the limited CG models of previs. And then we talk about it shot by shot and we talk about it as a whole. Then people can have the opportunity for questions. We talk about motivations and what we're trying to get scene by scene and how it fits into the movie. Then we'll break it down and say "OK, these three shots are going to so and so animator and here's the continuity that we're looking for here." "Play it subtle, or play it broad." "Be aware that so and so character is listening in from another room." Whatever the aspects are that the animators need to have in mind, and always at that point, we'll have the actors' voices cut in so we can talk about whatever it is we see on the little "lipstick cams" we have set up on the actors. Like, we can take a look at Gerard Butler's expressions are in this and they might be really funny and useful in this scene, etc. It's kind of a broad "Here it all is!" They have their camera movement and there's always a representative from layout there who can answer any questions about whether or not another camera angle might help them do the animation that's separate from the previous one its going to be shot in. It's a group hand off though.

Tony: I think that's a great way to do it. I know nowadays there are a lot of directors who would issue scene by scene, one animator at a time. I think there's a lot of value in doing a hand off with the whole team focusing on the overall sequence of shots.

Dean: Yeah, right. There's a weird thing that happens in animation, that I've noticed from the movies we've worked on, that I almost think comes down from the top, where they want to limit the knowledge that any one person has of what the whole movie is. I don't know if it's because they are nervous about the movie not being very good or if it's just the way they've always done it. Like, I'm always wanting

to give the voice actors, for example, the whole script and tell them "Read this, mark it up, give me your notes on it and we'll talk about it." Then maybe we'll end up doing lines differently or something like that because I want them to embody the character and to own it. And they are always like, "Oh no, no, no – we don't want to give the actors the whole script." I don't think it's because they are afraid they're going to leave it on a plane. I think it's more about that they don't want us to give them too much information. I wonder "Why? Why don't you want them to have it?" I don't really agree with that and I think it may be a lack of confidence in the material sometimes. That they don't want to discourage an actor because the story's not working fully yet. But if your overall story is working, why not let the actors in on the process because it's only going to get stronger. Another thing that we did, we tried it out on *How to Train Your Dragon*, we would bring actors into the booth together and mic them across from each other. It was great! Voice recording for animation is usually not done that way because, technically, they are always looking for that "clean recording" so they can have ultimate manipulation of the lines separately. But I love the idea of just letting the actors run a scene together and get some believable build and step on each other's lines if they need to and then animate that! Because that feels real! It's like those *Creature Comforts* segments [by Nick Park] that Aardman used to do. They always felt so funny and felt so real because they were running a mic and the person would just say whatever. More often than not you get the actors saying that they don't think they'd say the thing that's written and then tell you what

> **I love the idea of just letting the actors run a scene together and get some believable build and step on each other's lines if they need to and then animate that!**

they think they'd say as that character. Then you can tell them to go with it and try it out; you really get them trying stuff out and making it more real as opposed to what's written for them.

Tony: What do you look for from a first pass by an animator?

Dean: I really like looking at rough first passes – as rough as they want to show it because you can really get a sense of what the basic statement is. Again, if it reads as a postage stamp, it'll read as a bill board. It's a moment to have a conversation about the basics. It's harder to go back when it's finished and say that the statement isn't strong enough; subtle enough; or there's something that isn't quite believable in this movement here or in this character's posture, etc. You can have that conversation in the first pass and it's not going to require a ton of work to go back and fix it.

> **If you surround yourself with people who are better than you are, you're almost always going to be surprised by what they pull off.**

Tony: What do you look for in a creative team? Art Director? Editor? Storyboard artist? Animator?

Dean: I'm always looking for them to be better than I am at whatever they do. If you surround yourself with people who are better than you are, you're almost always going to be surprised by what they pull off. I'm looking for enthusiasm; I'm looking for people who like each other and like working with each other. Also, I look for people who believe in the story and who aren't going to try to be subversive about it or mutinous! So far that's never happened to me! There are people

From *Lilo and Stitch*. © 2002 Disney.

who are grumpy for whatever reason but they tend to be grumpy in general. I love to hear from everyone and I especially want people on the movie to have "can do" attitudes. We are moving into a whole new software module on this next Dragon movie and there are certain people that we interviewed that we're like "Oh gosh, it's going to be such a nightmare! There's going to be bugs everywhere! And that means that if you've planned for six months, you better plan for a year and a half." They were such wet blankets. I can tell in one interview if that person is just going to drag everyone down. I want the person who says, "You know, it's going to be tough, but I know we

From *Lilo and Stitch*. © 2002 Disney.

can do it and it'll be amazing when we do!" That's the first person who I want to work with.
I think if you surround yourself with people who are really optimistic and really believe in what you're doing and are also great "people" people, who can rally their team, then it goes so smoothly and you have a great team and you have a really nice experience.

Tony: How much responsibility is given to your creative department heads on one of your projects?

Dean: I'm of the opinion that the more creative control you can give your department heads, the better. They feel more invested in the movie, they feel more satisfied as artists and they feel like they are making more of a contribution. And if you've done your job well as a director, and picked people who are way better than you are in all those various departments, then it's serving you as well. You are able to be in awe of their work. I love that idea because it gives me more time to focus on the story and making sure that all those pieces are coming together well, if I can charge the responsibility to every one of those department heads and say, "You know what you're doing. You govern your team and I'll show up for approvals." I tell them to take control of their team and in turn, they'll love you for it and you'll all be happy at the end of the day with the job that you've done.

Tony: How do you combat the "Us against Them" attitude that can arise on a production between creative management and crew?

Dean: That's one of the balancing acts of a good director. You have to be the "go-between," hear people out on their frustrations and then very quickly try to deal with them. I think being forthright about it is the best way to go. Sit down with somebody who is creating trouble and tell them that they have to work things out in a better way. I think you have a much more smooth production if you have everyone respecting everyone else. I try hard not to harbor an "Us against Them" attitude by inviting everyone's critique into the room, so there is no feeling among the executives (certainly here in my experience at DreamWorks) that inhibits what we do. I tell the executives that I want them to be looking at what we're doing. I'll let the them take a look at the script at whatever point they want to see it because I believe that whatever feedback they give will either prove my argument (as a director) or prove their point in wanting changes. It's an open discussion and I like it that way. Everyone wants to make their mark on the film in the end and it makes everyone feel totally invested in the project. And that only behooves you in the end. If Jeffrey Katzenberg felt he had as much say in the creation of a movie as much as we the artists did, that's just going to make him go to bat for it in a bigger way. He's going to afford more money to make the film, he's going to set aside more money for marketing and make a bigger statement about it out there and he's going to support it better if he feels like "This is as much my movie as it is the artist's." The danger in it all, as we know, is that when you get 15 plus people in a room, you can only agree on a cliché, so you have to make sure that the result of that collaboration is agreed upon and doesn't end up becoming something that is so milky and watered down. I think decision based on by committee is dangerous. Hearing everybody out at least making them know that you've at least entertained the ideas and gone down the path of somewhat addressing it, sometimes finding different solutions than the ones they came up with, but still addressing it is a way of saying "I heard you, I respect you, I've changed it as a result of your observation" but I've also kept it in the voice of the movie with this very singular perspective.

Tony: Do you find it difficult to be true to your original vision for the project as time goes by?

Dean: That's a tough question. I think over time everyone loses perspective a little bit. It's probably why the audience testing process is a bit of a revelation. I don't like the leading ways a focus group leader tries to get a group to come down on a certain element of the story, i.e., "Tell me what confused you." "Tell me what you didn't like." "I know you liked this but what

didn't you like?" Sometimes that can be a little bit manipulative. Sometimes just hearing an audience laugh or not laugh in areas where you were expecting the opposite is pretty informative. It gives you perspective. Its work to try to hang onto the idea that you were excited about in the first place or the joke that was really funny the first time you pitched it. Or the moment that was really tearful the first time you saw it, wrote it or pitched it. All of those elements get really dulled to the senses over time.

Tony: We all know that budgets and schedules are a part of life for the filmmaker, but how do you look at them personally? Friend or Foe?

Dean: Both. I think budget restrictions force you to put the money where it counts and it can be a friend in a sense, like if you've run out of time and money, you have to make decisions that people will stick with. The more time and money that you have, it's the danger of being on the front end of a three-year production and people second guessing everything to death; there's a lot of time wasted. Whereas, when Chris [Sanders] and I were dropped into *How to Train your Dragon* with only 14 months to go before the release, and we had to rewrite the script from scratch, we had to make decisions in those first weeks that everyone had to stick with. We told the crew "You've got set resources. We can't afford to build new characters or build new sets. But what we can afford to do is alter these sets and alter these characters, and here's the story we want to tell. Are we in agreement? Are we holding hands and moving forward? No one can come into this room in three months and say that they don't get it." I really do think that having budget constraints and time constraints can really help you. I'm really a procrastinator so I don't really do any good work that's worth anything until I'm down to the wire. Then for whatever reason, it's like that high school mentality of "my paper's due tomorrow" so I have to stay up all night and do it. For whatever reason that's how I've always worked and it turns out to be my best bit of work.

Tony: At DreamWorks, do meetings help make the film or do they distract from the creative process?

> **I'm really a procrastinator so I don't really do any good work that's worth anything until I'm down to the wire.**

Dean: Had we not nipped a certain problem in the bud, it would have distracted from the creative process. That being that there are meetings about meetings – this is a "meeting happy" studio where people want to get together to talk about what they are going to talk about in the meeting. We saw that happening in the first few months of being here and we finally said, "OK, if you guys want to get together that's great, but we won't be in the room. We'll show up in the meeting to talk about what we need to talk about and then we're done." We didn't have time to be in all those meetings. We were under the gun and we needed to take advantage of every hour we had in the day to work out the story, write a screenplay and then push it through all stages of production. Meetings can be very helpful, especially upfront when we are getting everybody on board. I really do like to get everybody's opinions aired and make sure that nobody is holding back so that we can address it upfront while it's still malleable because when things are in production, things are much more rigid.

Tony: Do you have to interact with a producer, studio executive or investor on a continual basis?

Dean: Here at DreamWorks, Jeffrey is the guy that writes the checks. He is as much in the room as a creative force as he is in a sort of overseeing force. He's very candid too. He'll say, "Guys we need more dragons. We need something more to market. Can you put a scene in your movie that is going to give us play sets to sell later." So it's like there is a certain marketing that we are a part of. We'll say, "No we can't or maybe we can." And he accepts it. There is an honesty about it because he's trying to come from a marketing standpoint so that there is a movie to sell. It is nice to be tapped into that because you're looking at how franchises are built and you're not so much in the dark. If we do *this*, then these retailers are going to want to pick up our movie and the toy line and that is going to help us get a *bigger* foot print out there which will allow us to make more movies. There is strategy in it all. It is limited because Jeffrey wants us to be focused on making the best movie that we can make. Elsewhere, I've made little independent films where we had limited amounts of money where we had to interact directly with

> **Here at DreamWorks, Jeffrey is the guy that writes the checks.**

investors and with producers who write the checks. It's just about being responsible; doing your part to make sure that you aren't wasting money or time.

Tony: What is your definition of the perfect producer?

Dean: What I like in a producer is someone who can block for the creative process but I also think it's somebody who isn't going to try and be another director. The producer is somebody who supports the director and the idea of a single vision and not of a committee-built film. I love a producer who is gutsy and who isn't afraid to bite the hand that feeds them if it comes down to it; who will put up a fight on behalf of the movie and care passionately about it. And somebody who is looking out for the things that are just as important like marketing and promotion and giving us the visibility that we need; within the studio and outside too. A producer is a big job and they have a lot to govern, they have to be a real people-person and know how to create harmony on the movie, and not to disappear when times are tense. Nobody respects that. If you're going to head to the beach when you're asking everyone else to work over the weekend, it doesn't sit well. They have to be in the trenches! Be the biggest cheerleader!

Tony: How important is it to keep up with current technology?

Dean: I think you can get distracted with the constant change of technology. It's important to be aware of it but there's also the danger of being so caught up in new techniques that you don't pay attention to the classic old ones. Which are: tell a good story, draft characters that are believable, real and will stick with people. You don't need the latest software to do that. From a directing standpoint, it's good to be aware of them because a lot of that stuff comes up in conversation. It's good to know what kinds of tools are out there to work with but don't make it your emphasis.

> The producer is somebody who supports the director and the idea of a single vision and not of a committee-built film.

> So identify your goal, work hard and know that it's not going to be all sushi lunches and Academy Awards.

Tony: Any last words for aspiring directors?

Dean: Identify the goal. Certainly know what you want to do and do it for the right reason. Not for the false glamour of it or the credit of it. If it's something that you really passionately want to do, that you want to be the person who envisions a story and moves it through with a large team of people and you think you can inspire them to carry out those visions, then by all means, pursue it. Identify it and find whatever means you can to move toward it. One thing that James Cameron said when he was here [at DreamWorks] lecturing at the beginning of last year, he said that a lot of younger film-making students fresh out of the gate, come to him and kind of glom onto him and his success in hopes of kick-starting their own career. He always makes a point to them of "Don't look at me and don't look at the people who've already made it as your avenue towards success. Look at your fellow film students or your generation of film makers because they are the ones that are going to replace us. They are going to be the one with the big names years from now. You want to pair with them and start making movies with them." It's the inevitable turnover of talent in this industry. So identify your goal, work hard and know that it's not going to be all sushi lunches and Academy Awards. There are a lot of long hours and sacrifice that goes into it. But if you are driven to do it, you can't help but do it.

Tony: Thank you for your time Dean and good luck on *How to Train Your Dragon 2*.

4

TEAMWORK

I have always been pretty vocal about how much I hate sports. Alright, maybe not hate, but dislike may be a better word. It's not that I don't like throwing a ball around with a bunch of friends . . . well . . . actually – I don't. I mean, what's the purpose? One thing I do like about sports though is it's a great analogy for teamwork. Football, America's new national pastime, is all about the team working together to make progress (yardage) down the field and getting one of those "goal thingys." Vince Lombardi is one of the most loved and winningest football coaches of all time. So much so that they re-named the NFL Super Bowl trophy after him. Lombardi often credited his successful football wins to teamwork on the field. He was often quoted for his philosophy on teamwork and managing a team. Here's some words of wisdom from Lombardi:

> ❙❙ People who work together will win, whether it be against complex football defenses, or the problems of modern society. ❙❙

> ❙❙ The achievements of an organization are the results of the combined effort of each individual. ❙❙

The great American inventor Henry Ford is best known for creating the assembly-line process so that he could keep up with the huge demand there was for his automobiles. Ford knew that his process would collapse if not for the specialists he employed to work every phase of the line and to bonding them together as a team was his primary goal. If the guy putting the lug nuts onto the wheels didn't do his job properly, it would have ill fated results when the automobile rolled off the factory line. The wheels would

> ❙❙ Individual commitment to a group effort – that is what makes a team work, a company work, a society work, a civilization work. ❙❙
>
> Vince Lombardi

fall off! Ford, too, had a lot to say about teamwork. These are some of my favorite "Fordisms":

> // If everyone is moving forward together, then success takes care of itself. //

> // Coming together is a beginning. Keeping together is progress. Working together is success. //

> // A market is never saturated with a good product, but it is very quickly saturated with a bad one. //

> // I am looking for a lot of men who have an infinite capacity to not know what can't be done. //

> // If there is any one secret of success, it lies in the ability to get the other person's point of view and see things from that person's angle as well as from your own. //

Most of these quotes have to do with Ford's strong feelings about team work and the individual's realization that hard work will lead to success. He felt that nothing was impossible with hard work and the right team. He certainly proved that out in his lifetime.

So, you may be asking, "that's great for Mr. Lombardi and Mr. Ford but how does it apply to animated projects for you the director?"

Animation is the ultimate team sport! It is the ultimate assembly-line process! It is where the director must sometimes play the role of coach, leader, friend, psychotherapist, counselor, boss, captain, and servant. It is a huge undertaking to make an animated television show, video game, short, commercial or feature. As we saw in Chapter 2, the *process* is very much about having the best people doing their best work as part of the overall pipeline. For me, the single most important element is your crew.

Building a Crew

When I start on a project I like to know exactly what my resources are. I need to know the budget and schedule for the project because that will play a large part in answering the most important resource question: Who do I have on my team? If you work at a studio with a built-in crew then that question is already answered for you. If you are independent and have the freedom to hire a crew then you have the added pressure (good and bad) in choosing your team. It's kind of like when you were back in grade school. If you ever had the responsibility of being a team captain in PE then you know the pressure of choosing a team. There they are lined up against the wall. Do you pick the little scrawny kid struggling to lift his backpack or the kid that looks like he could bench press a small tree? Of course you want the best on your team. But how do you know and how do you get them?

From the beginning of a project, I like to start formulating a wish-list of talent I know and have confidence in. Several factors play apart in choosing the best talent for one of my projects.

How are They to Work With?

I can't put enough emphasis on this. Many new artists coming into the industry think that their stellar portfolio showing their amazing talent will be enough to get them the top jobs in our industry. Well, I'm here to tell you that is just part of the equation. How well you work with others and if you are reliable is better than half of the employers' decision process! No one wants to work with prima donnas or huge egos.

When hiring, I will usually turn to people I have worked with before first. When you are in the trenches of production you want someone you know will be reliable and who you work with well. I already have figured out their strengths and their weaknesses. That is a tremendous help in getting started quickly and on the right foot. Most likely we have been to the edge of despair on a film and made it through that's the kind of "soldier in the trenches" you want on your team. But on any production I will still take a chance on some new talent that I have never worked with before, too. That is important in developing new relationships for future success. Those new relationships will just take more time to foster. This giving of new opportunities are where happy surprises happen.

Are They Right for the Role?

You might be best friends but if the artist can't fulfill your expectations of the job then you have to move on. The needs of the project are what you are there to protect. Also, you may be tempted to hire someone you believe has great potential for the job but unless you have time for training in your budget and schedule you better served by experience. Become an expert at reviewing portfolios. Try to see "behind the lines" in their work they present. Does the work look expert or does it just show great promise? Promise is good but not if you need someone to knock it out of the park in one shot. That's where familiarity and experience is what is necessary. Remember, a portfolio is the artist's work that they have edited down to the pieces they feel represents them at their best. It may not be the level they can consistently perform at. What will you get when they sit down to work on your project on a daily basis? That's what you need to look for.

Are They Available?

As is the case in most industries, the best people are in high demand. Animation is all about what you can do not what degrees you have, so the highly skilled people with a strong reputation for being reliable will probably be in jobs working at the major studios. If you are fortunate, your project will be casting during another studio's lay-off period after a project just finishes. Then you may be able to pick up a very seasoned team that all have experience together – a definite plus! It is possible to woo them away for a short-term gig or maybe even a long-term feature but it will be difficult. Generally, what matters the most to artists (even more than salary) is the project and their role on it. This is where you the director need to put on your salesman's hat. If you can convince them that your film, commercial or video game is unique and different from any of the schlock they are currently working on and that they will be an important asset to its success, then you may have a chance. Of course, salary may be the tipping scale here . . .

Can You Afford Them?

They may be the Michelangelo of animators but if they charge five times more for their time then an average animator, then you have to walk away. This is where you will have to work with your budget to determine how many artists you can afford and what your salary averages will have to be. My experience is that it is best to have several hardworking animators that are at an affordable rate than one prima donna animator that is always threatening to break the bank.

After you have cast your roles for the film, if they are new to you, become a student of what makes each artist's work unique. Learn what makes them tick as an artist, what challenges them, and what excites them creatively. The more you know your team's strengths and weaknesses the better you can cast each one on particular parts of your project. Cast them for success!

The Importance of Casting

In live action, casting means choosing which actors will play the roles in your film. The right cast can make the film hugely successful. Similarly, casting is key to an animated film's success. Once you know who your team is, the next step is to assess their skill level and what they are best at. I like to spend some time in the beginning days of production looking very closely at portfolios, animation reels, paintings and any other past work of all my crew. It takes time, but knowing your crew's skill sets is crucial in setting them up for success.

Just like live action actors, animators are cast based on the character types they have connected with best in the past. Some animators are better at comedy sidekicks, villains, the heroic male or some the heroine. You can call it

Tony Bancroft, *Mulan*
Supervising Animator Mark
Henn and Barry Cook.

type casting, but when it came to casting an animator to lead the role of Mulan (for Disney's *Mulan*) for Barry Cook and me, there was really only one clear choice: Mark Henn – "Disney's Ladies Man." Now, I don't know if Mark likes that nickname (although I think it's probably better than Disney's "Girlyman") but it is his performance type for sure. He is responsible in large or small part for Ariel, Belle, Jasmine, Mulan, and Tiana. At Disney anyway, there is no better animator, male or female, at connecting to the elusive and sophisticated feminine mind than Mark Henn.

Casting is important in every facet of your creative team. If you need help in bringing more comedy to your script, it is a good time to look for a comedy writer that makes funny dialogue come to life on the page. If you know you will need a production designer that will bring a unique take on the visuals for your project that is dark and graphic, then look for someone that is the next Tim Burton for design. Every creative resource you will need is available out there somewhere. These days, you need not look past the Internet for your next big creative talent. I spend much of my week looking at blogs and websites by some of the top talent around the world. It helps me know what's popular style-wise and think outside the box when looking for the next new design star for a project. If you are a young artist, it is mandatory that you have a blog or at least, a website showcasing your work. Links to your digital portfolio is what employers request the most these days. Hard portfolios that you have to lug around to studios and that could be damaged or lost by employers are a thing of the past for the most part.

Support Your Team

Give your creative team some freedom. Don't micro-manage!

Once I have made my casting choices, I do my best to make sure they work. For me, that means not just giving them the regular directorial inputs that all artists need to do their work but beyond that giving them the room and time they need to succeed in their role. This is where the director must protect his or her choices of casting and his or her belief in his or her crew. You may have to go to great lengths to stave off executives or producers who are eager to make quick changes based on seemingly lackluster results. For example, back when I had my own animation studio I had a job directing a direct-to-video short for a major studio. They allowed me to hire my own crew even though the producers really wanted to suggest some of their own people. I hired two very talented animators of whom I had a good knowledge of their draftsmanship ability and performance skills. They were professionals but with little experience at this particular studio and less familiar with their creative practices and expectations. The work they produced for the first pass of the animatic was just what I asked for as director but the studio producers were less than enthused. Their immediate reaction was to suggest that I fire the two artists and replace them with two new storyboard artists who understood what they wanted in the way of polish in the drawing. I told the producers that the fault was mine as I was new to what their expectations were for an animatic too. I assured them that now knowing what the marker was I could get them to rise to the standard that they desired in the boards. I was adamant that my knowledge of these two artists' skills was right for this job. I promised the producers that if they gave me another pass to make changes on the animatic that I knew I could get the artists on board with their (newly expressed) expectations and they would blow them away. The producers were confused by my allegiance to my crew. To them, the rule of production was: if someone wasn't working out, you immediately fired them and moved on. The producers stood by their proposed solution to fire the artists but begrudgingly admitted that they did agree to let me hire who I wanted and left the choice up to me. I went back to the artists and had a long sit-down with them. I blamed myself for not communicating clearly the standards and expectations of these producers and that we would all have to re-approach the boards again. The artists were professionals and attacked this new pass of the animatic with hard work and new inspiration. When the studio reviewed the second pass at the animatic weeks later, this time they were thrilled. They couldn't believe the day-to-night change in the work and assumed that I had followed their advice and replaced the offending artists. I told them it was the exact same artists but with better direction from me. It was a very real risk that paid off. If that second pass at the animatic didn't work out, then those two artists, I and my studio would have been out of a job. Know your team's abilities and give them room to succeed.

. . . But Make a Change if Needed

There are always times when your casting choices may not work out. Sometimes changing your approach with the artist, re-communicating your direction and/or giving them more time is not enough. Sometimes an artist may just bite off more than they can chew in the casting opportunity. As a director on a major studio feature, I remember a time when I gave an opportunity to a friend who I felt confident, if given the right opportunity, would blossom into a superstar. So, I cast him in a supervising position on an important role in the film. After a few months, it was becoming obvious to the producers, studio executives and other artistic crew that he was not working out. I urged all of them that all he needed was more time and specific guidance from me and he would thrive. "Trust me" I said. They did, but after a few more very precious months, he still was not at the quality level expected for his role. The producer of the project sat me down and had a heart-to-heart with me. It was made clear to me that it was time to make a hard change. I believed in this artist still, but it was now even clear to me that he just wasn't going to survive the production if I didn't make a change. It was one of the toughest days in my career when I sat down with my friend and told him I had to demote him. He was not fired but we found a new area for him to succeed in. It was not a good thing for our relationship but it was the right choice for the film. At the end of the day, the film – not your relationships is what you are there to protect.

Allow Your Team to Own Their Work

I've worked with directors that like to hover over their team and I despise that sort of micro-managing style. They want so badly to do it all themselves that they don't trust their artists to make many choices on their own without their constant guidance. They treat their crew like an extension of their own hands. No artist likes that. An artist wants to be given the director's thoughts on the scene and desired outcome but then freedom to create – to make it their own. As a director myself, I love to see the unexpected happy discoveries that are offered up when an artist truly gets inspired by the work given to them and brings back to me something more amazing then I ever expected from the scene. As a young animator on Disney's *Aladdin,* I had an experience with this kind of creative freedom. I was assigned to work on the character Iago the parrot under Will Finn's animation supervision and the directors Ron Clements and John Musker. Finn had been very generous and given me a whole sequence of Iago scenes to animate. It was the sequence in the film where the evil Jafar is coming out of his secret lair and is confronted by an upset Jasmine there to question him about the arrest of Aladdin in the village. Jafar is surprised to see her and quickly slams shut the sliding door to his secret lair. What he doesn't know is Iago was walking out behind him and gets stuck in the door. As the dialogue between Jasmine and Jafar escalates, the sequence is accentuated by cuts to the comic Iago trying to get out of the tight spot. Just as Jasmine storms off leaving Jafar, Iago finally squeezes out of his trap and gasping and coughing flies up to Jafar's shoulder to deliver the line, "So . . . how did it go?" in a composed manner. The two last scenes were issued to me by the director, John Musker with his notes to make a gag out of the last line, "So . . . how did it go?" In the story reel the last scene never got much of a laugh but Musker knew it should, so he suggested a funny drawing of Iago might do the trick. After spending some time with the scenes, thinking them over, reviewing the audio, going over the animatic, I knew there was something more missing there. A funny drawing or pose from Iago was not going to be the funny "capper" that the sequence desperately needed. So, I proposed to Finn and Musker the idea of taking some of the funny coughing and hacking that Iago did in the previous scenes and moving it to the head of the final scene. That way when Iago enters the scene he is hacking, struggling to fly, losing feathers, almost falls off Jafar's shoulder then quickly composes himself in a pose with his hands clasped and calmly says, "So, how did it go?" Both Will and the director loved the idea and allowed me to change the cut, shortening the previous scene and opening up the head of the final scene for the extra animation to make the gag work. One of my greatest joys was at the next screening of *Aladdin* and hearing that final scene get a huge laugh! I never forgot the trust that Musker had in me to make that change. He trusted me as a young animator to do my job and "plus" what I was given. That's one small example of a director allowing his crew to own their work – the movie *Aladdin* was better for it.

Serve Your Crew

This brings me to a motto that I try to always follow: **serve your crew and they will serve the film.** Serve your crew? Most people think that a director is the big creative boss so therefore the crew is to serve him/her. Not so! Artists have been known to work with all kinds of horrible bosses and at low salaries if a project is interesting to them. Often times the leader is secondary to their interest in the creative opportunity. Even if you are a Spielberg, Scorsese, or Cameron and can command hordes of people dying to work with you, you need to realize that you need them more than they need you. You need the talented artists that are on your crew. And more than that, if you give them the creative freedom they deserve and fuel them with your passion and vision for the project you will be rewarded with a film better than you could have ever expected. They will not only serve your vision of the subject but add their experiences, ideas, and inspiration to the film. Suddenly your ideas are multiplied exponentially by the creative universe that is your crew.

Knowing your place is below the needs of your crew will help you to know how to serve them best. This is a good place to start. You should be asking yourself, "how can I best give my team the tools they need to do their best work on the project?" Sometimes that maybe listening to their issues with say . . . their workspace. If an artist feels uncomfortable at their desk they will be less productive. How about their need for more or less light? Maybe they don't have the right software on their computer to deliver the effect they are trying to produce? Sure, these are all issues probably best handled by a production manager, an office manager or human resources, but they came to you first. Help them get the issue resolved. Step in and engage yourself, even if it's suggesting they talk to someone else.

You are their creative supervisor so these things will come your way, because they are issues that interfere with them getting their work done on your film. Mostly, your job will be fueling the team with the creative input they need to produce the brilliant work you hired them for. That means, giving them your thoughts into whatever they are assigned to do. The earlier you can give them your inputs to create the box for them to work in the better. There is nothing more frustrating to a creative person than to feel like they are spinning their wheels endlessly or going the wrong direction. Give your team the direction they need to do their job and then know when to back away and let them go. They will thank you for it and the project will too.

Barry Cook stands ready to serve $1000 worth of donuts during *Mulan*. Art director Ric Sluiter approves of the sugar goodness.

Go Team!

Positive reinforcement – every artist craves it. Who doesn't right? Sometimes your primary role is cheerleader. There are times in the production when everyone is busy and the production train is charging forward. The worst thing you can do is step in front of it and slow it down. I could never understand directors that were always yelling and angry at their crew. Don't they realize you catch more bees with honey than with vinegar? Instead, encourage your team! Let the artists know when you are thrilled with the work they are doing. Praise them generously. Be amazed by their talents. Throw a party when the team's goals are met. Give out crew shirts to create unity and pride on the team. Pay out bonuses when expectations are far surpassed. Whatever it is, make sure your team feels appreciated. For example, when we reached 1,000 feet of animation done on *Mulan*, Barry Cook and I hosted a $1,000 donut party the morning we reviewed dailies together with the animators. You would be surprised at how many donuts a grand can buy. We had a tower of glazed joy all the way to the ceiling! It was a fun breakfast party that helped the artists feel appreciated and gave them a break from the grind before hitting the desk again. No matter how you "show the love," make sure it is felt because an appreciated artist is a productive artist. And a productive artist helps your project get finished!

interview: jennifer yuh nelson

After studying Illustration at California State University, Long Beach, Jennifer Yuh Nelson decided to follow her sister into the world of animation. Academy Award nominated, and two-time Annie Award winner Nelson started her career as a storyboard artist at DreamWorks working on *Spirit: Stallion of the Cimarron*, *Sinbad: Legend of the Seven Seas* and *Madagascar*. It was on *Sinbad: Legend of the Seven Seas*, and by the urging of her friend and mentor Brenda Chapman, that she accepted the position of head-of-story. A long-time fan of martial arts films, Nelson requested to work on the original *Kung Fu Panda* where she was responsible for developing many of the exciting fight scenes through her storyboards. It was on *Panda* that Nelson received her first Annie Award for her leadership and skill in storyboarding. After establishing herself comfortably as a supervisor over storyboards, DreamWorks asked her to take on the directing chores for *Kung Fu Panda 2*. The film was not only Academy Award nominated for Best Animated Feature but also won Nelson her second Annie Award for Best Director. Besides awards, the film was a worldwide box office smash making it "the most success film ever directed by a woman." And with that Jennifer Yuh Nelson has been on many lists of the most powerful women in Hollywood. It was my pleasure to meet her for the first time and interview her for this book which we did over lunch at DreamWorks Animation in Glendale, CA.

Tony: Thank you for your time Jennifer Yuh. Let's start at the beginning, how did you get into the animation industry?

Jennifer: My sister was working at a very small, little animation shop called Jet Lag, that did direct-to-video and stuff, and they were working on *Conan the Barbarian* for TV. They needed, essentially, an intern to come in to clean up, make photocopies, and help with model-pack assembly for sending it overseas, and since I was still in college, I needed a summer job. I said, "Sure. I'll do whatever. I don't care. I'll make coffee." My sister got me in there, and I made photocopies for about a week, and then they saw that I could doodle, so I was cleaning up other people's drawings for a couple more weeks, and then a producer came by and saw I had been doodling on my desk, and he saw that I could draw, so . . .

Tony: Did you draw before that or was that your first time in an art environment?

I've been drawing forever. All my sisters and I have been drawing, essentially, since we were born.

Kung Fu Panda 2 © 2008 DreamWorks Animation LLC, used with permission of DreamWorks Animation LLC

Jennifer: Oh, yeah. I've been drawing forever. All my sisters and I have been drawing, essentially, since we were born. It just was a matter of finding a job that allowed us to draw. But since the producer saw that I could draw he had me do character designs, and by the time I was done with that job, I was only there for about six months, from there I went to Hanna-Barbera. Hanna-Barbera is the first time I did story, and from story I went into all the other stuff.

Tony: What do you like most about working in animation?

Jennifer: I just like how mellow the people are. Seriously! Because people in animation were, kind of, like, the outcasts at school; they were the geeks that, you know, didn't do all the hip stuff. They'd sit on park benches and doodle weird pictures on their school notebooks and stuff, and, since everybody's like that, you're just surrounded by people like that, and that's been really nice. People who're all very artistic and,

their minds just roll in an artistic way. It's not like working in a bank or something.

Tony: What were some of the steps you took to become a director?

Jennifer: I've talked to interns nowadays, and they tell me, "I want to be a director," and I think, "Wow. What drive! What focus!" Because

> I was thinking it would be impossible for me to be a director – that I just should not even think about it.

I wasn't like that at all, you know? In fact, I was thinking it would be impossible for me to be a director – that I just should not even think about it. I was completely happy being a storyboard artist, because that's what interested me in the process,

> **I'm a very introverted person.**

and I thought, actually, that I would eventually go to live action and not be in animation at all, but . . .

Tony: Why did you think it would be impossible for you to direct?

Jennifer: Because I'm a very introverted person. I'm not the kind of person that likes to call attention to myself, and my image of a director was one that would, you know, storm into a room, take control right away, ordering people around, and kind of bossy, and that's what my image was, and I couldn't see myself doing that. I thought I'd be perfectly happy to stay in my office and just drawing boards. Fine. So, when Brenda Chapman told me, "You're gonna be a head-of-story," I fought it pretty hard.

Tony: Which film was that on?

Jennifer: That was [DreamWorks] *Sinbad: Legend of the Seven Seas*. I fought [the promotion to head-of-story] pretty hard, because I was thinking, "I really don't want to go on that path, because I'm not particularly interested at the end of that path."

Tony: Wow . . .

Jennifer: Yeah, and Brenda basically pushed pretty hard. I'm glad she did, because, again, it's very much against my nature, you know, but she said, "You need to do this." And I thought, "OK," and I ended up liking it after a while.

Tony: What are your day-to-day responsibilities as a director here at DreamWorks?

> **So, when Brenda Chapman told me, "You're gonna be a head-of-story," I fought it pretty hard.**

Kung Fu Panda © 2008 DreamWorks Animation LLC, used with permission of DreamWorks Animation LLC

"Kung Fu Panda 2" © 2008 DreamWorks Animation LLC, used with permission of DreamWorks Animation LLC

Jennifer: Well, every day is different for every part of the production. In the beginning you're sitting with the writers, head-of-story, and the producer, and just really coming up with the story — the bones of it. As production ramps up you're in a whole lot of meetings with every single department, looking at everyone's work, and it's just all meetings, all the time, because there's 350 people working on this film and they all need to know what's happening. So, you have to have a lot of meetings.

Tony: They need feedback and approvals, so that they can do their job, right?

Jennifer: . . . and guidance and reassurance. All sorts of stuff. And it's also polite to make sure people see you.

Tony: What is the best and worst part of your job as director?

Jennifer: I think the best part [of my job] is when people say that they feel inspired,

> the best part [of my job] is when people say that they feel inspired, that they're doing their best work, and that's all I ever wish for as an artist

that they're doing their best work, and that's all I ever wish for as an artist, you know. You don't go into one of these jobs thinking of anything other than, "I want to do something that I'm proud of doing." It's not for any other reason. And when others say that they feel happy about what they've been able to do, then you feel like you've made a little bubble of positivity in your job. So, that's the best part. The worst part is, again, going against my nature of being a very introverted person and getting up in front of a room full of 35 people, and telling them something that might not be popular.

Tony: What's the most important tool in your director's toolbox?

Jennifer: I think it's . . . gosh, that's a tough one. I guess, it's being able to read people. Because, as a director, you don't actually do that much of the work. You have to get other people to do the work, so, being able to try to see what people need to do their best work.

I think that's been useful, 'cause, it's different for everybody, so, you can't just treat people the same. That listening ability, I think is important.

Tony: What do you start with in developing the story for your project?

Jennifer: It is the character, really. It's gotta be about the character, because the character will tell you what he wants to do. So, I think that's the number-one first thing, is find out who this person is that you're gonna be following around for a couple hours, and then that character will make the plot for you.

Tony: How do you develop engaging characters? How do you develop those characters?

Jennifer: I think it's to make sure that they have something that they really want, that they're not a passive character, you know; they're a character that has an actual interest in something, and then you want to see them either get it, or learn something, or find something else, or change, or whatever. It's like your friends, if you have an interesting friend that is interesting, you watch them. You base your characters off people you know, people you've observed to make your characters as real as possible, because then it's identifiable.

Tony: How do you work with a script writer to develop your vision for the project? Or do you?

Jennifer: We do.

Tony: Do you write scripts yourself?

Jennifer: Oh no, I don't write scripts myself. I write, but certainly not professionally. I write as a storyboard artist would write, but, for the sake of a script certainly, we do use writers. We use them very early, you know, we just sit in the whole beginning stage of the idea trying to work it out

> You base your characters off people you know, people you've observed to make your characters as real as possible, because then it's identifiable.

together. I think starting with writers is important because then everybody's on the same page of what we're going for. Of course the script is a guide, but it has to be fluid during the process of making it, so, we allow the storyboard artists to add to it and other departments have comments too. Then the writers would come back in and write new drafts, or they might make adjustments, and it's all incorporated. It's very fluid, like braiding yarn.

Tony: How important is the animatic to you?

Jennifer: The animatic is very important because the process has changed so much from before, where we just went off of exposure sheets, but one thing that an animatic does is, especially for something insanely complex, it gives you the ability to see something and make sure that you can catch problems early, and allows you to treat a movie as a whole. Then you can really adjust the pacing of something, add nuances, and then ultimately only animate what you really need, instead of having to do as many re-dos.

Tony: How do you issue a scene to an animator?

Jennifer: Well, usually I start with a paper, writing down: What are the character's objectives? What's the point of the scene? What's the most important moment? Out of everything in the sequence that you're getting, what should it be going towards? So everybody who's working on that sequence is clear on what's the most important thing, because I expect everybody to have the same level of information so that they can feel comfortable adding to it. You can't add if you're blind, so, they probably get more information as far as what the emotional intent is or what the story intent is, and stuff like that, than they may ever need. Then they can give you subtlety you couldn't even have asked for, just like, you know, dealing with actors, you gotta tell them what they're trying to do. So then, once we do that, the animators will be clearer about what they're trying to do. They get their shots divvied up depending on the movie: either character shots or entire shots with all of the characters in the shot. The way we've been working is pretty much all the characters in the shot are done by one animator simply because of complexity. Then we do rough passes, and final passes, re-dos, all kinds of stuff.

The way we've been working is pretty much all the characters in the shot are done by one animator simply because of complexity.

Tony: So that first meeting you were talking about is a kind of a sequence meeting, everybody that's working on that sequence comes and then you may have a secondary meeting too with individual animators?

Jennifer: We might. We have drive-bys, you know, like, at their desk, working stuff, but the first meeting's always with everybody. Then they know what to hook up to.

Tony: What do you look for from a first pass by an animator?

Jennifer: Choreography, you know, making sure that the general intent of the scene is right. I'm not looking for all the nuance of the acting yet, of course, but if the general idea is there, then it's fine, and, also I look for any input, like, if they have a completely different idea for the shot, if it

if you're insanely talented but you just piss everyone off around you, I mean, how can you be a team that way?

works for the point, then that's when I'd like to see that.

Tony: What do you look for in a creative team: an art director, editor, storyboard artist, an animator?

Jennifer: Well, first of all, ability, because, you know, they gotta be able to do the job! But almost right up there is just their ability to work in a team, you know, that everybody plays well together. Because if you're insanely talented but you just piss everyone off around you, I mean, how can you be a team that way? What I hope for is that people can come in without any sense of their own ego or any of their insecurities and they can focus on the movie, and I've been very fortunate that everybody I work with is like that. They're very much like, "I want to make something great." It doesn't matter if it's my idea or that person's idea, or that other person's idea, or if the, you know, a guy from the mailroom walked by and said, "Hey, I have a good idea. We should try this . . ." It doesn't matter whose idea it is, as long as they can make something really good.

Tony: How much responsibility are your creative department heads given on one of your films?

Jennifer: A lot. I strongly believe if you're just following orders, it's just gonna look like crap, you know, that you have to be engaged in the process of making a movie. You have to feel it is your movie, and it becomes a personal project for you. When you get like that, it becomes a passion project. It becomes something, you wanna do something, and that's why I wanna make sure that all the heads of department are essentially ruling their kingdom in their department with the clear intent of what I'm asking them for, but they have full autonomy to get it there, whichever way they want. And amazingly that doesn't lead to chaos. It leads to really, really streamlined, really on-point, and amazingly subtle additions that they add.

Tony: How do you combat the "Us against Them" attitude that can arise on a production between management and crew?

Jennifer: I think you make sure you explain why things are happening. I think that when you have a vacuum of information, you fill in that vacuum with assumptions of the worst-case scenario. With communication you find out, no, they weren't just trying to mess with us, they had a reason to do that and then you don't get that level of animosity. So it's part of all those meetings you had. You explain decisions to the crew. You explain the thought processes behind

tough decisions, and why it's gonna be ultimately better for everyone involved, and everyone goes, "OK It hurts now, but I can see why you're doing it. So, let's do it."

Tony: Yeah, as the director, you have to ride that rail between the creative side and the production side, because you're in those meetings where you're talking about budget, schedule and quotas. You have to agree to those things, and then spread the word out to the crew to get everyone on board with the plan. Is that difficult for you sometimes? Do you feel like you're constantly playing both sides?

Jennifer: It's certainly difficult, but I wouldn't agree to something, ultimately, as a director, unless I believe it's better for the movie. So, once

> I wouldn't agree to something, ultimately, as a director, unless I believe it's better for the movie.

Kung Fu Panda 2 © 2008 DreamWorks Animation LLC, used with permission of DreamWorks Animation LLC.

you've decided that, then you have to go in, and you have to defend your decision, but all those decisions can't be ever treated like decisions from on high, given by somebody over there, you know, it has to be assimilated into, "Is this something I want to do? Will this make the movie better?" And then it's easier to explain to the crew. But sometimes it's still hard. It's like getting a vaccine, you know, "it hurts, but it'll keep you from dying of a disease." Then you explain it to the crew and they go, "OK," But it's still hard. You don't want to, you know, mess around with people's time, and their efforts, and you want to make sure that it all goes to something good, but sometimes you have to do difficult things to do that.

Tony: Do you find it difficult to be true to your original vision for the project as time goes by, and, if so, how do you keep things on track?

Jennifer: Well, sometimes you lose track. It happens. These are long projects. They take years, but, for me, what makes me gravitate towards something is, it sometimes comes down to a moment, or a single emotional idea, and how you get there, it really doesn't matter, and so, that's one of the reasons why I don't get too finicky about too many details about stuff, because I know a lot of people are gonna handle it, and it's gonna shift one way or another, because a lot of people have their input. But if you know where you're going, and it's a simple thing to keep your brain on, then, you kinda know "we're four degrees off, we've gotta pull it back." If you have 20 points you have to keep in mind, then it's gonna be hard to keep in mind. But if it's a fairly simple thing you just go for that. You can feel it instinctively, whether you're heading for it or not.

Tony: Do you have an example of that, from maybe *Kung Fu Panda 2* where maybe you felt like things were going off from what they should have been?

Jennifer: No, because I think every movie ever made by anyone goes through this process of in the beginning, everything's great! The ideas are great! It's gonna be amazing! And then a year and a half in, everybody's tired and saying, "Ugh, what were we thinking?" And then, in the end, you go, "Oh, this is great again." I mean, that's just the way it happens.

Tony: We all know that budgets and schedules are a part of life for the filmmaker, but how do you look at them personally? Friend or foe?

Jennifer: I actually think of them as a good thing, because if there were no parameters to what we do, we would probably take 20 years to make one of these things. You can always make it better, or you don't think of creative solutions unless you have some sort of limitation that you're up against, it can be paralyzing. So, to an extent, I think a budget and schedule can be a really positive thing. If they're brutal to the point that they keep you from making anything, that's a problem, but I think they can be used as a driver, you know, it's a deadline. If you don't have a deadline you just might never actually get yourself to do it.

> **I think a budget and schedule can be a really positive thing.**

Tony: At DreamWorks, do meetings help make the film, or do they distract from the creative process?

Jennifer: They totally help make the film. I mean; again, it's how 350 people know what they're working on. But I think it's important, 'cause otherwise you don't know what you're working on, and you could be making the most brilliant thing ever, and you have no idea if it hooks into the whole thing, so the more people know the totality of the process, the whole project, without too many details to make them really overwhelmed, but, as long as they know generally what they're doing, I think those meetings are invaluable to, sort of, tap back into that energy. Otherwise it's lonely, in your office by yourself.

> **I'm a hardcore gamer. For me it's so I can see the speed that people are seeing things in.**

Tony: Do you have to interact with a producer or a studio executive on a continual basis working at DreamWorks?

Jennifer: Oh yeah,. . .

Tony: What is that relationship like for you?

Jennifer: It's wonderful. I mean; I've been very fortunate in my producing partner, Melissa Cobb is just amazing. She worked on the first *Kung Fu Panda* too. She's super supportive, and very smart, and we work very closely together. It's very much a team, yeah. It's great.

Tony: How important is it for you to keep up with current technology?

Jennifer: Desperately. Desperately, I mean, not necessarily technology, like what's the next program used for animation. I don't think like that. It's more like a, sort of, cultural thing, like, I need to know what's going on right now, as far as, what kind of games are happening out there. I play games all the time.

Tony: Oh, do you? You're a gamer.

Jennifer: I'm a hardcore gamer. For me it's so I can see the speed that people are seeing things in. How is that changing? What are they getting input-wise, you know? How are they interacting with the medium? That sort of thing, I'm very interested in it, because I think it helps us from becoming stagnant.

Tony: Do you go to Siggraph and things like that? Do you want to know about the latest software, tools that are available?

Jennifer: No. I'm not really a software and tool person, and again there are great and very smart people who are really into that, and that's all they do. I'm more the aesthetic side. I'm very grateful that on one movie you can only do a certain thing [like fire or cloth], and then the next movie you find out that's not a limitation any more. You can do so much more, because of how technology's moving along. Ultimately, if it frees us to make something without worrying about the technological limitations of doing it. That's great. I mean, you know what it's like; you can't, like, do characters with hair, or flappy clothing, or, just, like, how in 3D, you can't have a ton of patterns on clothing, because it just would kill somebody [by giving them a stroke].

Tony: Any last words for young artists that want to be a director one day?

Jennifer: I'd say, it's more of a plea. Try to become the kind of director that other people would like to work for . . . because I'll probably be working for you someday.

Tony: Well put. Thank you Jennifer Yuh.

> **Try to become the kind of director that other people would like to work for . . . because I'll probably be working for you someday.**

5

EXPRESS YOURSELF!

What Makes *You* Unique as a Director?

My *Mulan* directing partner, Barry Cook, grew up in the backwoods of Kentucky which was evident if you spent more than 10 minutes with him. He is the smartest good-hearted hick I have ever known. On a daily basis, he kept me in stitches with a different funny story about one of his crazy, country relatives. It did not matter what phase of production we were in, what important subject we were discussing, without fail, he would break into a story about "Uncle Zeb" or "Granny Gertrude" or some such character from his childhood. Besides always being good for a laugh to break up the tension of the day, his crazy stories about characters from his past quietly influenced the movie too. You can see evidence of that in the scene form the film in which Mushu wakes up Mulan's ancestral ghosts and it turns into a dysfunctional family reunion filled with colorful personalities just like his kin. That's just one very specific example of how one's past experiences can shape the way they see things. We are all products of our upbringing, morals, and experiences. Our worldview is shaped by the things we have seen and heard around us – good and bad. These are the things that form our opinions and guide how we translate information. That's why when I speak about your "vision" for your film, it shouldn't be a daunting thing that you have to acquire, it's something you already possess.

I love to go to lectures where famous directors talk about their process in creating. It does not matter what college they went to, how well-read they are; without fail, at some point in the talk, they will admit, "and when I couldn't figure it out, I followed **my gut instinct.**" What an odd American phrase when you think about it. I don't

❚❚ Trust your own instinct. Your mistakes might as well be your own, instead of someone else's. ❚❚

Billy Wilder

Barry Cook in his natural environment. Playing fiddle, in the back woods, with some crazy characters around him.

117

know who, in the history of anatomical study, deemed "the gut" as the origin of all common-sense thinking but I think they're right. It's tapping in to that basest of natural instincts that are in our core being. Following your gut simply means: when in doubt – rely on your instincts.

Following my gut is what got me through my first directing gig! But it did not start that way. When I first got onto *Mulan* as a co-director, I was afraid of making a mistake. Since I was the second director onto the film after a year of the story process had elapsed, the train was already rolling with an all-star story team led by the legendary Chris Sanders. The team had developed a good working relationship with my co-director partner Barry and I didn't want to be the new guy that came in and messed it all up. I allowed my fear of doing or saying the wrong thing to hamper my own creative instincts. I told myself, "I'll just take a back seat and listen in to the creative brainstorming, if I have a big idea then I'll chime in." It's a survival instinct to play it safe but there is no safe in directing. You have to be all-in. That's certainly no way to be involved with a creative brainstorming session. In a non-ego driven creative session everyone adds to a concept with the universal goal of coming out of the meeting with forward movement on the story issue discussed. Every idea big or little adds to the overall consciousness of the team.

Me on a lighter day with the *Mulan* story team pretending to be in a Gap clothes advertisement. From left: John Sanford, me, Chris Williams, and head of story Chris Sanders. Photo probably taken by co-head of story Dean DeBlois.

I learned that my approach was wrong when I would hear other brainstorm members suggest ideas that I had been thinking but was too afraid to add. Then I looked like a useless echo in the room when I would say, "Yeah, I was just thinking that." Use the common sense that was given to you through your upbringing and education and go for it! What better way to make entertainment for a general audience than to tap into this universal "common sense." When confusion arises, it's your "gut" that should be followed, not the dull roar of your fears.

Every Director Has Their Own Vision

What makes a Steven Spielberg film different from a Brad Bird film or a J.J. Abrams film? It's their vision for the material. In the film industry you hear the word "vision" thrown around a lot. "He had a clear vision for what he wanted." "She had a unique ability to vision-cast." "They had a shared vision of how to make the process better." When I first started in the industry, the phrase "vision" was confusing to me. Maybe I'm just too literal sometimes, but my question was always, "what are these directors *seeing* that seems to be invisible to me? Where do they get this special *sight* that gives them the ability to "see" a finished film out of nothing?" "Is *vision* just another name for **imagination**?" The answer is yes and no. Imagination alone can only help you guess at the final outcome of your project. Vision, in this case, is not only what you see as a final image of your film in your mind's eye but a way of making it too. Your unique creative vision or "take" on something is a combination of imagination marrying with your past experiences to create your own personal **preferences** of how you like to see something come together. That "vision" for the creative elements and the order in which you choose to display them becomes your blueprint of how you want your project to be presented for others to receive. The clearer your vision, the clearer it will be received by your audience. There shouldn't be the scratching of the head or the "I didn't get it" looks on the audience's face as they exit the theatre. In short, **your vision is a product of your unique view of the world shaped by your past influences filtered through the material before you.** It's the reason why you can give 10 different directors the same script and come out with 10 unique movies.

Keeping Your Vision Clear in the Chaos of Other Voices

If I have not made it clear up to this point, making an animated project takes a lot of people. The crew on a big budget feature can swell to over 350 people in the heat of production. Guess what? Each one of those people has an opinion about how the movie *you're* directing should be made! One of the greatest principles of Disney Feature Animation was that anyone and everyone on staff should be able to share their ideas. From the lowest position all the way to the top! The concept being that **a good idea can come from anywhere or anyone.** The added benefit, besides improving the project, is the crew feels listened to. It is a great principle, in theory, but difficult to put into effect as a director.

The usual time we directors would get people's notes on our film was right after a screening of the storyboard animatic. The story was still in a pliable state and any last thoughts should be voiced then before the gears of the unstoppable production started up. This was a great and awful process at the same time. Some presented ideas were supportive and helpful to your vision of the film and while others were supportive of a different film that you did not want to make. You had to take the good with the bad. What a director developed in this Disney system was not only a thick skin, but also to become an "idea filter." Like a filter you allow many ideas in but only the best out. This is not an easy thing to do. The thing you must always hold onto is that **the filter is your vision for the film**. If it's not strong, then it will be next to impossible to filter out the bad ideas and ultimately you will end up with a soupy mess. That's the

The director as idea filter.

ultimate culinary example of the old adage that "too many cooks in the kitchen can spoil the soup"!

As if your own creative staff wasn't enough, you will have to deal with executive opinions as well. They need to be addressed on a whole other level of sensitivity. There is no ignoring a note from say, Michael Eisner or Jeffery Katzenberg as I had to deal with on Disney's *Mulan*. The pressure to succumb to your boss's whims are normal in an office environment but when you are making a multi-million dollar movie and you have opinions tossed your way by executives that have the reputation (and power) of Hollywood gods, it is a whole different kind of stress. Many times, it can feel like the executive just wants to be heard through his notes. Deep down, he may not even be sure himself if his note is helpful or destructive to the overall but he has to give it with all of the confidence and authority that his position warrants. It would be refreshing to hear an executive say something like, "Ya know guys, I'm not sure if it's just me being preoccupied with my blackberry, but the scene's pacing feels slow." That would be honest but not likely to happen. No, the truth is that executives come into a screening of your film after dealing with numerous corporate trials, personal problems, with unknown amounts of focus or enthusiasm, and after watching it just once, they make huge course-changing comments that you have to deal with. That's your job as director. It's time to be an "idea filter" all over again.

How Do You Know When an Idea is Good or Not?

Among other things, an animation director has to be critical of the artists he/she oversees. Critiquing other creative artists' work can be intimidating to say the least. Especially if they are legends in the industry.

Back in 1995, I was promoted from a first-time supervising animator on *The Lion King* to director of *Mulan* so quickly that I had not yet developed the confidence in critiquing my own work, let alone someone else's. The toughest challenge I had on *Mulan* was the weekly animation

The animation review room on *Mulan*. Supervising animator, Barry Temple (Cri-Kee) getting ready to discuss his scene with Barry Cook and I. Photo taken by Tony Bancroft.

meetings where I would have to judge the work of the animation crew. Especially intimidating was my review time with legendary animator Mark Henn (I wrote of his sensational career earlier in Chapter 4). For some context, it is important to point out that Henn was my mentor when I first began in animation. I was hired at Disney to work at the, now defunct, Walt Disney Florida Animation Studio. I was one of many assistant animators who worked under Henn and other senior animators to "clean-up" their scenes and prepare them for color. (A clean-up artist takes the animator's rough drawings and makes a refined single-line drawing that can then be colored.) Fast forward a short five years later and now I was his director on *Mulan*. It was hard enough for me to come to terms with, I think it was even harder for Henn to rationalize. I say this with all due respect because he is really one of my closest friends now, but the first six months of directing Mark Henn were hell. Every time I would have a comment, even the smallest, Mark would give me "that look." He respected my title but not me artistically. I hadn't earned my place at the table – and he was right! But whether I was ready or not, I was determined to make it work. I knew I had the one thing a director should always have in working with creative artists; a passion for excellence. Through time and hard work, Mark and the rest of the animators realized all I wanted was to get *their* best work out of them and up on the screen. I didn't care what was said about me after they left the room but I made sure they knew their work mattered to me and it had an important impact on the film.

The ability to step back from a specific creative element and see it in the context of the project as a whole is an essential skill the director must command. It is being able to judge something in the micro and macro all at once. The big picture is the constant goal but each individual creative element is the building block of the project. But so much

From *Mulan*. © 1998 Disney.

of what we do in the art of animation is **subjective**. It's in the eye of the person judging to say if it is "good" or "right" in the context of the project. Over the years I discovered a good litmus test to judge someone else's creative contribution – whether it was an animated scene, a story idea, background, character design, etc. I call it the "**is it better or just different**" test. Anyone can judge if something is better or worse but the real job is when something is just a different shade and doesn't change the overall. The goal of the director should be to always seek the "better" and not be dissuaded by the *different*. The *different* is what makes something muddy and convoluted. If an animator came to me and said, "I have this new idea for my scene," I would listen to it and then quickly put it in the context of, "does this new idea seem to make the moment in the film better or is it just a different direction with no benefit one way or the other?" If the answer in my mind is the latter than I would have to tell the animator, "no, let's keep the scene going in the direction it was intended." If to me there was no perceived benefit from an entertainment perspective than it made the choice rather simple. If the idea made the scene resonate more, be funnier, or clearer then it was definitely a better way to go. Either way, by this "better or just different" deductive reasoning I could have more confidence in my ability to judge other artists' work. Even Mark Henn's.

Don't be Just the "Approval Stamp"!

Traditional animation at Disney relied upon model sheets to illustrate what a character should look like as a guide for all of the animators to follow. It was the final design approved by the directors and was to be followed by all the animators to insure consistency. As a director we had an ink stamp made that was our very own mark, like the kings of yore, so that if we approved of the drawing we would place our stamp on the sheet next to our signature to deem it the official final model. Hahaa! On a good day, I loved to stamp a model sheet approved. I felt like I had helped contribute in the process to get the model to the

point where it was good enough for me to approve. But on a bad day, a director can feel like the person that is the quality checker in a shirt factory. Is the quality OK to move through the factory? Yes, then stamp it approved and move it on. Where is the creativity in that?

The feeling of being an approval stamp is common amongst directors as you move into the schedule-driven phase of production. In features, each department has an associate production manager that is waiting upon your every breath looking for the magic word "approved" so they can quickly move the finished shot onto the next department and make their weekly quota. No matter what the department, the weekly quota can become the driving force for the production staff on a film. The pressure to compromise your vision, to turn a blind eye to imperfections, or just stop searching for a better idea is immense as the production bears down on you. You will feel it from everyone around you at some point. In all honesty, you do have a responsibility to help the artists to move their work along in the river that is production. You are not a dam that stops the flow of creativity but a bridge that helps it pass through. Think about the reason you love the project. What makes it work for you. Never give up on that. There may be economies that can be made that will help the production move forward but you will stay stead fast on the things that really matter. You will not give up on your film because when it is all said and done, **no one will remember if the project was done on time and on budget but they will remember if it was good or not.**

Don't Give Up Your Authority in the Room

When presenting an element of the film to a producer or executive, it's important to always keep your opinion known, even if you are not leading the presentation. For example, if you are directing a television show and the "look" or style of the project must be presented to the executives in charge for their approval, it is most likely a

meeting that would be prepared by the art director. This is his department and his domain after all. Many directors would just allow the art director to present his or her team's work and just be there in the background. But the reality is by not running the presentation or standing beside the art director as he presents, you lose your voice and may be less likely to be heard the next time. That seems harsh, I know, but the truth is that the same rules of corporate politics are as true in animation as in any other business. On the surface, when the said director was in the background of the presentation just nodding or whatever, it didn't seem like a big deal – at first. It's where that leads through time that can be destructive to your control over your vision for the project. I have seen it lead to executives feeling so comfortable with their new relationship with that art director that they would just simply by-pass the director and carry on discussions about the project in the art director's office. An innocent "drive by" meeting by the executive and feeling the freedom to suggest changes that the director hears about latter. Now that director has no way of dealing with the notes except to go on the defensive.

There is a way of nipping this problem in the bud from the beginning and still allow your department heads and creative leads the empowerment that they deserve.

First, as director, you should never present an idea or concept to an executive, client, or investor that you do not support. If the person you are presenting to turns to you and asks, "do you like this?" Never should the word, "I don't know" come out of your mouth. Even if it's a new idea and you are unsure of the impact on the project but you like it well enough to develop it more never sound uncertain or negative. You should only respond with, "Absolutely, I am 100 per cent behind it" or at least, "I like it and I'm excited to see what he/she will do with it as they develop it more." Now you are being supportive of someone else's idea but making sure that your bosses know you are also involved with its development.

I like to always have a pre-presentation run through with my art director or creative lead that will be doing the majority of the presentation. Let them run you through all of the elements of the presentation. Catch any ideas or images that you disagree with and edit them out or fix them right then and there. Between the two of you work out your chorography of who will say what in the meeting and what elements will ultimately be presented.

Second, when the meeting starts it's best to give an opening preamble yourself before turning it over to your creative lead. It sets the tone of "all that you are about to see, I have been involved with and approve." This is a way of keeping your authority over the project in the forefront and also making it easier for you to walk beside your creative lead as he/she delivers the presentation.

Finally, if there is an "out of left field" question or comment that comes from one of the executives you should try to field it if it's appropriate. If it's clearly a financial question that would be better answered by the producer then let them catch it. But if it's something that is at all appropriate for you as the director to answer don't let it fall to someone else to answer.

I realize these suggestions may seem overly paranoid to some. Is it really such a big deal exactly how you are perceived by your bosses in any one meeting? Absolutely! The animation industry is littered with directors that have been fired off their projects and replaced by other directors who completed the project. Every studio has had experience with the "director shuffle." Some movies go through as many as four sets of directors before they are completed. The sad truth is that the only directors that are remembered are the ones whose name are in the final credits. Balancing between the perceptions your bosses have of you and your team may be the difference between finishing your project or not. Make sure you finish the project or you may not get another one.

interview: pete docter

Raised in Bloomington, Minnesota, Pete Docter is one of the most humble Academy Award winners you will ever meet. Self-described as a "geeky kid from Minnesota who likes to draw cartoons," Docter enjoyed success early in his animation career having won a student academy award for shorts he produced during his college years at California Institute of the Arts (CalArts). He graduated and the next day started as employee number 10 at the fledgling Pixar Animation Studios. From there it was to infinity and beyond! Working his way up from story, animation, to screenwriting on such films as *Toy Story*, *Bugs Life*, *Geri's Game*, *Toy Story 2* and *Wall-E*, Docter is now one of the top directors at Pixar having directed *Monster, Inc.* and *Up*. The latter film winning him the Academy Award for Best Animated Feature in 2010. Currently directing an untitled new feature for Pixar and executive-producing *Monster University*, Docter is also part of the exclusive Senior Creative Team (also known as Lasseter's Brain Trust) at the company. I am proud to say that Pete and I were in the same class at CalArts and I am glad that we had this time to catch up over the phone for this interview.

Tony: Pete, how did you get into the animation industry?

Pete: Well, I started doing flip books, because I loved movement, you know, there's always that guy who draws all the time. That was not me. I was kinda intimidated by drawing, but I loved movement, so, you know, any spare book, old books, or notepads, I would fill with little flip books, and I started working at a commercial house outside of Bloomington, Minnesota, where I grew up. I got a little experience there: painted

cels, did some inbetweens, then I got into CalArts, in, what year was that we started? 1987?

Tony: Now I feel old. Yeah, must have been 1987.

Pete: Yeah. So, then I spent three years there, and then, in the time there, over the summer, I did an internship at Disney, which was pretty cool, and worked a little bit at Bob Rogers and Company, and then, pretty much the day after graduation started up at this strange software computer company that eventually became an animation company, so, I've been here for over 20 years now at Pixar.

Tony: And you were employee number?

Pete: I was about the tenth person in the animation group. I think there were about 80 people there total. Then, maybe a month in to me working there, I saw Steve Jobs. He came and fired half the company! I remember thinking, "Gee, maybe this wasn't such a good idea."

Tony: "It's so unstable here at Pixar!" [laughter]

Pete: Yeah, exactly. But what he was doing was, kind of, refocusing the company. What they were doing up until that point, was making these image computers which were losing money. They were the industry standard, at the time, the Pixar Image Computer.

Tony: What do you like most about working in animation?

> I think most animators, and certainly directors, are frustrated closet actors,

Pete: I've always loved making stuff, even as a kid, before I started getting paid for it. I loved doing my own films, and then watching people's reactions, you know. I think most animators, and certainly directors, are frustrated closet actors, and so we may not have the facility of Jim Carrey, to make our bodies do what we want, so you, kind of, express that with your pencil or your computer, or whatever.

Tony: What were some of the steps you took to move up to the director position at Pixar?

Pete: Well, you know what, I remember writing to, this may have been even at CalArts, wrote to Frank Thomas and Ollie Johnston, and asked them, what was required to get into animation at Disney. Frank wrote a bunch of different things, things like solidity of movement, design, strong draftsmanship, study of motion, and he said, "and like everything in life, it requires a little bit of *luck*," [laughter] and I certainly feel like that was the case with me. I just, I happened to get to this small, up-and-coming studio at a time when it was growing. They were desperate for talent. I mean, frankly I think I would have trouble getting hired here now, based on the portfolios we see coming in, but I was, you know, there right

as we were, sort of, discovering a lot of this stuff, of how, computer animation used the principles of animation that were developed by the Disney guys, so it was a really exciting time, and I got to really sit right next to John Lasseter who was really very generous with how he shared what was going on on *Toy Story*. As he was directing, you know, Tom Hanks, he would drag me and Andrew Stanton down there, and we would shout out suggestions, and, so, it was helpful to him, but it was also really helpful to us, because then, later on, we really had a better picture of what was going on overall, and I think animation, especially at big studios, you plug yourself into one, small, little spot, you know, that one area of focus, you know, just design, or just movement, or whatever, and, for us, at that time, we were really just thinking about these things as films. We were doing, kind of, all parts of it, which is really great, and I would recommend to people, especially just coming out of school, you know, I know a lot of people are keen to get to Disney or Pixar, or whatever, but I'd say, man, go find a small studio where you have to do everything. That's really a great way to learn.

Tony: Working so closely with Lasseter, seems like that was a good training ground for you to become a director one day.

Pete: Absolutely. Yeah, the thing that shocked me the most, and this is not meant to demean John at all, but I always had this idea that directors, you look at films, like, *Pinocchio*, or whatever, and you feel, like, "Ugh. The director has it all in his head," and he comes in, and he tells you, "I want it to be an upshot, three-quarter,

> go find a small studio where you have to do everything. That's really a great way to learn.

with a, you know, this happens at exactly this frame," and stuff. That's the sort of myth that you're taught or that you pick up somehow, but the reality is that this whole process is a discovery, from the concept on, you're constantly re-focusing, and changing, and shifting, and, yeah, the director's definitely got it in his head, but, it's not, like, it's all there from the get-go. It doesn't all just come as a big flash of inspiration, which is, kind of, the way I thought of it, and, so, John was pretty open about what he knew, and what he didn't, and, yeah, it was a great training ground.

Tony: He sought help from the guys around him . . .

Pete: Absolutely. That's something that, you know, Andrew Stanton has put in words, that, you know, "the director's not necessarily the smartest guy in the room, he just knows who is," you know . . .

Tony: I like that.

Pete: It doesn't all have to come from you; in fact, a lot of it comes from other people. It's just that you have the ability to, kind of, assess what certain people are capable of, and what they can bring.

Tony: What are your day-to-day responsibilities as director?

Pete: Well, around here, and this differs from studio to studio, but, around here, Pixar's made a commitment to trust the director, and so, really, even before we come up with a concept, people are given the, you know, we talk to up-and-coming directors, and say, "Hey, go develop something. Come back and pitch a couple ideas," so, you know, from, at the beginning of the process, like, year one, I'm just sitting in a room, bangin' my head against the wall, reading, drawing, whatever, coming up with basic concepts, and then, then I'll bring in a small group to work with. Now it's different with

everybody, Andrew, and Brad Bird, I think, tend to work more independently, just on their own, close themselves off and start writing. For me, I like having somebody else to bounce ideas off of, so I do a certain amount of writing and drawing and stuff, and then I'll get together with, you know, like, in the case of *Up*, I worked with Bob Peterson, who was a great collaborator, and brought a ton to that picture, so he and I would sit, and chat, and we'd, kind of, refine, and hone the idea. Then we'd split off, and each of us would write, and then we'd get back together, and so, it's almost like psychotherapy, where you're analyzing, "What is it about this concept that's really grabbing me?" It might be the subject matter, or it might be something deeper, something that resonates some sort of life lesson, that you feel emotional about and that other people will feel as well.

Tony: And . . . the tough thing about it too, I guess, is that if you over-analyze something, you can, kind of, kill it, right? Kind of, like, over-analyzing a joke, and it's not funny anymore?

Pete: Yeah, I guess so, although, there's a season for analyzing, and really, I mean, it could be that we over-analyze, but, we certainly do, and then we just, kind of, forget analyzation, and just dive in and trust your gut, and go, go, go, go, and then you get to an event, like, say, a screening, or a script pass, or whatever, and those are the times where you, kind of, step out of the pool, and look on the sidelines, and say, "OK, here's where we took a wrong turn. And this is what we need to do to fix it," and then you jump back in, and splash around again, and try to get to the other side, so, anyway, back to your question, I guess, then, you know, there's different seasons, obviously of directing a film, so those are the early seasons, and then mid- about

> **"the director's not necessarily the smartest guy in the room, he just knows who is,"**

year one to two, we're starting to build the story reels, so, in the case of, again, in the case of me, I do some amount of writing, but, then I like having a writer as well to collaborate with, and, you know, I'll take their pages and re-write stuff, and vice-versa, again, in some cases, Brad, or Andrew tend to write on their own, but, for me, I guess, I feel, like, I'm not smart enough to be able to get in there and write, and then also step on the side and analyze what works and what doesn't, so, it's, I think a director has to be a really good editor, so that you know what's crucial to put across, and what can you cut out. And then, later on, as you go into production, it's just full-time, you know, from, like, eight to six, or seven, it's going from meeting, to meeting, to meeting, to meeting, and you're looking at every phase of production, from lighting, to, animation, modeling, shading, art direction, everything, so, that's a crazy time, and it just gets more, and more intense till, finally, you're done, and then you can't quite believe it. [laughter]

> **I think a director has to be a really good editor, so that you know what's crucial to put across, and what can you cut**

Tony: What is the most important tool in your director's tool box?

Pete: I think you just have to be a good study of human nature . . . I remember at school, looking around at everybody, and going, "Oh, that guy's gonna be the best animator around," I mean, my thought was it's all about your skills, as a draftsman, or in terms of movement, and all that, and now that you get out in the world you realize how much just social skills are really crucial. The fact that somebody can communicate clearly to someone else, and corral a group of people getting

them all focused on the same page, I mean, that's all really crucial skills that a director needs, and, at the same time, I feel like, as soon as you're conscious of that, like, as soon as I stand in front of a group of people, I say to myself, "OK, Pete. You gotta lead these guys, and rev 'em up, and get 'em excited," then I just become self-conscious of it, and I think people can sense that, you know. I think it's just gotta come from you. Hopefully you have a sense of enthusiasm and passion for what you do, and an ability to communicate the emotion that you're trying to get across, and then I think, really trusting your team. And again, different people like different things, but, I feel like, the more I can tell, let's just say, an animator, the essence of a scene, and the feeling I want, and what's going on in a character's head, and let them worry about the specifics of, "Where's his hand on frame forty-seven," and "How fast does his elbow move," and all that. They know that stuff, and they're gonna bring all these great acting ideas. My job, at least initially, is just to make sure they're focused on the right thing, and that they have the right information in their heads so that they can do their job and bring their own creative ideas to the thing.

Tony: What do you start with in developing the story for one of your projects?

Pete: It's different every time. With *Monsters* it was just the concept of, "OK I know there are monsters in the closet . . . just, like, there're toys that come to life when I leave the room." That concept is what we started with, and then, from there you start asking, "Why? Why do they scare kids? What do they get out of it?" and all that.

Tony: What was it with *Up*?

Pete: *Up* it was more just a feeling of, having directed *Monsters*, wanting to get away from everybody sometimes. For me, I'm not a natural-born extrovert, so I definitely need my downtime at the end of the day, and a lot of times I would just wanna crawl under my desk and hide there for a little while, so we were starting to develop different ideas on "escape and getting away from people," and then, of course, in the end, realizing that really what life is all about, is community, and connection with other people, so, it might seem enticing at the beginning, but, by the end, you really need family and that was Carl's journey in the end. It was more of that idea that led to the specifics.

> **I'm not a natural-born extrovert, so I definitely need my downtime at the end of the day, and a lot of times I would just wanna crawl under my desk and hide there for a little while**

Tony: So, you're kind of like Carl? Is that what you're saying?

Pete: Yeah, exactly . . . Yeah, I think you have to be, you know, you have to be your characters, 'cause they all come from you. You and the team, of course.

Tony: How do you develop engaging characters, such as Carl?

Pete: We've tried a ton of different things. I remember on *Monsters* we actually . . . do you remember that, you took it in high school probably, the, Myers-Briggs personality test?

Tony: No, I don't remember that.

Pete: . . . you know, you're an I, S, T, J, or an introverted, sensing, thinking, judging person. That, kind of, personality test?

Tony: Oh yeah, I do remember that. I think I failed that test. [laughter]

Pete: So, we actually gave those tests to all our characters, you know, we answered them for Randall, and for Mike, and all that, you know, just trying to find out who these guys are, and how they would operate with each other, and, I mean, the only purpose for that was that sometimes those tests would ask us things that we wouldn't

have thought of on our own. I don't know how much that helped. A lot of times, it's almost, like, improvisational actors, where you put the characters together in a situation, and say, "Alright. The two of you." I remember we did this for *Monsters* as well, "Mike and Sulley: Sulley's on a job interview, and he has to pick out a tie, and Mike's helping him. Alright, go!," and we'd send all the different story artists, and, I think in that case, we teamed them up, and they would do these little, almost, like, improv, kind of, comedy sketch things, and, we came up with some great stuff, and it really helped us define the characters. Something else that, I remember we really struggled on that was just finding out who Sulley was, and it was only once Mike's character became clear that Sulley then, in opposition, started to emerge. So, a lot of times, characters come out of contrast, or conflict with each other, but again, every time you start one of these, you're left, kind of, scratching your head, and sometimes things come from inspiration from the voice actors, or your daughter, or sister, you just never know.

Tony: How do you work with the script writer to develop your vision for the project?

Pete: Right now I'm working with Michael Arndt, who wrote *Little Miss Sunshine* and *Toy Story 3*, and so, we sit in a room, and we'll, kind of, beat out the basics of the story, and we'll spend days talking about the general themes and concepts. Then what we usually do is say, "OK, let's write an outline. Let's figure out the specifics of what happens where, and where the characters go," and all that kind of thing, and then we'll review that, talk it around, and then, we'll start to pick out specific sequences that he'll write, or that I'll write, and then, you know, look at each other's work. I'm also working with Ronnie del Carmen, who is this amazing story artist, and he really thinks visually, so a lot of times even before we have script pages, we'll talk about story beats, and he'll just start drawing, and, so, pages will, kind of, emerge out of drawings, which is great, because then you're not relying so much on a character standing, and talking, you know, you just, instinctively as you draw, start to think more about action, and how can I show the audience this story point through movement, through character intention, instead of dialogue.

Tony: How important is the animatic to you in the process of making your movies?

Pete: It's pretty key, I mean, I'm really interested in history, animation history, and, from what I've gathered, I don't know that the Disney guys, back in Walt's day. I think they built reels, they built Lyca reels, maybe you [Tony] know something about this, but, for us today, we really use that thing as, like, if it's not in the reel, most of the time it's not in the movie. We have all the nuances of what the characters do, the beeps, the pauses, and the sound effects. It really becomes, for us, a very close blueprint of what the movie's gonna be.

Tony: How do you "issue" or "launch" a scene to an animator?

Pete: Yeah. We call 'em, "handouts," I guess.

Tony: Handouts . . . OK.

Pete: And that is probably one of the most key meetings for the director. I know John Lasseter, as he's been pulled in all these directions on his films, he feels, like, if you're gonna pull me from any meeting, that one has got to stay. Even if somebody else finals the shot John wants to be there in the handout meeting with the animators, because that is so crucial to communicate what you're looking for, so, you know, usually you have some, sort of, sheet of paper with a little image

of the storyboard, and whatever information that is going to the animator, and you run the reels, and by that time we have layout with all the final dialogue in there, and he'll, I mean, usually we watch the storyboards, 'cause there's oftentimes really great acting ideas in there, and then we watch the [CG] layout version, which is, kind of, like, chess pieces sliding around on a chess board. But then, between the two animatic versions, then the animator will turn to me, and he'll say, "You know, in this scene, the character's really feeling, you know that feeling when you have just run a marathon and you're so exhausted you can't even breathe? It's like that. It's just, you know, he's completely out of breath," and whatever other, kind of, analogies I can use, and sometimes I'll just instinctively, kind of, act it out, do some facial stuff that, that will probably inform them, and then they go off, and analyze, and do whatever their process is. Different people work different ways.

Tony: What do you look for from a first pass by an animator when they first come back to you and show you what they did?

Pete: I just try to see whether, do I feel what I want, what I was looking for, you know? Does the movement that this animator has putting across here, even though it's clunky, and missing inbetweens, or however it's presented, you know, you try to see through all that, and just look for the acting ideas, whether it's communicating clearly, and do I feel what I want to feel?

Tony: And then, as a director, what do you do when an animator just isn't getting that? What do you do to resolve that?

Pete: Well, yeah, it's, I mean, in 99% of the times, you can, if it's not there the first pass, then, in just talking through the second pass the animator will go, "Oh. Oh. I'm sorry. I misunderstood," and then, you'll get it, but sometimes it is just a slow process . . . You're saying something that the animator just doesn't understand, and in some cases we've actually, you know, gotten to a certain point and said, "OK, thanks. Let's move you on. We need you on another shot," and reassign the scene. But most of the time, if the animator did something wrong, I feel like I did something wrong, you know, I didn't communicate properly what it is that I need in the shot. Because one of the worst things as a director, is knowing that this guy or gal, has gone off for and worked on the scene for a week or two, and I'm not gonna use any of it. Wasting people's time — I hate that. Both for them, and for me, because that's basically throwing money away.

Tony: What do you look for in a creative team, art director, editor, or storyboard artist?

Pete: What I look for is a kind of a two-part thing. One is that they resonate in some way with what I'm trying to do, and, you know, I wanna, I want them to be excited about what I'm putting across, so if they, if I pitch the story to them, and they go, "Hmm . . . meh," then, you know, that's a bad sign. But, also, I feel, like, the more I know myself, and my own weaknesses, the better off I am, because I can augment, and supplement that with the talents of these other people, so, you know, I feel, like, I'm pretty clunky when it comes to camera, and staging, like, I have basic things that I know what I want, but, compared to some, some people I just don't know that I have that, "camera gene," and, so, I've always had really strong artists, like, you know, Ronnie del Carmen is amazing with that stuff. He just has an instinctive sense of where the camera should go, and, so, he brings a great deal to that, in the case of *Monsters*, Lee Unkrich, who was co-director, he brought a lot of the staging and camerawork to the project. So, I feel like, the more you know yourself, and where you're lacking, then you can find that

help, you know, have other people help bring that to the screen.

Tony: Kinda the motto of, "Always try to hire people that are better than you," right?

Pete: Yeah. Yeah. Well, that's for sure, but then also, people that are, that have strength where you have weakness.

Tony: Yes, absolutely. Well, speaking of which, how much responsibility are your creative department heads given on one of your films?

Pete: As much as I possibly can! I would love to have people that can just read my mind, and can run the departments on their own, and a lot of the times, they really do a lot, but, in most cases it takes, especially, like, we were talking about with the handout, it's, like, communicating what's needed for the story, because, as complete as the story reels are, or the animatics, there's usually something crucial missing in there that the director has to, kind of, communicate to the rest of the team, but, you know, from art, to animation, to layout, I really try to, as much as I can, empower the guys that are gonna be leading those teams. I don't remember who said this, but it was a live action director talking about, you know, 90 percent of his job, he felt, was in casting the right actors, and then, once you have 'em, you just, kind of, let 'em go, and I kinda feel, like, that's true of your leads as well. If you get the right people, it can really make things so much easier, and so much better.

Tony: Right. Well, that, kind of, plays into the next question I'll ask you, which is: Do you have direct contact with all of your staff on your project, or do you rely on department heads, or leads to communicate to the crew?

Pete: I think it's pretty crucial that you have direct contact, and it's not possible all the time. Sometimes during certain phases, or check-ins, you have to, you have to delegate, but, as much as you can, as we were talking about the handouts

From *Monsters, Inc* © 2001 Disney • Pixar

for sure, and, you know, I like to check in along the way. Both, I think it's good for the artist to hear it right from the horse's mouth of what it is you're looking for, then also, it gives them a sense of whether they're succeeding or not, you know, 'cause hopefully you're excited about what they're doing, and you can pass that enthusiasm along to them.

Tony: Do you kinda walk the floor if you have extra time? I'm sure you don't really have extra time, but . . .

Pete: I do as much as I can. Like, in animation, we have this system that has grown over the years where, the morning we have dailies, and that's everybody sittin' in the screening room, and looking at each other's work, and this came right from the beginning on *Toy Story*, that John was really, he ran that room very openly, so anybody at all was able to speak up. It wasn't like, I was expecting him to kinda rule, and say, "Here's what I want you to do, and la, da, da, da," but it was much more of a conversation, so that's pretty cool,

and everybody, we try to do that as much as we can, 'cause that's where a lot of great discovery comes from, and then in the afternoon we do walkthroughs, which is more of, it's me and the lead and the animator, so a very small group, and we're looking at, we can step through frame by frame, and this is, you know, that's where you get into the stuff that is completely contrary to what I was talking about, of letting the animator do whatever they want. Hopefully they've done that, and they've brought some great ideas, but, usually by the end there's some little thing that you're feelin' like, "Eh. That's not quite working, and let's just get in there and take a couple frames out," or "I wanna push this pose a little more," or whatever, and that's the time to do that.

Tony: How do you combat the, "Us against Them," attitude that can arise on a production between creative management and the artistic crew?

Pete: For me, I mean, I've had great producers on both the films I've directed, and on the one I'm working on now, it's Jonas Rivera again, and he and I just click on so many levels that we're both after the same thing. So he doesn't try to do my job, I don't try to do his job, and yet, we both contribute to each other's, so, he'll come in and say, "OK, Pete. Here is the schedule. We have a screening day here, and this is all the work we need to do. I was thinkin' maybe we could do this, but what do you think?," and, so, we'll kick around things like that, and I trust that the information he's given me is right and accurate, and then, once we agree on a strategy, I trust that he'll be able to get there, and similarly, creatively, you know, he'll come in and say, "Hey, I watched the reels, and I had this thought. I don't know . . . ," you know, he'll be very deferential, but, he'll kick in some ideas, usually more one-on-one than in a large group, so, that way we kinda contribute both to each other's job. And in large part because of him, and who he is, he tries to get a real focus from the other managers that, "OK, first of all, we're all making a movie. We're not producing footage in animation, right? That's secondary. We're making a film," so, you know, the focus has to be right. And secondly, his thing is, "Let's pretend this is our own cash, so, when we say we want to spend X number of hours on this, if it was my money would I still spend it? Yes, or no," and that kind of helps make decisions as well.

Tony: That's a great way of looking at it too. Makes it more personal, for sure.

Pete: Yeah. Exactly.

Tony: Do you find it difficult to be true to your original vision for the project as time goes by?

Pete: Yeah. It's tricky because, on the one hand, if you just hold doggedly to what you first came up with, you're gonna fail, because, I think, the nature of, especially these studios, were set up to have these projects evolve, and change, and grow, and hopefully they get better, and better. Sometimes, you have this track laid in a straight direction, and it kinda bends a little bit, and sometimes that might feel, like, "Hey. We're going in the wrong direction," but other times, you know, by the time you get there, you feel, like, "Whoah, I'm glad we took that turn," you know, so, it's both a matter of holding on to the, kind of, feeling, or the nugget of what it was you were trying to say, but also, take into account, especially the audience, you know, as you show this thing, what do people react to, 'cause that's ultimately why you're doing it. It's not an exercise in therapy for yourself; it's making entertainment for people, so, you wanna be really aware of what people are reacting to and what they respond to.

Tony: What do you do to make sure your vision is being communicated to your crew?

Pete: Whatever it takes. Just a couple days ago, I brought in this piece of music, that had literally nothing to do with anything but, it just had a feeling that I wanted in this scene, and so you give it to the story artist, and say, "Listen to this while you're boarding." Sometimes it'll be acting something out, or writing up a document, you know; almost every film, there's these, kind of, a, what do we, what do I, these, sort of, mandates, you know, two page documents, like, "OK, here's what I'm really looking for in the design of the thing," or whatever, so, you know, sometimes writing things helps you kinda crystallize, and distill down what it is you're trying to say. "If I had to jump around naked, I'd do that," you know, I mean, really, it takes, whatever it takes.

Tony: Would the naked thing be inspiring for the crew?

Pete: I don't know. I think that would be scary to them. [laughter]

Tony: We all know that budgets and schedules are a big part of life for the filmmaker, but how do you look at them personally, as a friend or foe?

Pete: Both. I mean, from a distance, I think, "Oh, it's crucial. It's essential that every creative endeavor have a deadline." Otherwise we'd never get done, which I think is true, but, then when you're in there, you're, like, "Ahhh, this sucks! Get this schedule outta here! I just want more time! I need time!," so, it's both. I think having the schedule in mind, it really helps for me, kicks me in the butt, because I do, at the beginning, tend to . . . the world has so many possibilities, and, so, it's the schedule that limits you, and says, "OK, you have two weeks. Out of all these possibilities which ones do you want to allow yourself to explore?," and it forces you to make decisions and choices and I do think none of our films would have been finished had we not had a deadline.

Tony: Back in the day when I was at Disney and working on *Mulan*, we never talked about the budget for the film. By your answer, you've mostly talked about the schedule, is that how it is for you, too?

Pete: Yeah. I mean, to be honest, I don't even know what our budgets are, you know. The producer does, but, really what it comes down to is weeks and time, so I know that I have Artist A for three weeks and that's it. So, what do I want him to do before he goes away? I'm sure many companies are like this, but Ed Catmull, who's the president around here, is very analytical, and, so, he likes to, from time to time, step back, and say, "OK, where is the studio going, and how can we do things better?," and, so, we noticed that the man-weeks from *Toy Story* to *Bug's Life* jumped huge, and that it kept going up, and up, and up, and we realized, this is not gonna to be attainable at some point. It's gonna take so many people, and so much time, that we're gonna outprice ourselves. There's no way we can make enough back for the time invested, so they've been trying to correct that, and on every picture they ask to come in a little bit smaller, a little bit smaller in

terms of the number of weeks, which is, you know, it's a good challenge. Sometimes it's untenable, but I think it almost makes you try to think smarter about how to get that up on the screen.

Tony: Do you have input into the budget and schedule on one of your films? Probably more schedule I would think, right?

Pete: Yeah. Yeah. More schedule, and like I say, the budget is really, it's a function of time, and then the specific people, and that's why I think they don't want us to feel, like, "Oh. You don't want to hire the seasoned guys, because they're more expensive, so we're gonna go for all the cheap guys," you know, they just say, "OK, we want you to come in at this number of man-weeks, and that's what we're really looking at," so, then that becomes the source of many, many meetings, a lot more that Jonas, the producer, has to be in, but I sit in on a couple of 'em, and, kind of, at least have a sense for, "OK, the work that you guys have done, you've allocated this amount here, and this amount there, and my feeling is, based on the story, we really have to spend more on balloon development," or whatever, "because that's gonna be a really key element. I know you don't see it on the boards yet, but it's gonna be huge. We need to have those things look right," so, it's that, kind of, back and forth.

Tony: At Pixar, do meetings help make the film or do they distract from the creative process?

Pete: Yeah, It's funny. I remember talking to Marc Davis, before he died. We got to go over to his house, and we had dinner, and we were talking about Disneyland, and how they did *Pirates of the Caribbean*, and we asked him about meetings, and he said, "Meetings!? We didn't have any meetings! We just did it!," you know, and, "If I wanted something, I made the call, and there weren't any budget meetings," and all this. That may, or may not be true . . .

From *Up.* © 2009 Disney • Pixar.

Tony: Yeah. I find it hard to believe.

Pete: But we definitely have a lot of meetings around here, and I think the bigger a studio is, and the bigger a production is the more meetings you need to have, because, when it's small, you can just say, "Hey guys, come here!," and then you can blab out what you're looking for, but, when it's big, you can't do that, so you have to structure it, and as soon as you sense a meeting is going nowhere, then we try to just either correct it, or disband, you know. I like to, especially as a director, I want to come in with a sense of, "What is this meeting about and what do we have to accomplish?," So, right at the beginning, kind of, explicitly state your goals, what is supposed to happen during this hour, or half-hour, and if you don't make it, then that's you. Sometimes it might be creatively that you just haven't solved what was necessary, but, you just don't wanna go off the rails and start thinking about some other thing that's not the point of this meeting.

Tony: You spoke to this a little bit earlier, and this is a product of being a director in a big studio, I'm sure, but, do you have to interact with a producer, or studio executives on a continual basis and what do those relationships look like for you?

Pete: Yeah, both. At Pixar, we're certainly lucky, because there's not a sense of adversarial nature there at all. Everybody's very collaborative, and supportive, you know, but, having said that, whenever we hear, "Oh, we have a John check-in," that you know, John Lasseter's coming over to look at what you're doing, well, your blood pressure goes up, because you want it to look good, you know. He's gonna bring great ideas to it. I've never been to a meeting with him, where it wasn't productive, because he's just brilliant. But it, I think in a good way, makes you, step up a little bit. I hear a lot of people, especially, you know, at other studios, that feel, like, "Oh no. This guy came in, and I just got these awful notes, and now, what do I do?," you know, "The movie's getting worse because of these executives who are coming in and suggesting things," and we've been pretty much sheltered from that, which is awesome, and I know we're spoiled because of it.

Tony: What is your definition of the perfect producer? You've already talked about your producer, Jonas Rivera, that you've worked with on the last two films, and maybe he's it, but, what is your definition of the perfect producer for you?

Pete: Yeah. I think that person needs to, definitely, be a close confidant and friend, and somebody who understands creatively what you're trying to do, but doesn't try and do it himself or herself. Both Darla Anderson, who produced *Monsters*, and Jonas Rivera, who produced *Up*, have that ability, and it's gotta be a thankless job, because, of course, as the director, and the creative staff, they get most of the glory at the end, right? The press wants to talk to them, and the producer's, kind of, this invisible, "Oh, yeah . . . Let's talk about schedule and money," and, of course, that's not really what their job is, but, that's the perception. I think the other thing that both Darla and Jonas have is this great easygoing personality, and they tend to attract talent, you know, and any time you have to fight away people from wanting to work on your film you know you're in good shape. You know that somehow you've chosen the right key people if they attract other key people.

Tony: How important is it to keep up with current technology for you?

Pete: Well, I always like it. I don't feel like it's a job for me. It's like, any time I can, going to these tool show and tells, or looking at new development, it's, like, having new toys to play with, because then, who knows how I'll be able to use that, and I do think it's pretty key, you know, if you have all these great tools it means you can think better, and more efficiently about how to put ideas across, or maybe that opens up a whole new creative venue for you, that you wouldn't have even thought of had you not seen this new tool that does X, you know?

Tony: Where do you find your inspiration?

Pete: There are a lot of directors and filmmakers here that talk, and reference other movies, and I do, to some degree, but more often I'll find it just out in life, you know, "Oh. That reminds me of this situation, or this guy that I met, or this incident that happened to me at the airport," or whatever. I think inspiration largely comes from real life, which is why it's important to have some, sort of, balance, as a director. If you spend all your time at work, then you've got no life, and that tends to limit you creatively.

Tony: I remember at CalArts you and a bunch of the guys going out, and just drawing, and recording people with tape recorders at the shopping center, or at the grocery store, and I remember you guys doing that on an ongoing basis. At the time I thought you guys were crazy, and wasting time [laughter]. But now I look back, and I think, man, you guys had the right idea, studying people.

Pete: Yeah, and I feel, like, I'm getting lazy now. I'm not doing that as much, and I think it's really important, because, you know, even just the way people dress, or talk, all those things change over time, and I wanna make sure that I'm not getting all my information off of TV shows, and movies, that I'm out there in the world, and observing the way real people act.

> **You know that somehow you've chosen the right key people if they attract other key people.**

Tony: That's your audience. You wanna be relevant. Along those lines, where do you see the animation industry going in the future?

> **If you spend all your time at work, then you've got no life, and that tends to limit you creatively.**

Pete: That's a good question. I'm never quite sure how to answer that, because I don't really feel, like, in some sense, I don't feel, like, what we do today is really very different than the way Walt Disney, and those guys were treating what they did back in the 1940s, you know. I think it's still a focus on character, and on storytelling, and getting something up there on the screen that the people in the seats look up there, and even though it might be about cars, or monsters, or toys, they still say, "There's something about that that I see in myself. I really resonate with what's happening up on the screen," and, you know, today's movies are a little, for sure, faster-paced, and the technology is totally different, and that'll continue to change, but, I think, at its core, that basic idea of speaking to the audience about what life is about, that's gonna remain the same as long as people are around, I think.

Tony: Any last words for the young artist that may be reading this book and want to be a director one day?

Pete: Just weird stuff that pops into mind is, keep drawing. I think a lot of people feel, like, "Oh. It's computers. I don't need to draw." It's really crucial. Being able to draw, it helps me see better, you know? I might look at somebody, or something, and go, "Heh. Heh. That's really cool. I love that," but, then if I draw it, then it sticks in my brain, and I notice details that I wouldn't have otherwise, you know, by putting it down, as well as, of course, just being a great tool for communicating. You get in, and talk to people, and, "Uhh. It should be . . . uhhh . . . Give me a piece of paper," and it just, you know, a picture speaks a thousand words, so drawing is crucial. And take *risks*! Don't just fall into being a big fan of fill-in-the-blank filmmaker, and trying to do what they do, you know, if there's some way that you feel, like, "Man, I can do this in my own way," or, "push things in this direction," or, "I don't know who's done this, but I think we can." Keep challenging yourself like that and stay true to your own strengths . . . What I want to see when I sit down in a theater is not some regurgitated product from a studio. I want to see what feels to me like a statement, that there was a soul behind this. That somebody felt driven to make this movie. Even if it might be flawed, I'd rather see the stamp, or the hand of an artist than a perfect bland film.

Tony: I think that's a great way to end it. Pete, thank you so much for your time.

> **I think, at its core, that basic idea of speaking to the audience about what life is about, that's gonna remain the same as long as people are around, I think.**

BE PREPARED

Know What's Coming and Prepare for It

They say that **if you are prepared for the worst then the worst probably won't happen.** That may not always be true but I know I've found that it helps to be ready for my creative team as the film goes down the production pipeline. Animation is a slow and laborious process but there is still plenty of time to make it even slower and more laborious by not being prepared. Lack of preparation can translate into budget and schedule overages, or worst, not making your delivery date! This is where it is crucial to have a keen understanding of the production process for your project. By knowing what comes next you can work ahead of the process and insure you are properly prepped for the next group of creatives coming onto the project. A great example of this is from Dean DeBlois's interview that he gave for this book. He mentions there that as he is working on *How To Train Your Dragon 2* he has told the producers that he does not want to bring on storyboard artists until he himself really knows the story inside and out. He is bringing them on at a much later date than the film's production schedule suggested – but for good reason. Many times a studio is eager to bring on the next department in hopes that this infusion of new creative minds will speed up the process by helping the director to search out solutions to creative problems. These new artists feel like they are wasting their time contributing ideas that usually don't pan out and the director gets frustrated by "more cooks in the kitchen" asking questions that he has asked himself months ago. DeBlois has the right idea. Make sure you as the director are prepared before bringing on costly others. It may seem to take longer but in the long run will save money and time.

> **"** A lot of directors don't know what they want to do. Every director I've seen that was a good director that I've admired knew exactly what he wanted to do. They didn't sit there and think about it. **"**
>
> – John Milius

Artists Need Answers

Every department in the production pipeline has their own unique needs so they can do their job to the utmost. The basic ones are obvious: What is the story? How much time do I have for my part in the process? What is the approval process? But there are so many more questions that will be specific to that department's skill set. An art director needs to understand what the emotional rhythms of the sequences are so he knows what palette to use. A modeler needs to know what the style choices are so he knows how to sculpt his shapes. A rigger, the limits that the model needs to twist and turn in any given scene. The director needs to learn what all those creative needs are so that your artistic staff can perform at the top of their abilities and give you what you want. The best way to learn what those needs are is to come up through the production chain yourself. The best directors are those that have spent years not only becoming expert in their given job in animation but also spent much of that time working and communicating with other artists in various departments developing an understanding of how they work and what their needs are. Some of the most successful CEOs started in the mail room and worked their way up. The needs of every department are too numerous to list and change based on the project but one good example is the **animation department**.

Since I was an animator and have directed animators this is the one area I feel very qualified to speak about. An animator's questions for the director are exactly what an actor in a live action film would be: to know who the character is they are working on and what that character wants in any given scene. **A bad animator cares only about the physical action of getting the character from point A to point B. A good animator wants to know why the character is doing what he is doing.** But an animator is concerned with technical elements too. Is the style of animation more limited or full? What is the camera doing in this scene? Does my scene hook-up to some other animator's scene that has been previously animated and I need to match too? So, to answer these questions: enter the director's "issuing" session. Some studios call this a "launch" or "scene start" but no matter what it's called, this is a crucial meeting between director and animator where they sit down and discuss the scene or group of scenes that the animator is about to start to work on. The director will usually start by showing the most recent cut of the storyboard animatic. Then they will discuss it. First, the main focus (or importance) of the scene.

Supervising Animator, Tom Bancroft (right) gets a Mushu scene issued to him by the directors on Disney's *Mulan*.

What is it about? What is the motivation of the character? Next, perhaps discussing the actor's voice performance and any elements that the director wants to accentuate or "hit" in the dialogue. Is there subtext that needs to be brought out through the visual performance? Then the director can discuss the staging – including how the characters' movement should be choreographed to move the audience's eye through the scene. And finally, adding any detail that is not readily obvious in the storyboards such as expressions or poses that could be funnier. This is the time for the animator to take notes and, just as crucial, ask questions. Therefore the director should be prepared to answer these questions or at least get the answers if not readily available. By the end of this meeting the animator should know exactly what the director wants from the scene and how it fits into the larger sequence and film.

I have been a part of hundreds of "issuing" sessions on both sides of the table and one thing is for sure, if the director doesn't communicate the scene's purpose, the animator will create their own. I remember working freelance as an animator on a commercial where the director gave me such loose direction it was ridiculous! It was just, "it's all in the boards just make it funnier." OK . . . So, I went to work. First, I did my homework: I looked at the animatic watching for scene continuity and hook-up poses that I needed to match to; then I listened to the dialogue over and over to glean any fun expressions that would make the scene funnier. I thought I did everything asked of me but upon turning the scene in for director review I found out he was upset with me. He was mad that I didn't accentuate the product that the commercial was all about. I told him that was never mentioned by him in the issuing session and it wasn't emphasized in the boards either. The director thought that it should have been obvious but never bothered to communicate the most important element of the scene to me. And it was **my** fault that I didn't read his mind! Assumptions like this happen at every studio on productions large and small. They are part of a lazy, unprepared director's daily regime and cost the production a lot of money in changes later. This commercial was ultimately completed but that director has a hard time finding the creative staff that will work with him a second time. I know I'll be busy when he calls.

Give Clear Direction

One of the things you can't help is how information you give to someone else is translated. Case in point, a director can give the insight to an animator that a character is "excited" thinking that will help describe the **outward physicality** of the character but the animator could translate that word as an **inner emotion** and make the character happily thoughtful. Worse yet is an example of a director that I worked with (whom shall remain nameless) that, when reviewing an animator's first rough pass of a scene, would be so unclear as to what bothered him that it made the animator feel confused and insulted. The animator thought that he did everything asked by the director in the scene but the director would just look at the scene and say, "Nope, that's not it! I don't like it!" and summarily dismiss the animator to figure out where he miss-stepped. How does that help an animator? A director has to give **some** direction! It's the "I don't know what I want but I'll know it when I see it" syndrome that is the worst kind of lazy directing. If you don't know what you want, then don't expect others to know for you. A director should be keen enough to assess the scene and imagine it to be what he wants it to be and understand the difference. Often times, the difference between liking the scene and not are small changes. It could be just an adjustment in the staging, a stronger pose or more comic timing. If you are a director with limited animation experience or can't draw and therefore don't feel comfortable getting technical, then it's best for you to describe how the scene should make you *feel*. Things like "I want to feel like the character is more torn between his choices in this scene" or "I'm not feeling like the character is excited enough." Whatever the problem is, be as specific and clear as possible and your team will get you what you want.

The Real Pressure Cooker: Working with Voice Actors

You really learn to appreciate how easy going and humble animation artists are to direct once you get to the recording phase with professional voice actors. I'm not saying they are all horrible to work with but, wow . . . some definitely are! I've worked with a bunch of big "name" actors in my career and some have been a pleasure and some a personal hell I don't want to revisit anytime soon. But whether the actor has a big ego or not is not the biggest problem in recording the talent for your film. The real pressure comes from making sure that session goes as smoothly as possible. This is especially true if you are directing at a large studio on a big budget feature with an A-list voice cast. Talk about pressure!

Your time with big "name" actors is minimal and you must be overly prepared for recording sessions. For a main character in

The great Patrick Warburton (Kronk) pondering the readiness of his spinach puffs for Disney's *The Emperor's New Groove*.

a film the studio will usually only have 5–8 recording sessions agreed upon in the voice actor's contract to be used over the term of the movie. Each recording session takes forever to schedule with the actor's agent and by the Screen Actors Guild (SAG – the actor's union) rules, a session can only go for a maximum of four hours with any one actor. The studio is paying a lot of money for that actor to come in and probably pulled a lot of strings to make it happen. The studio heads and executives will be anxious that everything goes well so they may request to be in the recording room with you. Their stress slides down to the producer and then her stress to the director to make sure that session runs efficiently. The concern is not only that the actor is happy but most importantly, if you do not get all of your script material recorded in that session, it may be months before you get that actor back again.

When recording Eddie Murphy as the voice of Mushu for Disney's *Mulan*, scheduling was horrible. Murphy was busy with filming several movies during the duration of work on *Mulan* (most notably *The Nutty Professor*) so getting him to commit to a schedule was near impossible. This back and forth of schedule requests went on for months until the production couldn't wait anymore. We had to record him or we were in jeopardy of not finishing animation on time. It finally came down to his request of us flying out to his home in New Jersey where he would give us some time. He had a small recording studio in his basement that he used to record some of his music. We quickly rigged it for our specific film recording needs and he came down in his bathrobe and recorded his lines. It was where he felt comfortable and at the end of the day it was worth the hassle because that's what gave us the great performance of Mushu for the film.

I have learned a few dos and don'ts over the years of recording various actors that can really help in making the sessions run efficiently and make the actor feel comfortable.

Before the recording session
- Go over the story animatic and discuss all of the scenes you will be recording. Know why every line is there

thinking over the subtext or meaning behind each one. Bring in a separate "comedy punch-up" writer, if necessary, to add more comedy to the dialogue if it is lacking.

- Work over the script one last time. Put together a "pre-recording" meeting with you, the producer, the writer, and any recording PA that will be in the room with the actor on the day of the session. Review the "highlighted and numbered script" only (the PA should have already gone through the script highlighting the actor's lines and numbered them so it is easy to discuss a specific line individually). Make sure to highlight things like laughs, coughs or impact noises that you will need from the actor but maybe forgotten because they are in the script description but not the line.

- The recording PA should staple all of the actor's pages on individual cardboard pieces for ease of use during the recording session. If the pages are just loose paper alone they make noise that can be picked up on the microphone as the actor turns pages. Rustling noise during a take is a lost take!

- The day before the recording session make notes in the margins of your script on lines that you feel may need

Production assistants ready the recording studio for the voice-over actor. The script pages are adhered to cardboard sheets to reduce noisy page turning during recording. A missed take is a mistake!

The director should review the recording script the night before a big recording session to make sure he is prepared.

extra coaching for the actor to get the read you want. I will write acting instructions like, "as if hearing this for the first time," "like you just got punched in the gut by this news" or "like a bratty kid teasing" next to the lines to remind me of what I am going for in the read. I try to paint an emotional picture for the actor with the notes. Stay away from technical notes like "should be fast" or "staccato read." More on this below.

- Just before the actor arrives talk with the recording engineer about how you like to call out takes or any other procedural business so that it is not wasting the actor's time later.

During the recording session:

- Don't assume that just because the actor has done years of television and movies that they feel comfortable in front of a microphone in a dark room by themselves. Although your producer or the casting director should have communicated how the session will run and should have asked about any specific personal needs the voice talent might have in advance, you should still "roll out the welcome mat" to make your voice talent feel comfortable upon his or her arrival. Talk briefly to the actor about the environment of the recording room.

Does this lighting work for you? Would you like a bottle of water beside your stand?

- Decide whether to show the animatic with scratch dialogue to the actor or just pitch the scene to them on boards. The latter approach is preferred by the more sensitive actors because to hear the sequence with someone else doing scratch for their character can throw them off their ideas of what they want to explore in the character reading. I really only show the edited animatic if there is a pacing or cadence to the dialogue that I think is important to point out. Even at that I always prelude the sequence with, "what you are about to see is very rough and performed by non-actors around the office . . ." That way the actor won't be under the false impression that you are showing something they are to imitate in some way and they feel like they are necessary to the process.

- Some actors may be a little put off by the fact that they are alone in a recording room and everyone else

Make sure the actor is coming into a comfortable environment.

is in a sound-proof engineer's room talking about their performance in-between takes. I like to ask the actor before starting if they would like me to sit in the recording booth **with** them to read against them. Because acting is so much about *reacting*, many actors prefer to have someone to play their lines against so they can get better reactions and pacing. This is a great way to make the actor feel more comfortable and develop a trust report. The director must be very careful though as their voice will be picked up on the microphone too. If the director comes in too quickly after the actor's line, you will have an unusable take. If the actor would prefer not to have you in the room than hiring a "professional reader" or another actor to be in the room reading against them may be a good idea. On *Mulan* we did this many times for Ming Na Win (Mulan) and her performance really benefited from it. Although Eddie Murphy never seemed to like it. "He slows me down," Murphy would say.

- Remember to keep the energy up in a sequence. Slow readings are trouble in editorial because there is not much to do editing-wise to speed them up without making them lampoonish.
- Be conscious of the time. If you spend two hours of a four-hour session just going over the first 10 pages of script then you will have to rush everything else.
- Lastly, do whatever you have to do to get the performance recorded.

On that last note, I once recorded a very famous actress (whom will remain nameless) who had done literally, hundreds of voice-over recording session in her career. She was the sweetest person I had ever worked with but when she got in front of the mic we couldn't hear her voice over the rattling of her jewelry. I literally had to ask her to take off all of her jewelry so we could record her "jingle" free. Being a professional she agreed to do it but was perplexed about why she needed to saying that she never had to before. After seeing the 10 pounds of gold and silver she laid on the table, I was perplexed as to why she thought she **wouldn't** have a problem!

Albert Hitchcock showed his disdain for the Method actor when he jokingly said, "When an actor comes to me and wants to discuss his character, I say, 'It's in the script.' If he says, 'But what's my motivation?' I say, 'Your salary.'" But the truth is that most voice-over actors rely on the same Method approaches that theatre actors do to find their character so it's important for the director to understand that training. The actor wants to know the emotional **why** behind a line or scene. If an actor is struggling with a line, it's usually a good sign that it is either the wrong line for the character or the actor needs to understand a change that has occurred to the character in that given scene. A director needs to communicate differently when working with professional actors. To give a technical note such as "can you give me that line twice as fast?" can be confusing to an actor. The actor wants to know **why** the character is saying the line faster. Is she rushed because of an impending calamity? Is she hurried because she has important information to get out? Is she speaking fast to avoid revealing a deeper truth? You can see that all of the possible answers to these "why questions" would take the line reading in a variety of unique and interesting directions then just "read it faster."

Be Prepared to Throw Away Your Preparation

The biggest problem with preparation is that you can miss the moments of spontaneous inspiration that arise. In animation, spontaneity is usually hard to come by but when it happens you have to grab it. Many of the best little gems about every film I have ever worked on were discovered in an off-handed comment, a funny scribble, an improved line or an unplanned hall meeting. The director must be flexible enough to recognize a better idea when it happens and have sense enough to roll with it. Be in the moment. That is to say, **don't think so hard about what comes next that you miss the greatness in front of you.**

interview: eric goldberg

Legendary animator and director Eric Goldberg was born in 1955 in Bucks County, PA and grew up in Cherry Hill, NJ. Goldberg studied at Pratt Institute, where he majored in illustration. While still in college, his work impressed master animator Richard Williams who hired Goldberg to work on the mid-1970s feature *Raggedy Ann and Andy*. Williams, eventually moved Goldberg to London to join him at his studio where Goldberg animated and directed commercials for over four years. During the 1980s, Goldberg started his own London-based studio, Pizazz Pictures, to produce television commercials on his own. Walt Disney Animation came calling in 1990, persuading Goldberg to jump the pond again to work on a string of feature hits at their Burbank, CA studio. Utilizing his love of comedy, Goldberg, supervised two of Disney's funniest characters in the Genie (*Aladdin*, 1992) and Phil (*Hercules*, 1997). Goldberg also became co-director of Disney's 1995 feature *Pocahontas*. Soon after, he received an Annie Award nomination for his work directing the animation for Warner Brother's 2003 live-action/animation hybrid feature *Looney Tunes: Back in Action*, where he also provided the voices of Marvin the Martian, Tweety, and Speedy Gonzalez. In 2011, he was given the Annie Award's top honor, the Winsor McKay Award, for his achievements in animation. Besides his animation feature work, Goldberg is a multiple award winner for directing the animation on numerous commercials and short films throughout his career. I was able to interview Eric Goldberg in his office at Disney Feature Animation.

Tony: How did you get into the animation industry?

Eric: Oh, boy. Well, I was always an animation geek, from when I was very young. I was a TV boomer baby, you know, and, started doing flip books at a very early age, and eventually got a Super 8 camera as a Bar Mitzvah present, and started making my own Super 8 films, which eventually found their way to Richard Williams, who was directing *Raggedy Ann and Andy* in New York, actually bi-coastally, New York and LA. A friend told me that they were hiring. I was still in college at the time, but I went down for the world's worst interview, because we didn't have DVDs, we didn't have, you know, links to our online websites . . . no, I lugged a Super 8 sound projector with me. The reels are clattering all over the floor. Fortunately, Dick Williams saw something in me, and decided to hire me anyway, and once *Raggedy Ann and Andy* was finished, eventually he invited me to go to his London studio, and do television commercials, so, I packed my bags, and went to London.

Tony: What do you like best about what you do?

Eric: You know, the thing that I like the best is seeing, or *feeling* an audience respond, you know? Joe Grant [legendary Disney artist and mentor] used to say, "Animation is monk's work." He never had the patience to actually animate which is why he stuck to design and all the other areas, but, at the end of the day, we are, kind of, cloistered, as directors, as animators, hunched over our desks, working things out, and putting in an awful lot of labor-intensive hours, hoping that the alchemy of all of that will actually result in somebody sitting in an audience in Peoria, and making them laugh, and that's huge! To think that you could orchestrate worlds from blank sheets of paper, blank computer screens, and still have somebody who's never seen the work before respond, whether they laugh, whether they cry, you know, whether they're moved in any way. That's a pretty amazing thing, so I think that's really what I like best about it and if I was gonna split between animating and directing, well, animating's like being in front of the camera, and directing's like being behind the camera. So, as an animator you get to really push performance, and as a director you get to see the big picture.

Tony: What were some of the steps you took to move up to directing animation, specifically for commercials?

Eric: Well, I always knew I wanted to animate – from the age of six, making flip books and drawing. I just kept at it, and kept at it, and knew that eventually it was gonna lead to other things. One thing that was quite impactful on my early

years was the Kodak Teenage Movie Awards, where they would award you a prize for your film, you know, if it made the cut. They held the awards at the Plaza Hotel, in New York every year. My first year, I won a second prize. Two years later I won a first prize, and then two years after that I won the *grand prize*, which was, you know, a summer course at USC in filmmaking. In that grand prize year I roomed at the Plaza Hotel with David Silverman, who then became a lifelong friend, and, of course, he went on to do *The Simpsons*. But it was those Kodak Teenage Movie Award that got me thinking about filmmaking: "OK, how do I construct these shots? How do I time them out? How do I stage them for clarity?" all that kind of stuff, so I was a nascent filmmaker in my teenage years. And, truth be told, even in my flip books, I was doing that. I'd have about five *scene cuts* in a flip book, you know, and really be, kind of, directing it, and when *Raggedy Ann and Andy* finished I contacted Dick Williams, to have him write a letter of recommendation for me, and he said, "Well, come to London. Come to London. I have a commercial with a pot-bellied kangaroo in it."[laughter] So, I did. I flew to London and the Monday I get in I get handed a schedule by Jill Purdum, who was the producer, and it said, *"Director, Eric Goldberg*: Schedule three weeks."

Tony: Director?

Eric: Yeah, I was immediately *promoted* . . .

Tony: Wow!

Eric: . . . and it's a kind of thing where, with the knowledge of that, was the fact that if I don't deliver on time, the ad agency will sue the company because they'll miss their air date! I was 21 at the time-talk about being thrown

> animating's like being in front of the camera, and directing's like being behind the camera.

into the deep end! The great thing about doing commercials, at that time especially and at a place like Dick's is, you're surrounded by all this amazing talent. You had Richard Purdum, Russell Hall, Tony White. You had all these, really, really great guys. You had Roy Nesbitt doing the layouts. And Dick himself, who was the world's greatest mentor, as well as, so passionate about the medium, and he'd also bring over the elder statesmen animators, like, Ken Harris, and Art Babbitt. I got to know them, and work with them, but, aside from that atmosphere, it was sink, or swim. You got that schedule, and you had to do everything. You had to stage it. You had to lay it out. You had to animate it. You had to pick the colors. You, basically, had to do everything! It was total immersion filmmaking, and that trains you pretty quickly, you know. It's a, kind of, thing where, normally I would turn out about five minutes of animation a year, so, that's maybe ten commercials, and that's a fairly sizable chunk for anybody to turn out.

Tony: At that young, inexperienced age, were you working directly with the ad agencies and client?

Eric: Absolutely. The agency guys would come in, and tell us what they wanted, and at that time, and, actually, it still occurs to this day; their storyboards would be very, very loose. So, the very first thing that would happen, is that you would re-board it to, first of all, give it some character, and personality, and, second of all, stage it correctly, so it would actually work, and you'd know where the scene cuts were, and all that. That's the first *directorial* part of the process, in commercials, is taking it from an agency storyboard, and making it into something

> **I don't deliver on time, the ad agency will sue the company because they'll miss their air date!**

that actually feels like a 30-second film with a beginning, a middle, and an end. Regardless of whether there's a pack shot [product shot] in it, or not, you're still communicating in a very concise amount of time, all of this information that has to get across, and be entertaining at the same time. When I finally landed at Disney's, and did the Genie [in *Aladdin*], commercials were fantastic training for me, because I already had years of experience learning how to make something read in a split second, which was helpful for doing the Genie. I could use all of that stuff that I learned to get it to read. Yes, you don't get a character like the Genie coming down the pike every day, but, the fact is, that I had all that commercial training, and I knew what I could achieve with the fewest number of frames.

Tony: Have you directed animation in any other mediums, other than 2D drawings, and, if so, what do you prefer?

Eric: I've directed all sorts of media. I've done some stop motion. I did some pixilation with a live actor. I've directed CG animation. So, it's, a kind of thing where all the same principles prevail no matter what the delivery system. You're still making things work based on all the classic principles, even if you're using something different. Now, I can't animate on the computer, but I can direct computer animators, you know, because you're still talking about acting, and weight, and timing, and performance, and all the other stuff . . .

Tony: The basics of animation.

Eric: Exactly. So, that's not a huge stretch for me, and, in fact, because I can draw, I can help the computer animators. I can draw mouth shapes for different blend shapes. I can draw turnarounds

From *Aladdin.* © 1992 Disney.

for the characters, you know, and, it's a, kind of, thing where my drawing will inform what they do on the computer animation, so, it's really not very different. My favorite, of course, is hand-drawn. Always will be, but, hand-drawn sounds, at least these days, like it's a limited thing. But it's not. Working at Dick Williams, and then later at my own company, Pizzazz, I learned that hand-drawn encompasses so much. You can do any style. You can do any graphic style in hand-drawn. You can make it painterly. You can make it sketchy. You can make it, you know, with the heck rendered out of it on a frosted cel. You can do anything in hand-drawn. It doesn't necessarily have to look, like, cliché Hollywood design, you know. Russell Hall, who went on to animate Jessica Rabbit,

in *Who Framed Roger Rabbit*, used to be one of my roommates at Richard Williams, and we had a couple of jobs based on the artwork of Ronald Searle. So, late into the night, Russell is sitting there with a dip *ink pen*, and animating on cel with a dip pen, so it looks exactly like Ronald Searle drawings, and the jobs were stunning! Russell said something that always stuck with me. He used to smoke these very unfiltered cigarettes, and, he'd take a drag, and say [with British accent], "You know, it probably took Ronald Searle about 40 years to develop this style, and we have to do it in three weeks" [laughter].

Tony: That's the job of a traditional animator: you are always adapting to the style of the commercial, the film, commercial or whatever it is.

Eric: It's a challenge, you know. Every now, and again, you know, you would be called upon to animate something that preexisted, you know, like, one of the commercials we did at Pizzazz was based on a faux Patrick Nagel style, so I staged the whole thing, and drew it, and animated it in the most minimal fashion possible to actually suit the style. It's nowhere near the same kind of animation that you would do if you were doing *Tom and Jerry*. It's the kind of thing where you adapt the style of movement, and the style of staging, often to the design that's being utilized, rather than the other way around. Now, often it's an organic relationship. You want to stage something that way, because it looks like that or you'll know what the content of a commercial is supposed to be from the ad agency, and the client.

Tony: One thing I'm missing in your background is: How long were you at, at Dick's, and then when did you start your own studio [Pizzazz]?

Eric: I was at Dick's London studio from 1977 to 1981. That was four years, and we had our own studio, Pizzazz, from 1984 to 1990, so, basically, it was about six or seven years . . .

Tony: And that was in London? You started it in London?

Eric: Yeah, and in between that time, you know, I had come west to direct the animation on *Ziggy's Gift*, which we also did commercial-style. We did it Sharpie-on-cel, and it's a, kind of, thing where most of the industry that was working on it would say, "You're not animating on cel. Nobody animates on cel." Well, we did, and to my knowledge it was the only way we were gonna get it done, and get it in style. You could use a Sharpie, and get that crinkly Tom Wilson ink line on there perfectly. It would look just fine, so, it's a thing where, better to do that than Xerox it. The other thing, too, is, that it was a complete time saver, because, many times, if you had a complex

piece of animation, you might rough it out on paper first, and then tie it down on cel, but you'd leave the in-betweens just to be done directly on cel, you know, and you'd flip the cels. There'd be tissue in-between, and you'd get a very accurate in-between.

Tony: That's so interesting. I haven't done a lot of cel work, so, to me, that is an art form in itself.

Eric: When we had Pizzazz, we had the luxury of having our own ink and paint department. While in London at the time, the ink and paint departments were filled with people who wanted to be something else. This person wants to be a poet. This person wants to be a rock star. So on, and so forth, but they found that they had steady hands, and so, we had these beautiful colored ink lines on our cel, you know, when we were doing commercials at Pizzazz, yeah, we'd do some stuff directly on cel, but color was starting to come into design, much more than it was during the 1970s, and so, we had this great ink and paint department that could do these colored ink lines, you know, and really give our stuff production value.

Tony: How do you answer the question: What does a director do on an animated commercial?

Eric: The director, basically, controls the staging, the timing, and in large degree, the content, and I think that's what people don't quite understand, is that, if you're an animation director, whether you're on a feature, you're on a film, or on a commercial, or whatever, you know, you will get something, in many cases, that's just raw material, OK? "This is what we want. This is where we want the pack shot. This is the general idea here," but, it's up to you, as the director to make that into something: A) Cohesive, B) Entertaining, C) Interesting to look at, and D) answers all the things that the agency wants.

Tony: Like selling the product . . .

Eric: Yeah, selling the product. So, it's a, kind of, thing where, let's say for example, you've got a commercial where they want Tinkerbell to fly in, alright, and they indicate Tinkerbell flying in on the boards. Well, if I re-boarded that, I'd say, "Well, how 'bout she flies in and takes a little bow?" you know, and it's those little personality touches that you can work out fairly early, and they go, "Oh. That's what it's going to become," and usually on commercials, I'll set it up very thoroughly with pose drawings, so that if I can't animate it, the people that I hire can animate it, so the pose drawings are your bullet points, and I work out rough timing that way too. It is not unlike the way the old shorts directors used to work, the way a Chuck Jones or a Tex Avery used to work, where they would make a bazillion pose drawings, time out the sheets, but, it doesn't stop there. See, there are certain people who think, "Oh. And then the animators just take it, and inbetween it." No, they don't. They have to perform. They have to make it alive, you know, Chuck Jones used to do great pose drawings. If you give it to an animator, like, a Ken Harris, or a Ben Washem, they'll give you gold. If you give it to a lesser animator, he'll just inbetween the poses, and it'll look stiff. Well, once, then you have something to show the agency and the client what you're thinking. You cut it together, and they can see the acting that's going on. They can see the staging that's going on, and by the time you've done an animatic, they have a pretty good idea of what they're gonna be getting when it's animated, and then when it's animated you get all the bells, and whistles, and the flourishes, and all that great stuff, so, they can buy off on it at that early stage.

Tony: Which is key for you.

Eric: Yeah, which means we don't have to do 28 million pencil tests, because they're not getting something that they thought they were getting. We already determined that earlier in the boards. Then the poses serve as layouts for the other artists I'm working with, so, it's a, kind of, thing where it was immensely useful in a film, like, *Looney Tunes: Back in Action*. Where we were working with characters over live action, you know, and those poses, which were done on a [Wacom] Cintq, you know, basically, where they were there for the producer buyoff, and the director buyoff. They then became our panels for the workbook that circulated around the studio, and then they were blown up to be the layouts for the scene. So, it's a, kind of, thing where . . . features are different. Features you don't necessarily have to pose everything out, and nor would you want to . . . sometimes the performances get a little richer if the animators bring more to the table, you know, and I've learned that being at Disney's over the years, and working on features, and most of the directing that I do with animators is verbal these days, not visual. If it's something that has to be done under time pressure, or with very specific artistic, and technical needs, I'll pose it out. So, I can work both ways. Many times what I'll do is a very thorough storyboard, and that will become the roadmap. There's some commercials that I did a few years back. They were for Disneyland's 50th anniversary, where the Disney characters were animated in CG, and it was done down at Digital Domain in Venice. I did very thorough storyboards, which, basically, became the keys for the animation. Without the roadmap, we never could have gotten it done. I've been in too many situations where the posed out storyboard isn't done, and then the agency, and the clients get upset, because they have no idea what to expect, or why it's turning out a certain way, and all that, so, while it may seem a little paint-by-numbers, what it really is, is insurance. It really, is my insurance to make sure everybody is on the same page, and that when we get into the grueling process of actually creating the animation, and the rest of the film, the hard stuff's already been figured out.

> **the most difficult part of the job is actually the stress, and pressure of getting it done at a very, very high speed, and rate of turnover, without sacrificing quality.**

Tony: What is the most difficult part of your job as an animation director?

Eric: I think the most difficult part of the job is actually the stress, and pressure of getting it done at a very, very high speed, and rate of turnover, without sacrificing quality. That's the toughest thing. I mean, yes, if you do crap, you can crank it out fast, but, if you don't want to do crap, then you have to find a way of doing quality just as fast, and so, that, that's the rod I create for my own back most of the time.

Tony: I know your quality standards are of the utmost, so it must be very difficult.

Eric: It is difficult.

Tony: How long are you on a commercial, usually?

Eric: Usually a commercial schedule is a couple of months, you know, which is very, very tight. I mean, I remember, when we were

From *Pocahontas*. © 1995 Disney.

at Pizzazz, a standard animation portion of the job used to be six weeks. Just the animation itself. Not to mention ink and paint, and, you know, shooting, and all the post. Yeah. So, these days, you know, it's getting tighter, and tighter, and tighter, and, because of that, what you have to do then is overlap all the stages. Back in the day you would have approval of an entire pencil test, by the agency and then by the client. Only after that would the scenes go onto ink and paint. Now, you have to get half the film approved, and it goes immediately into ink and paint, and while you're animating – the second half, and it's a, kind of, thing where you're constantly having to hold hands and sing Kumbaya with the agency, and everyone else saying, "Trust me. It's all going to work," but they will not have seen anything beforehand. One shortcut that I take, which I learned from my Richard Williams and Pizzazz days, is that I'll animate clean. In some cases, what I'll do is, I'll animate and Susan will follow me up. Susan will do the color palettes on most of the commercials we've done, but what will happen is, what they will see is a clean pencil test. When they're approving it, it's already to go into ink and paint, and that way it saves a huge amount of time, rather than approving something rough, then getting it cleaned up, then having them approve it again, and then it going to ink and paint. So I save time by working as cleanly as possible. Now, not every animator can work that way, but some can, and I can cast them accordingly, knowing that they can. Other people, OK, they're rougher.

Tony: What is the most important tool in your director's toolbox for a project, especially on a commercial?

Eric: My brain. That's the most important tool, because you're constantly thinking: How can I "plus" the material? How can I get what they want, and make it readable? How can you dissuade them from something that doesn't really feel like it's a particularly cohesive idea? Often,

> **you're constantly thinking: How can I "plus" the material?**

I have to think on my feet, which is not a bad quality for people to nurture, because, it's one thing just to sit there with a sour puss and say, "Oh, that's not gonna work!" but, if you say, "You know what? That may not work as well, but if you try this, you know, you may get what you want, and we can do X, Y, and Z," and usually they buy it. They buy it because you're offering them a positive alternative.

Tony: And they're not always just artistic issues. Sometimes there is diplomacy that you need to have to negotiate those waters of working with others.

Eric: Yeah. You don't want to tell anyone they're an idiot, you know. For example, here's something I never understood about many people working in commercials: they would make fun of the agency or make fun of the client, and, yeah, OK, sometimes that's valid, but, at the end of the day – they're *paying* you, buddy. They are paying you to make their spot, and so they have a point of view that you have to listen to. It's their grief that has to be answered, and so, you know, you can't dismiss what they say. You have to take it seriously, and if it's something that really is anathema to you, then you better find a way of presenting a positive alternative so that you can both live with it.

> **at the end of the day – they're *paying* you, buddy.**

Tony: How soon do you get into storyboarding? Is the script locked from the ad agency, or do they give you boards, rough boards first?

Eric: I've been on a lot of commercials where they haven't locked the dialogue, you know; they have dialogue written, and roughly staged, but they haven't timed it out. They usually write more than you can squeeze into 30 seconds, and so, really, you start as early as you can, and you start to realize what some of these problems might be, and many agencies will require you to pre-time your boards, just so they can see how much time you're actually spending on each shot, which is very useful, because then they'll see how much dialogue is supposed to fit in a certain scene, and then they may have to edit it down, and so on, and so forth, or, you know, if they're not getting their "legal" breakfast on screen long enough, you know. That's why it's a kind of thing where you do it as early as possible, and then as soon after that, you do the animatic, and that's really the roadmap. In the same way that it is for a feature film, it is for a commercial. That's your Bible – once you have it up on reels. And only then can you really tell if your timing is working, if the soundtrack is working, if things are clear, or they're confusing, you know. There're some people who go to the lengths of actually pre-animating the animation, and they'll put after-effects, and stuff all over the poses and things like that. I hate that. It's better just to read these clear poses to me. I don't care if you can make it dance around the frame, you know. In fact, I'd rather you didn't! Just so it presents a view of clarity to the people we have to show it to. I'd rather put in more pose drawings, and make the boards more animated, than have somebody put a lot of after-effects into something that doesn't show much performance.

Tony: I understand in a commercial you probably do a lot of the animation yourself, whenever possible, but when you do come up to a situation where you have to hand off to other animators, what's a hand-off look like for you?

Eric: I'll get together with the animator. First of all, I'll find out who's available, and cast them accordingly, write them down for each shot I want them to do. I'll show them the animatic, and usually give them a digital copy of the animatic to take away with them, which will also have the soundtrack on it. I'll give them their sound as a separate file, and they will have a complete layout with poses. My poses are both on-model,

in character for the acting, and, you know, in proportion for the layout, so, they've got their roadmap already set, and I often will make indications down the sheets [exposure sheets] on timing, you know, if a character is walking at a certain rate, or if a certain musical accent needs to be hit right there, you know, I'll indicate that on the sheets, and I'll explain it verbally, and explain the performance verbally, you know. With all of that, it doesn't take more than a couple passes for them to nail it. One thing that's great in this digital age is that many people have home setups, so what they can do is shoot it at home, send me a QuickTime movie file, and we can talk about it

From *Hercules*. © 1997 Disney.

on the phone, and they can make their changes right then, and there, and, you know, while we're both looking at the QuickTime, and it's, it's amazing how efficiently that works. Back on *Pocahontas* we were working with Disney Florida Animation, but with fax machines, ¾-inch tapes, played simultaneously, bi-coastally over a satellite conference phone system. It was grueling.

Tony: You kind of answered this briefly, but maybe you have a bit to add to it: What do you look from a first pass by an animator?

Eric: I look for it to hit all the right beats. On a first pass I don't necessarily expect it to be perfect, but given the pressure of how we have to work on these things these days you want it as close as possible, but, you know, if the first pass hits the bullet points the right way, and is entertaining, you know, that's really what I look for in a first pass, then you can finesse it, then you can say, "Ok, add a few more frames here," or, "This needs a little more cushioning here. It pops a little." So on, and so forth, and then you can finesse it from the first pass, so that by the second pass it should be pretty nailed.

Tony: How do you know when an animator just isn't getting it for whatever reason, and what do you do?

Eric: If an animator isn't getting it after a certain amount of time has passed I will say, "Thank you very much," and will pay him, and then I'll do it myself.

Tony: Which is tough for you, I'm sure.

Eric: It is tough. Yeah.

Tony: It blows your schedule out of the water.

Eric: Yeah.

Tony: What do you look for in a creative team, an art director, an editor, a storyboard artist, an animator, when you're doing a commercial?

Eric: It's an interesting question, because often there isn't a team. Often there is who's available, you know, who's available in the freelance ranks to help you out on a commercial. You may not get your first choices, or your second choices, or you may get some of your first choices, and others not, so it depends. I mean, I'm fairly lucky because I can board, and I can pose it out, and I can design, and Susan [Goldberg] can art direct, and pick the color palettes, and do the clean-up, so, I mean, between the two of us, we've got a lot of jobs covered, you know. And, so that obviates the need to have to pass it amongst a million different hands. It's largely animation, clean-up, and effects animation that requires the freelance work, you know, and we have a core of people that we rely upon for all of those things, people we've worked with in the past. There's a battalion of great clean-up artists who are available to work. There's a ton of great effects animation artists, because every 2D job needs a million tone mattes these days. But the artists are all chomping at the bit to work, and it's pretty amazing how quickly, and efficiently, and expertly they can turn out that kind of work from their features experience. All the people I'm talking about are people who have features experience, and they bring that to the table, you know. You're not necessarily just hiring a student, and saying, "Here. Do this." you know. The sad truth is that, because of the compressed schedules, you need to have people upon whom you know you can rely. You know what they can do. You know their quality level. You know their turnaround level in terms of their speed . . .

Tony: They're reliable.

Eric: . . . Yeah. And so, you know, commercials usually are not a time to experiment, because there isn't the time. It has to be done right the first time.

Tony: How do you combat the, "Us against Them," attitude that can arise on a production between creative management and crew?

Eric: I've only really noticed an "Us against Them," atmosphere on commercials where the animation is combined with live action. Then it becomes sometimes, "Us against Them," because the live action director, you know, positions himself as *the* director, and the animation is post. But if your live action director is worth his salt, he should consider what the animation is going to be doing, and allow for it in his shoot. It's more like co-directing, but often because live action is far more glamorous than animation, the live action production companies, and directors often throw their weight around a little bit more than they should, but they're making comments on some things that they just don't really know anything about. If somebody hires me to be the expert on the character animation, I don't need Mr Yo Ho, who's animation experience might be his kid watches *Phineas and Ferb*, to tell me how my characters should be moving and acting!

Tony: I'm giving you a knowing smile because I've been there too. Do you feel that it's your responsibility to inspire, and motivate your crew?

Eric: I think a director has to motivate his crew, on whatever job he's doing. Now, often, money is a good motivator, you know, because people need to eat, so, if you do this, you get paid. "Great! Thanks!," but you're motivating the crew to do quality work. I think my ace in the hole has always been that the people I work with know that I can do practically anything I'm asking them to do. So, they know my quality standards, and they want to work to that, they enjoy working to my standard. First of all, it's your neck on the line, you know, you're the one representing the animation, and so, whether you're handing it to somebody else to be done, or whether you're doing it

yourself, it still has to be good. That's often, you know, something that comes back to bite you in the butt, because if it does come back [from the artist], and it's not good enough, then you have to take care of it yourself, before you show it to the agency, and the client – it just has to be right. But your drive for that quality is what can be inspiring to those around you. You shouldn't have the attitude of, "well, it's just a cereal commercial."

Tony: Absolutely.

Eric: You can still make it funny, and entertaining. Look how many iconic characters have come out of cereal: Tony the Tiger, Snap, Crackle, and Pop, the Trix Rabbit, Dig 'em Frog, but, it's a, kind of, thing where these characters last for a variety of reasons. The other thing is, I'm old enough to remember very early commercials from when I was a kid . . .

Tony: . . . they had an impact on you I would imagine . . .

Eric: They had a huge impact, and I see them now, and they're still good! All these commercials that Hubley used to do at Storyboard – the Marky Maypo spots, and the John and Marsha Snowdrift thing that Art Babbitt animated. I mean, brilliant, brilliant spots in design, conception, and animation.

Tony: Well, like you, these were guys that had done features films, and other things, that found that they enjoyed doing commercials. Because they were quick, fast money, or creative little shorts or whatever, but they still put their quality into it.

Eric: Absolutely, and there's no reason not to, and, and in later days Richard Williams was the same, you know, it's not just enough to sell the product, you know, he wanted his company to be the Rolls Royce of animation. If Disney was the Rolls Royce of features, Richard Williams was

From *Pocahontas*. © 1995 Disney.

the Rolls Royce of commercials. That stays with you, you know, you never knowingly go into a job, saying, "I think I'm gonna crap this out," or, at least I don't. I can't. That may be my curse.

Tony: Right. Being true to your vision: Do you find it difficult to be true to your original vision on a commercial? From what you first thought it should be, what it would be, schedules being what they are, is it tough to keep that going?

Eric: You know, using the word, "vision," with a television commercial, is almost an oxymoron, but let's put it this way: All film is collaborative, alright, and everybody's got something that they need to put forward. Now, I could say the same thing about feature films. Yeah, you wanna talk about a director's vision – but the truth is you've got a million people giving you input. People used to ask me, "What's it like directing on a feature like *Pocahontas* at Disney?" I would said, "It's like getting to wear the captain's hat while 28 people tell you how to steer the ship!" [laughter]. In

many cases, that is true, because the studio will have certain things it wants to put across with a movie. They might have advertising tie-ins, you know. Usually that doesn't rear its ugly head, but it has once in a while. They might have a certain audience they're aiming for. They might have any manner of things they want the movie to express, even if you are directing it, you have to take all of that stuff on board. You get to be a visionary when people leave you alone, you know, and they still like what you do, but that is very rare, either in features, or in television commercials. Television commercials have the same thing. They have things that the agency needs to put across for the commercial to be successful. I can't tell you how many commercials that I see where I go, "That was a pretty funny commercial. But what was the product?" where they've done all the job of make it entertaining so well, but I can't remember what the heck they were selling. So, it fails as a commercial, and that's not good either.

Tony: We all know that budgets, and schedules are part of life for the filmmaker, but how do you look at them – friend or foe?

Eric: Friend. I can budget things that I know I'll be able to deliver on, and by that, I know that A) Anybody I hire will be paid well, and B) We will still make a profit at the end, and not eat up all the money just breaking even. So, to a certain extent, the budgets are also our financial insurance. In other words, if I budget a certain way, for certain things, then I know that even if I don't make one animation drawing on the entire commercial, I'll still make a profit at the end of it, because it's my directing that they're paying for, and not necessarily my hand. You can't animate everything yourself a lot of the time, so, you know, you budget for what the animation would cost if you were, if you were going to hand it out to everybody, and not do any animation yourself, but then if you happen to be able to do some animation yourself, OK, that's *extra* profit for you. It's worked into the budget, you know, so, you're working it out so that, it still took that much time to produce that much footage.

Tony: Do you have input into the budget, and the schedule, or is it something that is given to you by a producer at the studio that hires you to direct the commercial?

Eric: I usually have input on the budget all the time. The schedule is usually not as moveable. It depends on how much the agency, and the clients are asking for. If they're asking for something with a bazillion characters in every shot you have to consider that. That's gonna take longer, and be more expensive, and it's at those early storyboarding, and animatic stages that are so critical, where you can plan something to have a crowd shot, say, as an establishing shot, but you don't need a crowd shot for the rest of the film. You've already established it, you know. You have

to plan smart so you can get it done, and still convey the impression that this is, an environment full of people, and that applies to features as much as it does to television commercials. We had a bunch of crowd shots in *Princess and the Frog*, and a lot of what I did on *Frog*, behind the scenes, was tell them how to simplify it, how to, "Put your money shot here, and then cut close to the two frogs, and just show confetti falling," sort of thing.

Tony: That's so important.

Eric: Yeah. It's very important, because, first of all, more often than not, it actually strengthens your storytelling. It actually focuses you on the characters, and the periphery is the periphery. You find ways of doing re-use, you find ways of repurposing things in a way that's invisible to an audience, and that's the best, is that it still looks full and rich, but the audience doesn't know what you know, in terms of having constructed the scenes.

Tony: I think you're a unique director. So many directors that I know of, they resist that kind of thinking. They work against the budget and yet, you see the value of budgets and schedule with a strong "less is more" value to your work.

Eric: You know, when Alfred Hitchcock did a film, first of all, he was a huge fan of storyboarding, and he did many of his own storyboards, and he only shot what he wanted, which also meant that he was an efficient filmmaker. Now, these days, everybody thinks you're inept, or a fool if you don't shoot coverage. You have to get the scene from 28 different angles so that we can fart around with it in the edit suite, because we're all Orson Welles now that the Avid [editing system] exists. At the end of the day, Hitchcock only shot what he knew he needed for the effect that he wanted, and it's, the same way with animation. You plan for what you know you need, and then you don't overdo the rest.

Tony: Often times, as a director of commercials, you're hired by a particular studio to come in, and direct that commercial, so, you're working with the producer at that studio. What are those relationships like for you, in general?

Eric: It depends on the producer [laughter]. Seriously, I think it's a, kind of, thing where some producers have a lot of experience with animation, and know what they're talking about, and will do everything they can to make your job easier, and more organized, and those are the producers I enjoy working with. While other producers, are neophytes, and that's tough a lot of the time. Here's an interesting example that occurs sometimes when you're dealing with an effects house. Effects houses always animate handles. They always animate an extra eight, or 12 frames, head and tail of a scene in case the agency wants to play with the editing. You don't do that in animation. Every frame counts, and every frame is labor intensive, so, you don't have the time, or the budget to animate an extra second's worth on every shot on a commercial. Moreover you're working with cut points that you designed yourself, and if you know you want a character to cut on movement, and you finish the movement in the next scene, then those 12 extra frames will just get in the way. But a producer should know and understand those things. Often producers are good as buffers for their director. You should be able to call your producer, and say, "This is a very elaborate scene. It's gonna be great when it's done, but I'm gonna need three more days. Can you call the agency and see if we can get a few more days if they get X, Y, and Z scenes on time?" For me, I don't really care that much if the internal deadlines slip a day or two, as long as everything is delivered at the end, on time, and of high quality. That's the deadline that I take the most seriously. I mean, the other thing that goes with

that corollary is there's never enough time to do it well, but always enough time to change it, and it's amazing how frequently that happens.

Tony: So, how important is it to keep up with current technology as an animation director?

Eric: I think you have to keep up with current technology. If you don't, you're missing a lot of the things that you can have in your toolbox. I remember when we had Pizzazz, and it was the first time digital compositing suites, and video editing suites were coming into play, where you could actually do all manner of effects work, and combination work, right then and there in front of you. I remember the times when a live action combo was an aerial image job, you know . . .

Tony: You're dating yourself! [laughter]

Eric: I am dating myself, yes, and I've done a few of those, but the fact that you could do it on video now that much easier and quicker was amazing. There's so much more at your disposal that way. Just knowing the technology, even to the point where, if I do a storyboard, if I do it on the Cintq I know that I can send the .jpgs immediately to editorial to cut into the animatic, as opposed to having to scan it, and then send it, and blahdablahdablah . . . So, you have to keep current with this stuff. Obviously the programs change minute-by-minute in technology, but if you have a healthy working knowledge of what will work for you, and make you efficient, then I don't think it's a problem.

Tony: How do you continue to grow as an artist, yourself?

Eric: Every job has its challenges, and many of those challenges are creative ones. "Oh. I've never animated an alligator playing the trumpet before. I guess I gotta learn more about the trumpet" . . . Or, "I've never directed anything in this style before." "I've never done consultations for CG animation before." There's all sorts of challenges that every job will present to you and that's how you keep fresh — by doing stuff you've never done before, and still relying on your knowledge of previous work to get you to the next level.

Tony: Part of that is that you enjoy a challenge, but it also sounds, like, you are a problem solver. That's what you really like, right?

Eric: Yeah, and, and problem-solving on the basis of interesting creativity, so that, when someone says, "Oh. You can't do that," it's because they've never done it and lack the confidence. People like to tell us about ourselves when they are really talking about their own fears. You're presenting them with something new that they've never done before, and they are uncomfortable confronting. But what that is ultimately doing is stifling the creative needs of the job that you're doing. If you feel, creatively, something has to be done a certain way, and people are telling you it can't be done that way, then the answer should be "Let's find a way." Rather than limiting what can be done, just make it doable. I mean, years ago, Susan and I did the Magic Lamp Theater for Tokyo DisneySea. Nobody had ever animated the Genie in 3D before, ever, in

From *Aladdin*. © 1992 Disney.

stereoscopic, ever, and we knew we had to make it work. Well, I had a great crew and we used a lot of hand-drawn roadmaps. I did, like, a 400-drawing Lyca reel [animatic] for it. We solved a lot of those problems when we were reviewing the animation. Like, what looked like the Genie, what didn't look like the Genie in action. How do you get it fluid? How do you make this work? So on, and so forth, and we got a Genie in stereo 3D that still feels like the Genie! Nobody had done it before. But you couldn't tell WDI Imagineering who tells you, "We're coming over and want you to do this job," that it can't be done. You just have to go, "OK, I'm plunging in!"

Tony: Where do you find the industry going in the future?

Eric: The short answer is: Damned if I know. The full answer is . . . the burgeoning technology is a blessing and a curse. It means more, and more things can be done in an interesting, unique way. It also means in many cases that people let the technology drive the artistry, which I don't think is right. I think the artistry has to utilize the technology to get across the stories, the characters, the personalities, the content, and, in some cases, it can simplify things, and in other cases, it can make it far more complex, just by giving you a toy box full of many more goodies than you had previously encountered, you know, and to that end it's, like, an artist choosing to work with a limited palette, saying, "OK, I have all these things, but which ones do I want to use, and why?," and that's a very good discipline to have, because otherwise, if you just sit there for hours on end, going, "Ooh! We can do this!," and, "Hey, we can do this!" you'll never get the job done. You use the technology for just what you need it to do.

Tony: I think a lot of young students, and animators getting into the industry, especially

wanting to direct for commercials might have this question: Do you have an agent, or someone representing you to get work?

Eric: I don't have an agent.

Tony: Never have?

Eric: No, I never have. And, at the end of the day, what really is your agent is your work. You send a reel around. You show people what you can do, and that's your agent.

Tony: So your reputation is your best agent?

Eric: Yeah, you know, but, it's not just verbal reputation. You have to have something tangible to show for it, you know, you build up a body of work that people can refer to, and say, "Oh. That's pretty cool. Oh. I didn't know he could do that," you know, and you not only give them what they expect, but you give them stuff that maybe they may not have known or seen before. That's really the only agent that you can have as a director, is how you do your work.

Tony: Any last words for the young artists that want to direct in the future?

Eric: Learn everything. Don't just learn what you're comfortable with. Learn all aspects of filmmaking — live action, and animation. Study things. The more knowledge you have at your fingertips, then the more creative you can be, because then that knowledge will become second nature, and then you don't have to concentrate on it. You can actually concentrate on creatively utilizing those tools, and I think that's probably the biggest advice that I would have for anybody. There's inspiration and knowledge to be had everywhere. I mean, just in animation alone . . . I come from an era when I had to buy 8mm copies of clips of Disney films in order to study them. Nowadays you can go on YouTube and find everything that was ever made. So, do it!

BUDGETS AND SCHEDULES

Budgets – Friend or Foe?

Ahh, the dreaded budget. The most basic formula for what constitutes a budget is: the number of days it will take to produce the project multiplied by the cost of the staff plus equipment and overheads. A simple formula that can be brewed a multiple of ways for different outcomes. Many a director has succumbed to its pressures while others have allowed the shackles of restraint to have a freeing effect creatively. By now we've all heard the story about a young Steven Spielberg getting his second directing opportunity on a low-budget movie about a shark attack on a small beach community. In 1973, Universal Pictures gave Spielberg a low budget of $9 million to bring the Peter Benchley novel *Jaws* to the big screen with much of that budget literally being eaten up by the constant mechanical problems of the film's star – the shark. The insufficient budget and the constant problems with his robot shark forced the director to make one of the most important and effecting choices in the movie's now legendary history. Spielberg decided to show the shark as little as possible. It elevated the movie from being a corny horror movie premise to one of the most thrilling movies of all time. In fact, *Jaws* went on to become the all-time biggest box office record holder (at least until *Star Wars* came out two years later). Besides, changing how people felt about swimming in the ocean, Spielberg showed that limitations don't need to restrain you creatively. They can be tools to push you to more creative levels than you thought possible. A low-budget curse can be made into a blessing by a resourceful director with a positive attitude.

> **Anxiety is the handmaiden of creativity.**
> – Chuck Jones

Live action budgets are different from animation in one very unique way. A live action budget puts greater weight on "above the line" production costs than "below the line." The "above-the-line" costs are the high-end creative staff that the studio is investing in. They will not green-light the project unless they have their "above the line" crew in place. They would include, but are not limited to the producer, screenwriter, director, and cast, the "above the line" being the majority of the expense in the budget. "Below the line" is everyone else working on the film. This group could be ten times the amount of people than the above the line group, but they are considered by the studio not as integral to the success of the film and therefore replaceable. In animation though the lines are blurred. Animation is all about the team as a whole and the costs even out a lot more in the budget. We all don't make as much as the score composer! I have worked on productions where certain animators took home more in their weekly pay check than the director and producer combined. In animation it's the "below-the-line" costs that can be massive in the budget. Really assessing the budget with a creative eye towards what you need and what you don't will help make the right choices for the film.

Prada or Payless?

A film budget is much like your home budget. When shopping for shoes you have a choice to make. Are you going to buy **Prada or Payless**? One may look great and be top of the line but the other still gets you where you need to go. Can you afford the extras? You will have to make creative and practical choices in making your film also. There are many ways to make a movie and a lot of pots to put the money into in the process. Do you care more about the quality of the animation? The look of the color and visuals? Is a greater majority in the script and storyboards? What about postproduction? Can you afford that awesome full orchestra you want for the soundtrack? Those are all creative questions you will have to ask yourself as you dive into the challenges of the budget.

Some studios are more open to the idea of the director being involved in budget discussions that are usually left exclusively up to the producer. Some directors are pulled into them whether they want to be or not. Sony held up production of *Stuart Little 2* until director Rob Minkoff, the producer, and studio could agree to a final budget figure that made sense to them for their sequel. Some directors have it in their contracts that they must not go over a certain budget number or the difference comes out of their pocket!

While still other studios don't want the director to be a part of the discussion of budget at all. In fact, on one film I directed, I never knew what the actual budget was and to this day still don't know what it cost to make. Sure, I have some ideas. I know it is one of the last from the 90s era where spending was over-the-top. That's most certainly why I don't know anything specific about it. The policy at some studios is to never officially announce the budgets of

Mulan's associate producer Rob Garber and producer Pam Coats. The film's budget was in good hands with these two.

their features. To this day, I feel that not knowing the budget for that film made it harder for me. In early discussions with my producer, I would ask, "Can we afford artist A or artist B?" The response was always the same: "Anything you need we can get." It was unsettling in a bizarre way. I liked the idea of the sky's the limit when it came to quality, but I kept thinking the door has to shut on the spending at some point. I would ask, "There must be **some** sort of limits, why not just tell me what they are?" The producer would just say, "I'll let you know when the answer is no." Well, that answer did come towards the end of the production when we were forced to "reevaluate" the complexity of the scenes that needed to finish so we could make our release date. We literally had to pull characters out of scenes that had already been planned before they went into animation. If you don't know your financial limits, it's hard for a director to creatively plan his film.

These days before I take a gig directing I like to get involved with the budget and schedule at an early stage. I may not have any control over how much money we have to spend on the project but I want to have a say in how it's spent. **Understanding the sandbox you're playing in will help you think outside the box.** Here's a process I go through in respect to the budget and schedule and how it helps me to solidify my vision for the film.

1. **Read the script.** Really take in the project as a whole. What is it that you react to the most? What are the "drivers" in the story that you react to and how many of those things are related to emotion scenes (usually cheaper to produce) and how many are related to big visual moments (i.e. songs, explosions, battles, crowd scenes, a lot of water, etc. = expensive)? This will already help you get some general figures in your head as to whether the story can be achieved on a lower budget or will need a bigger one.

2. **Find out the budget and schedule.** If you are being hired onto a project, then most likely it has a producer or production manager that has already worked up their idea of a budget and schedule and will want you to buy off on it. They will want you to either agree to it (and by agreeing you are saying that it is possible to make the project under those restraints) or give your input into it (a better situation to be in for sure).

3. **Think over the budgetary and schedule short comings.** Assuming the producer and/or studio is open to your opinions on both the budget and schedule, you need to spend some time balancing those figures against the initial visionary thoughts you have on how you want to tell the story you read in the script. Is there enough time to produce this film? If the time is limited for whatever reason than that will affect the budget. Less time on the schedule usually means more money is needed in the budget. A short schedule always translates to either extreme compromises in the quality of the film or more artists will be needed to finish by the deadline. Is there room to be creative with the money in the budget? Will you always feel like you're hand cuffed creatively with the dollar amount of the budget or should you seek more?

4. **Don't be afraid to kill your darlings if need be.** Better to do this is in the beginning of the process before you become too attached to certain elements. First, be realistic. Look at the story and try to make it submissive to

the budget. Do you have too many characters hanging around that aren't necessary to the story? Too many locations to design and build? Maybe some of the scenes could be combined in the same location? What about effects? Too many water, fire or smoke scenes? Are there a lot of long haired animals that could be styled differently or recast as penguins? At first some of these compromises may seem undesirable but on second look they may actually improve the story you are telling. Remember: an **over**-frosted cake is as bad as an under frosted one.

5. **Fight for the things that shouldn't be compromised.** Remember those elements that attracted you to the project in the first place? Those are probably the same elements that your audience will fall in love with in the story too. If it's a heroine with long flowing hair (Rapunzel) and the story revolves around that, then you may as well **not** make the movie if you can't work out that expensive CG effect and budgetary problem. Don't throw out the baby with the bathwater as they say.

6. **Do a script breakdown**. This is something that is usually done before a final budget is made and approved for production to start. Usually performed by a production manager, some technical and/or artistic leads and an accountant working together, someone will go through the script page by page to calculate the cost of every element written in the latest draft of the script. They will make a list of exactly how many characters, unique expressions or pose changes, locations, effects, scenes, camera moves, furry characters, costume changes, etc., there are and attach a number (usually in man-hours) to all of those elements to be designed, modeled, animated, textured, lit and rendered and how many minutes of film each will appear on screen. It's a huge task and the producer and director should be on hand to help define some of these elements as it develops.

7. **Creative scheduling can save a lot of money.** The cost involved with a schedule is usually related to man-hours spread over time. That is, when an artist comes onto the project how long he is on the budget until he is released,

multiplied by the amount that artist costs hourly or weekly to have on the project. Avoiding all of the artists in any one department coming on all at the same time and for the same duration is key to savings. Look at ways to ramp up to full staff as needed.

8. **Put the money on the screen.** While reviewing the budget, continually ask yourself, "will this money be used to make the project better or someone's life more comfortable during the process?" For example, you may have a robust travel budget because your main voice actor lives overseas and the crew will need to fly out to record him. It may be more pleasant to fly First Class (many of the big studios do) but Business still gets you there and saves money that can go towards something meaningful for the film . . . like another animator or rigger that you may want!

A Director's Responsibility

As the director of the project the budget and schedule may not all be up to you but you do have a responsibility to it. Many directors just want to be "creative only" and not get involved with the messy, boring stuff of the business of filmmaking. The smart director recognizes their responsibility to the production to creatively work within the parameters given to him. If you are a stubborn director that ignores the budgetary urgings of your producer and production manager I can guarantee that you will not complete the project. The trades are full of stories of studios firing directors over "creative differences." I bet most of those stories are public relations speak" for "that director wouldn't control his spending"! Delivering a project "on budget and on schedule" is a difficult thing to do but can be very positive for your career. But the quality of the project is what matters most! At the end of the day, no one will remember if your project came in over or under budget. They will remember if it was great or not.

Probably the best way the director can help to save money for the budget and best affect the schedule was discussed in the last chapter. That's right, **be prepared**!

Knowing what you want and communicating it effectively, not only makes for a content staff, but is the budget and schedule's best friend too! There will be less time spent in the mare of costly waste that comes from indecision and confusion. The production process relies on constant creative choices and approvals by the director to keep the art of animation moving forward from one artist to the next. Knowing what you want and expressing it in a timely fashion will keep the creative factory that is an animation studio going to the finish line. That creative momentum can be a huge asset to the success of the project too.

Alas, even in the best of worlds of preparation things can slip past the director's fingers. You're not perfect are you? Say, after reviewing a piece of animation several times you come to the conclusion that it's not the animator's fault the scene is not working, it's the line reading. It's flat and dull. You know you heard a better one in the list of takes but it was not put in the cut for whatever reason. Don't hold up the animator for long. Their time is the production's money! Quickly coordinate with the production manager and editor to listen to the various line readings to find the best version, cut it into the reel and get it to the animator. The clock is ticking when you have artists who are paid hourly. Save money by not having them sitting on their hands without work to do.

If things are not planned out well enough in advance, the inevitable will happen – cutbacks. This seems to always happen at the worst time in the process of your film making, right at the end when you are just feeling like the best work is being produced. Everyone is working like a well-oiled machine but it's still not enough. There is too much to do to meet the "locked in stone" deadline. This happened to Barry and me on *Mulan*. We had established the story as being about a girl joining a troop of men and fighting in a war to save China (and her father) but we had too many large group scenes left to finish. Just as our girl

© 1998 Disney. This scene from Disney's *Mulan* is a good example of the compromises a director must take into account even on a big budget film. How many of *Mulan's* troops end up by her side by the end of the film?

was going off to war – we couldn't afford the war! We had finished the big song "Be a Man" which is a training montage of Mulan and all of her group learning to be a soldier. In that sequence we establish that Mulan is part of a troop of about 40 men or more. Then as Mulan and her troop trek off to engage the villain in the first big action scene, we were told by the production staff that we had to make some big cut-backs if we were going to finish the production in time. It was a tough blow creatively but we decided to find ways to bring the troop number down as they traveled to the "burned out village" they come upon before the action starts with the villain. They start the walking off to war at about 40 but every scene we trimmed or hid the total number of men so that by the time the action starts it's Mulan and about eight guys running for cover from the Huns! At the time it was a devastating compromise to have to endure for me as a director but the funny thing is that the audience never notices! At least not in any letters or comments on the film that I've ever seen.

Let's Schedule a Meeting to Discuss the Schedule

"Does the schedule drive the production or the production drive the schedule?" This was a question I asked myself many times after my first year of directing a major studio animated feature. As a director at a large studio your time is never your own. I had a schedule that was printed out for me every morning when I arrived to my office. It was on a small piece of paper that I could easily slip in my pocket and take a glance at throughout my day. If I "lost" it (on purpose often) there was always a new one that would materialize on my desk as if by magic. The schedule had every moment of my day planned out in 15-minute increments from script review meetings with the writers to animation, to layout, to recording, to editorial and so on. Down to every 15 minutes was my day planned out on the schedule. The only thing that wasn't on there was bathroom breaks! When things got really hectic in the heat of production, the production manager instituted something

From *Mulan.* © 1998 Disney.

called "the director drive-by." By the name you would think that meant that myself and the other director could use that time to catch up with a department we felt needed more of our time. No, instead it was so that any department could come by if they saw us with some extra time in our offices and hijack us to ask a question or discuss a problem. Being a first-time director on Disney's *Mulan,* I thought is this how a movie gets made? When do I have time to sit and think about the picture and try to improve it if I am just too busy being whisked away to meeting after meeting trying to put out fires? After a while, my directing partner Barry and I had to force the idea of having some "office time" added to the schedule where we could process some of the creative elements of the film and actually work on making it better ourselves. In the studio system of the schedule driving the production it can feel like you are never really making the movie. The schedule should serve your needs as a filmmaker not the other way around.

The schedule is forever linked to the budget as the amount of time an artist in a particular department spends on the production directly translates to a numerical dollar value on the budget. The less time you have an artist on the schedule the more savings to the budget and, hopefully, you can use that money somewhere more necessary. Early-on the director should spend time with the producer and production manger to review the schedule with a mind towards analyzing how many artists are in any given department and when they come on and off the production. For example, it may be well and good that the story department is supposed to start in September with two artists and then three weeks later ramp up to six artists that stay on for three months while you work on the animatic. But if you see that the writers will still be working on the script into November than perhaps you can hold off the starting of the other four story artists. They may end on the same date as before but if you can push their start date even by a couple of weeks (multiplied by 4 story artists) that could translate into a savings of thousands of dollars. Maybe that is money saved that you can use for an after effects artist to help sell the storyboards to an executive or nervous investor. Money saved means you have more options. That's all from just looking at the schedule with a creative eye. The schedule and budget should be fluid things that will evolve as the production grows. **The only thing locked on a schedule is the release date. Make it work for the film's needs.**

A Good Producer is a Great Savings

In American football, you have blockers and you have quarterbacks. Many people would relate the producer (often at the top of the filmmaking food chain) to the quarterback. No, a good producer is more like the blocker for the director. Actually more like **a blocker and a cheerleader** combined! They are running ahead trying to keep the problems of budget and schedule away from the director while always encouraging and unifying the entire staff. A good producer is the "great protector" of the film. They don't get creatively involved in the minutiae of making the film but they know how to get the tools that the director desperately

The best cheerleader in animation, Don Hahn.

needs to make his or her film –the producer: "great protector" defined. A bad producer pulls the staff apart into two sides: "production" and "creative." I have seen this us-against-them attitude at many studios large and small. It is destructive to the larger goal of everyone making a winning project.

I was fortunate to work with one of the all-time best producers in animation on several projects at Disney and that was the legendary Don Hahn. Hahn was responsible for helping to bring to life such Disney classics as *Beauty and the Beast, The Lion King, The Hunchback of Notre Dame, Atlantis* and many others. He stands as one of the most revered and well-regarded producers in Disney's history. Hahn's gentle and fun-loving manner was a mystery to me. It seemed to fly directly in the face of the Hollywood image of a volatile producer. It always amazed me at how Hahn could seem so calm as the walls of the production were falling down around him. I never saw him shout or even raise his voice! He always had a positive "we can do it" attitude that was infectious to the staff. As long as Hahn was producing, the staff felt like kids in the back seat of the family car going on a long road trip. There was this feeling of "it doesn't matter where we go as long as Dad's driving." They say that the managerial style of the entire office flows down from the top guy. That was certainly the case with Hahn too. All of his support staff of associate producers, production managers, all the way down to production assistants all treated the creative artists and each other with respect. There was real unity. When there is a "we are all in this together" feeling amongst the staff, the process goes faster. It just magically does. The time usually spent grumbling and complaining instead is focused on the work! That saves money and makes for a better film.

Doing it the Independent Way

The big studios know how to spend money. They have such large overheads and costs from support staff that it's a wonder they make profits sometimes. Recently, I interviewed to do a 2D (traditional) short at Warner Brothers with one of their classic characters. The producer told me Warners had a year-long schedule and a budget of $2 million to get that one short done. You learn to be frugal when you have your own animation company as I did for over seven years, so I went to the producer and said, "You know for **that** amount we could overlap the schedules and crew and produce at least two or three shorts." She quickly shushed me and said, "Don't tell **them** that!" Maybe that is why I didn't get that job. What seemed obvious to me, to try and find a way to do more for less, to them, was a negative. Many times something that is priced low just seems like cheap quality to some big studio executives. The big studios have been dealing with their high-priced ways of doing things for so long that they can't see how to do things on the cheap **and** still achieve high-quality standards.

Developing and producing features and shorts independent of the big studios is something I know well now. For the last 10 years I have produced animation through my own studio and then at three other independents after that. The independent route can be creatively rewarding and financially challenging at the same time. On the positive side, you have few cooks in the kitchen. When you create an idea there are very few that will tell you that it is not marketable enough. It can be a much more artistic and personal experience. The sky's the limit! Until . . . On the negative side, you have to raise your own funds and resources. I worked at a studio for over two years and we spent some of that time creating some great feature concepts but most of the time was spent going to investor presentations trying to convince bankers and mutual funds that we had the next big thing. I traveled the world trying to find that illusive capital to make the features I wanted. The thing that keeps you going is the hope that you will be able to find that money to produce **your** film but the independent route is plagued by limited funds and resources.

The role of the director is key in the fundraising phase for an independent feature. An investor that knows little about the film or animation business (which is almost all of them) looks at two things to really convince them that the plan is a good one. You would think that one of them would be the actual **film concept** but that takes third place since the investors have a difficult time discerning a good idea from a bad one. The two things that are paramount to the investor is the **team** and the **plan**. The team is the "above the line" group brought together for the project. Investors will look at the experience and success of the screenwriter, producer, director, voice cast (big-name actors) and the studio's CEO and CFO. They are asking themselves, "Do I believe that these people know what they are talking about and know their market? Have they had success in making profits before for their previous employers? Does the studio have financial heads that can manage this team and my money (the CEO and CFO)?" Assuming they are impressed with the answer to those answers then they look at the next criterion. The plan is the practical way that you will make the film in as *inexpensive* manner as possible while making the highest amount of *profit* as possible for the investor. This plan would include the budget for the film, the schedule for completion, distribution possibilities and any other ancillary products (toys, music, games, etc.) that may bring in more profit for the investor. The director is a major element in both these elements of team and plan. First, to an investor, the director is probably only second to the voice cast as being integral to the success of the film so your reputation is massively important. It's important to be unashamedly confident as you list your résumé of credits and films you have directed. I always include the box office totals when I speak of the movies I worked on because that excites investors more than awards I have earned. Second, the director is important in shaping and selling the plan of the production to the investor. In creating the budget one of the primary elements in cost savings to be decided is where the production will take place. In today's animation world, there are far more options than doing the whole film in the US which may give you the highest quality standards but be far more expensive. These days, you need to look at overseas options for your production. Just as Illumination Entertainment, Disney and DreamWorks are all discovering these days there are handfuls of small boutique studios all over the world with various degrees of experience and price savings. Finding that jewel in the rough that can be a good partner to do the most expensive element of production is a huge savings for the budget and selling point to the investor of an independent film. Just by using an overseas studio you can shave millions of dollars off the budget which translates to more profit for the investor. That's not to say that the less experienced and foreign talent does not come at a quality price too. It certainly does! That is why the director must be part of those early budget and schedule discussions to figure out where to put the money and time to serve the story best. The head of the independent studio, production accountant, producer and the director all need to work hard to find that budget that "feels" right and will make investor's profits swell. Be prepared that the solution will most likely be a budget that is lower than you would like and half the time that you think is possible to produce the film. That's the independent way! If it seems like I am suggesting that impressing the investor is more important than creatively developing the film, then you are right! Get the money and then worry about making the film. Without the money there will be no film.

Once the elusive budget is obtained, whether you are working at a big studio or a small independent one, the job of the director doesn't change from that point on. Keep your objective clear: **make the picture that you would want to see and hopefully, the audience will want to see it too.**

interview: chris wedge

A pioneer in computer animation filmmaking, Chris Wedge was there at the beginning of what is now a multi-billion dollar business. Born in Binghamton, New York, Wedge received his MA in Computer Graphics and Art Education from the Advanced Computing Center for the Arts and Design (ACCAD) (formerly CGRG), under the Ohio State University. With a small band of animation innovators, Wedge co-founded and is Vice President of Creative Development at Blue Sky Studios. In 1998, Wedge and his Blue Sky crew received an Academy Award for their innovative and character-driven short *Bunny*. This caught the eye of Fox who purchased the innovative studio and gave them the opportunity to produce their first feature. Wedge directed the first *Ice Age*, nominated for an Academy Award for Best Animated Feature, which went on to become one of the most successful franchises of all time spawning three other sequels to date. Since then he has directed 2005's *Robots* in between his responsibilities as executive producer on everything Blue Sky produces. I caught up with Wedge over the phone while he was deep in development on his newest directing opportunity, 2013's *Epic*.

Tony: So, how did you get into the animation industry?

Chris: Well, I was interested in animation from the time I was a kid. You know, I grew up in the boondocks needing to, kind of, make my own fun and I got interested in animation. It was something I had total control over and I could just experiment and fuss with it from the time I was about 12. I went to film school and studied animation in a film program that didn't have too much animation

going on at the time, but I had a lot of support and I just continued to do the same thing, make my own little movies on my own, and, you know, I would spend sometimes two or three years on one little movie and just keep it alive, keep it going.

Tony: You started out doing traditional animation then?

Chris: Actually, I got tired of drawing 2D animation very quickly. I got into puppet animation and into stop motion. I got more and more into elaborate armatures, and characters, and rigs, and sets and I just loved lighting those little sets, so that you couldn't tell how big things were and I loved walking into my studio and walking around and turning all the lights on and not looking at the set until my eye was on the eyepiece of the camera, at the shot that I had set up, and just looking at it there and nowhere else.

Tony: And just imagine yourself in that world . . .

Chris: Yeah, just so that it, you know, it's a separate reality. I just always loved the 3D nature of stop motion and, I'm talking, this was, like, late 1970s, early 1980s . . .

Tony: You quickly moved into CG though, right? I know you were at the forefront of computer animation . . .

Chris: Yeah, you know, it was interesting. I was very interested in 3D animation, but, I grew up on the East Coast, and I went to school in New York, at Purchase College – I thought the animation industry looked pretty dismal. I had wanted to work at Disney when I was a kid, but I didn't really want to work at Disney when I got out of school. I had been introduced to some of the earliest 3D computer images from a friend of mine, Stan VanDerBeek, who's actually an experimental filmmaker, an avant-garde animator in the 1960s and 1970s. He was actually a father of one of my friends, and Stan introduced me to some of this stuff and it was blowing my mind, and this was the work that, Ed Catmull was doing at NYIT (New York Institute of Technology) in the late 70s. I looked at some of these images, and I couldn't believe they came from computers. They were very rudimentary by today's standards, but at the time, it blew my mind, and at the same time I landed an opportunity to work at a company called MAGI/Synthavision, nearby where I was going to school. And MAGI was a group of ex-IBM guys that had formed their own company to do simulation for the Department of Defense. They realized that some of things they were simulating, like, radiation simulations, and the effect of radiation on different materials, could be visualized, and what they ended up developing was one of the first 3D ray tracers, and they were looking to develop their presence in the entertainment market, in the entertainment world, and when I joined them, they had just done a test for Steven Lisberger, who was

just getting *TRON* on its feet at Disney – this was in 1980 – and before I knew it I was maybe the first traditionally trained animator ever to work on a computer.

Tony: Wow. That's great. Was that around the time Lasseter was getting Pixar started?

Chris: Well, it was about three or four years before . . .

Tony: OK . . .

Chris: . . . I met John in 1982. He was working at Disney and he was promoting, I think, their junior training program, and he'd won a student academy award or two. John's story, the way I understand it, is that he was working at Disney and he saw all this cool *TRON* animation coming through at Disney, but it wasn't being done at Disney. It was being done at these two or three little satellite companies where people were developing CG, and feeling that there was a resistance to pursuing computer animation at Disney, he went in pursuit, and he came by MAGI to meet us one day, and we became fast friends . . .

Tony: Fascinating.

Chris: . . . we actually did an animation test together for *Where the Wild Things Are*.

Tony: Did you work on that? I had no idea. I've seen that test.

Chris: Yeah, I did the CG on it and Glen Keane did the character animation, and John wrote and directed it. Well, you asked me how I got started, and so, I'll get to the interesting part . . .

Tony: No problem, it's all good.

Chris: You know, I was at this company, MAGI, for about three years, and we did the work on *TRON*, and I really felt like I was on the bleeding edge of something new. I thought CG animation was going to grow. We had a lot of ideas about what we wanted to do back then, but it was a very difficult technology to use. It was a very cumbersome. There was no interface at all, and,

'ICE AGE' © 2002

I saw that the people that were making the most interesting images in animation on computers were people that knew how to program computers. So, this is like, 1983, and, so, I figured the thing for me to do is to go back to school and learn how to program. I went to Ohio State University and worked with Charles Csuri who had one of the only programs at the time where artists could learn how to create computer animation, and I learned how to program. I hung out there in a very supportive graphics lab and did two short films in about three years. I got a lot of exposure to what ideas were out there, from an academic perspective, and a kind of creative think tank, I was able to

think about what the future of animation could be. This was at a time when for the first five or ten years of computer animation, there was a lot of experimentation going on. It was a lot of fun, because every time you did something, it was, like, the first time anyone had done it, so everybody involved back then got a pioneer moniker attached to them. Then in 1987, MAGI had gone under, and a group of the people that were left just sitting around thought, "We don't want to stop doing this. We want to start from scratch, and use what we know, our inspiration for what the future can be, and build a new technology, a new company," and so that was Blue Sky Studios.

Tony: That's awesome! From such humble beginnings . . . How about animation in general? What do you like most about working in animation?

Chris: What I like most about it is that it's a technique where you can communicate the most complete version of a fantasy from your brain to another person. I just love that you can divorce yourself from the world of physics, the world of what things are supposed to look like and the way things are supposed to move, and just go to places you can't see any other way. I mean, that just philosophically is what I like about it. You can heighten physics. You can heighten the color. You can stylize characters to exaggerate personalities, and . . .

Tony: Kind of make a new reality.

Chris: Yeah. That's what I like about it.

Tony: When people ask you, "What is a director for animation?" what do you tell them that you do?

Chris: I tell them somebody has to tell everybody what to do! You know, somebody has to be the person everybody can go to.

Tony: So, you see yourself as a creative supervisor then?

Chris: Well, yeah. I mean, it's my idea that they're doing. We make our films with three or four hundred people around us, and the films are so complex, there's so much work to do. It's a waste of my time to sit down and storyboard, or to sit down and animate, because all those disciplines are so time-consuming that I can't do that anymore, so that what I end up doing is talking the film to life. I talk, and talk, and talk, and talk, and talk, and I make little sketches every once in a while, and every once in a while I can pound out a page of screenplay, but, for the most part, I'm talking with other writers, or I'm talking with storyboard

artists, or I'm talking with character designers, or I'm talking with editors, or animators and, you know, just coaxing the film to life by describing it to people.

Tony: I've never heard that translation of what you do on a day-to-day basis as a director. I like that. What is the best and worst part of your job as a director?

Chris: Well, you know, I can't really, I mean, it's all going to be relative, because, well, the worst part of my job would seem silly to someone that has a real job.

Tony: Like somebody that tars roofs for a living . . .

Chris: Yeah, I mean, it's all relative but for me, the best part of directing is when you achieve something that is beyond what you imagined, and the worst part is when something doesn't quite get to where you wanted it to be. That's all it is. It's creative.

Tony: What is the most important tool in your director's toolbox?

Chris: I think it's gotta be my command over the English language at this point.

Tony: Communication, right?

Chris: It's just communication. And there's a lot that comes with it. You have to tune into a vibe that keeps everyone inspired, but, also keeps everyone calm. Keeping your imagination as fluid as you possibly can, having your ears open, and being willing to listen to anybody that's making any sense at all, and being willing to use new ideas. I mean, that's one of the first things I learned; just don't *ever* assume that somebody's an idiot, because of what you heard about them, or what their job is. You just always assume that the best idea can come out of anyone's mouth, even if it's a studio executive. You know, just try not to apply any judgment at all . . .

Tony: What do you start with in developing the story for one of your projects?

Chris: Well, everybody's different. I think that's where my habits could use some improvement. I always start with an idea for a place, or a world that I think will look cool in animation. I know a lot of people start with a story or a book, which is much, much, much, much smarter, but I just start with, you know, it mostly starts with images and moments in my brain, and that's all well and good, but at the end of the day, movies are about characters in stories. That's all the audience cares about really. They get used to the way the thing looks. The get used to the world. They want a ride, and so, a lot of my development process involves reverse engineering, you know, getting to the most important part last, which is character. "So, here's a world, what could happen in that world? . . . It could be this; it could be that; it could be a story about this; it could be a story about that. Who would be the characters? It would be somebody like this, and then, it could be somebody like that, and then . . ." You know, that's the hardest work in the whole process, finding the characters and then, designing the movie beat by beat, every step of the story.

Tony: Well, the next question is about characters. How do you develop engaging characters?

Chris: It's incredibly difficult work for me. You have to create characters that the audience can relate to very, very closely, and you have to put them in an interesting situation that keeps the audience engaged, and every character should be doing what you would do if you were them. Even if you were the bad guy, and you just did something awful, and you didn't want anybody to know about it, everybody knows how that would feel. You have to make sure everything's believable, and then, the most fun is developing the comedic aspects

of characters. That is absolutely the hardest stuff to do, finding the funny things that always comes from character. That always comes from somebody misinterpreting a situation, or the audience, being surprised by some character's perspective, or an ironic turn of events.

Tony: Along those lines, how do you work with a script writer to develop your vision for the project? Or do you? Do you work with script writers?

Chris: Yeah, we do. I work with a lot of writers. And it's usually, finding the person that you feel is gonna share your perspective on the tone, and can write characters the way you want them. Everybody's different, so, you know, every project is different, and sometimes every writer is different.

Tony: Is that trial and error for you to find the right writer?

Chris: Well, we have worked with a lot of writers over the years, and you go back to the same ones for some things, and some writing relationships are incredibly productive, and some are less productive. But, I think one important aspect of being a director is that you come to understand very quickly that although you may have done every job in the building, you haven't done it in a while, and in the meantime people have gotten a lot better at doing it than you ever were. So, with writers, you know, you talk out what the scene is, or what the outline is. You talk it, and talk it, and talk it, and it's a conversation between you and them. Then they go off and work and get into their own zone where they can pull the thing together, organize it, and write the voices, and then they bring it back, you read it, and . . . you know, hopefully it surprises you, and you take those fresh ideas, and you start building on them.

Tony: How important is the animatic to you in your process?

Chris: The animatic's important – we need it. It's like the scaffolding. Obviously, we try to tell as much of the story as we can visually, the way, you know, the story artists get to visually explore the script, really get to explore things. And it's also, for me anyway, it's the place where the ideas stick. It's the bones of the movie laid out on the table, and then everybody else gets to, kind of, move around and add what they add.

Tony: How about with animation? How do you go about "issuing," or "launching," a scene to an animator?

Chris: We call it, "kicking off."

Tony: "Kicking off." OK, every studio has a different term for it.

Chris: We usually go a sequence at a time; there's probably 30 or more sequences in a movie. We kick it off with a group of animators and, you know, the reels have been done for a while, and we've broken all of the assets out; we've broken all the shots and cameras out; we've been through our layout process. Since we're all 3D, we have a CG layout version of the reels, matched to the animatic, so that, the animators inherit cameras and character setup and roughly the right poses. All the information they need. Lately we've been trying to work it so, if you have 10 or 20 animators

'ROBOTS' © 2005.

doing a sequence that has 40 or 50 shots in it, each animator takes a contiguous set of shots so that they have the hook-ups between the shots in front of them. Then we do as complete a job as we can to pitch the sequence and all the intricacies of it. I'm a believer in letting everybody know as much as I possibly can, so, we screen the movie frequently for the crew, so that they know what they're working on, so, hopefully they all know the movie fairly well, and when you, when we kick it off . . . By the time the animators get a sequence, I've already worked with a group of animators to develop the characters, you know; we've already had a group of leads that have been studying the characters, and . . .

Tony: Doing acting tests and stuff?

Chris: . . . running tests and coming up with the physics, or the physicality, or gestures. Of course, we've already recorded the voice actor, and we have the dialogue ready so many times we have video reference from the sessions, if they want to look at it, depending on how specific or unusual the characters are, or the world. Sometimes we'll have reference of animals, specific animal motion that they can refer to also. This is the moment when you're pouring the concrete and you've only got so much time before it sets. An animation sequence will be in production for us, for sometimes as little as a week, sometimes as long as three weeks, but usually, in a couple of weeks you've got to make sure the animation is good and all the hookups are right, because then we have to move on to the next thing. We push a movie through our animation department — and we've only got one animation department — roughly about nine months to a year.

Tony: That's a fairly aggressive schedule.

Chris: Yeah, but I mean, we've also got pretty good at planning scenes out, so that the first draft the animators take is a blocking pass. We just put poses in and after a couple of days we've got the sequence, kind of, running and then we go and refine, and by the time the animators go into spline we pretty much have the shot. For my mind, at that point, it's up to the animator to finish it. It's mostly a matter of finesse.

Tony: What do you look for in a creative team – an art director, an editor, a storyboard artist, an animator?

Chris: You have to look for people that are incredibly talented, and have a tremendous command over their discipline. So, for the art director you want somebody who can draw and paint their butts off, and, editors who can work really fast, and, you know, share your sensibilities about the camera and cutting. Sometimes we use a head of story, sometimes we don't. I like to have a layer of lieutenants that are all just masters at what they do, and we meet together as often as we can on that level, and just talk about what we're going for. Our approach is to get to the end of every road as quickly as we can, as roughly as we can, so that we know what we're in for from each shot. Even if it's not the final camera, the final animation, or the final lights, but it's generally what we're going for that way everybody can see it as fast as they can.

Tony: Those lieutenants that you were talking about, your creative department heads — how much responsibility do you give them on one of your films?

Chris: I give them as much as I possibly can, I mean the trick is to delegate to people that can do their jobs better than you can. I also don't think it's interesting for them if they're just executing somebody else's orders, so, each one of these positions is another collaboration where you count on people to bring as much of themselves to it as they can, because then they feel accountable, and responsible, and they're gonna drive themselves to make it as good as they know how to.

Tony: How do you combat the, "Us against Them" kind of attitude that can arise on a production between management and crew?

Chris: I know that some of those rivalries exist (at other studios), but we all work in the same building, we live with each other, and we go from one project to the next together. We all know each other pretty well, so it's a pretty solid operation here. We have almost five hundred people at Blue Sky, but it doesn't feel like a factory. It's not as big as some of the other studios, and we try to promote as much as we can from within, so, maybe you were a unit animator on this movie then you may get an opportunity to be a supervisor on the next one. But you are right, there are two disciplines here, the creative/technical aspect, and then the management, or production aspect, but, I think if you put people that everyone respects in those important roles, than nobody will complain. If somebody has a rational perspective you can't argue. What, I mean is, if it makes your life hard, I mean, that's, you know, we're not doing this 'cause it's easy to do, we're doin' it because we love it, and if your life gets hard and you understand why, then you'll do the best you can. One thing I learned a long time ago, and it's not always easy to apply, is the only solution to conflicts is communication. I mean, no matter what the issue is, if everybody understands everybody else's perspective then it's a lot easier.

Tony: These pictures take so long, is it hard to keep true to that original spark of an idea? Do you find it difficult to be true to your original vision as the project goes on?

Chris: Yes and no. For me, when I start the film, I don't understand exactly what it's gonna be, because there's so many details, they're so

complicated, that part of it is you just have to let it become what it's gonna become. At the beginning of developing it, you enforce a lot of your own ideas on it, and you insist that it be this or that, but after a while you realize that there's a lot more to it than you thought. I mean, everybody feeds off of what came before them, so, you've got no clay to start with, and then you've got a little clay, and then a writer comes up with an idea, and then a designer draws a character, and then a writer sees the character and says, "Oh, it can be this," and then a story artist takes a moment and does a little trick with it, visually, and then shows that to a writer or a designer, and they say, "Oh, it could do that, it could be this," and it opens up. All the way through there's so much feedback that you can come up with big story ideas late in the process that wouldn't have occurred to you if you hadn't been cultivating the ideas for so long.

Tony: At Disney we called that process "plussing." It was a big thing that was handed down from the Nine Old Men that every department had a responsibility to make the work better in some way as it came across their desk, you know?

Chris: Yeah, but it also goes back to the people that came before you, so they can react to what you contributed and make their part better. It's a real back and forth too. So, when you ask, "Is it hard to hold on to your original vision?" It's good to let go. I come up with the initial idea, and I blurt out everything I can think of about it to the crew, and then they take it somewhere else. It's so much cooler, because here's a specific idea that opened up a whole other, better idea.

Tony: How about budgets and schedules? We all know that budgets and schedules are a big part of life for the filmmaker. How do you look at them, friend or foe?

'ICE AGE' © 2002.

Chris: Friend. Absolutely. Because when you've got a budget and schedule it means your film is in production, so, shut up! Shut up and stop complaining, I mean it . . . really . . . getting a movie greenlight is, like, getting struck by lightning on your head – twice in the same day! It's nearly impossible. So, when you've got a budget and a schedule, you've just gotta live with it, and, if anything it gives you limits that creative people need. They'll just sit there and dream, and twiddle their thumbs forever. You'll never finish anything if it's just up to you. The budget is like your parents keeping their hand on the back of your bicycle the first time you're riding a two-wheeler, you know, you just need the guidance. You need it. That's not the best metaphor, but, you do need boundaries.

Tony: It helps to have some kind of boundaries.

Yeah. I've found that too. Creatives work better with some kind of . . .

Chris: Gimme me a deadline. Somebody, please, schedule my day, you know. If you just leave it up to me I'll just waste my whole day.

Tony: Yeah. I don't know about you, but when I was at Disney, meetings were scheduled constantly. At Blue Sky do you find that meetings help make the film or do they distract from the creative process?

Chris: Well, I'm very fortunate because I've got a great production team around me, and my day is scheduled pretty rigorously. I think there's a great art in production management. You know, you put some deadlines together, like, a screening; we're gonna have a screening in two weeks, and we need to have this, this, this, and this done. So, if I can be put in front of someone with a nugget of a problem that we can solve together in a half an hour then that's a luxury for me. Just to have somebody tell me, "Solve this one now. Solve this one now. Solve this one now." I find that the schedules are another thing, like the budget, that's such a great crutch. It's very useful.

Tony: Do you have to interact with a producer, or studio executives on a continual basis, and, if so, what is that relationship like for you?

Chris: Well, I'm gonna assume that studio executives are gonna read this book maybe.

Tony: You can assume that.

Chris: I'm gonna be careful. Now look, here's where the rubber meets the road, because, you know, the studio's putting up the money, and they're gonna market it. Our movies cost a lot of money, and they put gigantic marketing pushes on these, and they're marketed internationally, and they count on a lot of people to come see them. So, not every idea that I've ever had is a broad audience movie. Some of my ideas are pretty weird. Some of the things I get excited about

wanting to see aren't necessarily things that are gonna appeal to a broad audience, and that means they're *not* gonna appeal to the studio executives. Movie studios are interesting places, because they are the places that dreams come true, sure, but they are absolutely, first thing's first, a business.

Tony: Yeah. It's called show-business.

Chris: That is the absolute bottom line. You know, film studios aren't run by directors and art directors. They're run by lawyers and businessmen, and, you know, that's just the reality . . .

Tony: That kind of says it all, doesn't it?

Chris: Yeah, I mean, that's just the reality. So, you find yourself constantly in that clutch between art and commerce. That's where we sit, and so, you're doing the best you can to persuade people to make it as cool as you can, but keep, you know, there's always some concession you have to make to the kind of movie house tropes that audiences expect.

Tony: Do you find that over the years you've gotten better, in how to communicate with studio executives?

Chris: Yeah. I think so. Look, I'll tell you a quick story . . . when we made *Ice Age* it was my first feature film, and I'd been looking forward to making a feature film all my life. I was pushing 40 years old. Blue Sky had been around for about 15 years and I had won an Academy Award from a film, a short film of my own design (Bunny), and I really didn't feel I needed anybody to tell me what to do at all, and, so, I was probably a bit of a handful for the studio. While we were making it I was pretty argumentative. I was sure I knew what I was doing. We had some difficult things to figure out, but we got 'em done, and I really didn't feel I was compromising much, and, so, we got to our first audience preview screening of the film, where you show the movie to a test audience, and you gauge their reaction. I went into this thing, and we had about, you know, 60–65 percent of the animation done; a lot of it was storyboard still, but, I went into it thinking, "I don't need this. I know what the movie is. I know how it works." As soon as the movie hit the screen, I could feel the audience engaging with it. I had this sensation that the movie was coming off of the screen and hovering over the audience, and I had a sensation that the audience was, kind of, reaching up into the space above them and interacting with it that way. I felt this palpable interaction with the audience, and, from that moment forward, I was willing to get down on my hands and knees and do whatever it took to keep them engaged and keep them entertained. If something wasn't funny enough I wanted to cut it or improve it. If a scene was running too long, I wanted to cut it. All of my high ideals . . .

what I considered to be my artistic prerogative, was thrown out the window.

Tony: From that moment, you became an entertainer.

Chris: Yeah, I guess. Yeah, yeah, yeah . . .

Tony: Right? I mean, an entertainer is all about their audience, and making their audience happy.

Chris: Yeah, yeah, no, it's exactly, it's like that moment in *Sullivan's Travels*, like, "What am I doin' trying to make art here?" I should just try to, you know . . .

Tony: Amuse people.

Chris: . . . try and entertain people.

Tony: Yeah. Entertain people, right? Nuthin' wrong with that in my opinion.

Chris: No. So, I guess over the years you just start, I mean, my inclination is to do things that are weird and dark, but, over the years you just, you start thinking, "Well, this character isn't working. Nobody's gonna like this guy. I gotta, I've got to

from *Epic*. © 2013 Twentieth Century Fox.

find a perspective on him that makes the audience engage." You just keep going back in and trying to make it more relatable for people, just finding ways to help them understand the character quickly, so, they can, kind of, put him in a box and enjoy who he is.

Tony: How important is it to you to keep up with current technology on an ongoing basis?

Chris: You know, I haven't sat down and animated in front of what we use for, like, ten years, at least. I just, I don't have to. I think if I were there, there'd be a natural progression of watching things evolve, and understanding what their capabilities are, but, as far as technology goes, my experience with it has been that when I started with computer animation you could do almost nothing but move spheres and boxes around on a screen, and to do that you needed a piece of graph paper, line commands, that you typed in words and numbers, and a super computer. You know, these days, they can pull off just about anything you can imagine, so, I don't know which pressure is more intimidating: trying to push your ideas through arcane tools or having people waiting for you to challenge them with a new idea.

Tony: Any last words for young artists that want to direct one day?

Chris: Yeah, for people that want to direct, they should make sure that they are great at what they do. A lot of people go to learn how to animate, or learn a 3D package, or put a demo reel together so they can get a job, but, you're just gonna get a job as an animator if you do that. Directors are people that have made their own films. The people that are gonna direct movies are the people that know a lot about movies, and watch a lot of movies, and know how to communicate cinematically, know how to tell stories, and just study every aspect of the craft from every perspective.

Tony: Does that include watching movies for you, I mean are you . . .

Chris: Oh, absolutely.

Tony: . . . are you an avid film buff yourself?

Chris: I love watching movies. I'm not kidding. I love to just sit and watch movies. It's one of my favorite things to do. There's nothing like sitting and watching a really interesting story, and feeling you're in capable hands with the director, and feeling as though the perspective is focused, and the filmmaker's giving you exactly what he wants. Yeah, for aspiring directors it's important to analyze them. You know, you're thinking about the stories; you're not thinking about just the technique. You gotta push that stuff out of the way to a degree, and just focus on how the film affects the people that are watching it.

Tony: That's good advice Chris. Good luck on your new film *Epic*.

YOU'RE ONLY AS GOOD AS YOUR LAST GIG

Keeping the Momentum Going

So, you finished your first directing job. Good for you! The hard truth is you will be forgotten before you know it. In the world of entertainment, you're only as good as your last project. It seems a little extreme and maybe it is, but in general the opportunities will come more readily if your last project was a financial and/or critical success than if it were a project that only your mom and her reading group enjoyed. If you had any success (and if you have read this book and done any of what I suggested, you should have) then the only issue is how to do it again. It seems simple enough doesn't it? Your first directing opportunity was difficult to obtain and a struggle to finish but now you have proven yourself to others and there is the new stigma of "yeah, but can he/she do it again?" You were under the radar before but now you are doing it with all eyes on you. The pressure rises exponentially the second time around. Ask yourself, how many directors have you witnessed that came out with inventive, risky and original films their first time out but then seem to hit the wall of mediocrity after that? And yet, consistency of excellence is the goal that we all should have for ourselves because that is the way to make a career.

Just like you hear actors talk in the media about taking their time to "pick the right role" a director must do the same. **Choosing your next project is more important than picking your first project.** Will the material stretch you into new areas that will showcase your skills more fully? Is the

> **My advice to young film-makers is this: don't follow trends, start them!**
>
> – Frank Capra

material marketable (will people want to see it)? Can you bring something to the material (through your vision for it) that is unique and will be notable? Is there some added bonus that the project has that will help make it more desirable (i.e. bigger-effects budget, big name actors, a writer, art director, or producer you always wanted to work with)? Notice out of all the questions you should ask yourself , there are none about making more money. The desire to make more money is the wrong motivation in looking for your next project. Those who have made that the priority have regretted it in the bigger scheme of their directing careers. Look for the elements that will make the project a success and the money will come.

Always Have a Fresh Idea in Your Back Pocket

OK, not literally in your back pocket but be prepared unless an executive, agent, or producer asks if you have any original ideas yourself. You should be able to pull out several ideas on a moment's notice that you have put some real time and thought into. The first project you directed might have been given to you as something developed in-house but the second opportunity may be yours to invent. The best way to continue directing (especially features) is to gain the reputation of being a creative artist that has

Even the director's phone doodles may spark the next big idea.

their own ideas. Sometimes your ideas are just concepts. Maybe you have a picture in your mind of a fairy tale world of fairies that fight a war against trolls. Maybe just one very cool action scene that you know would be spectacular. Maybe you have a unique location in your head that has never been seen before in animation. That's where stories begin. Think of something that people have never seen before, something that you would want to see in a movie and go from there.

When we were working on the film *Mulan* at Disney I remember our head of story, Chris Sanders, practicing little bizarre voices in the hallway and making doodles of a twisted little alien monster. He was playing with the ideas that would ultimately become his first directing gig, Disney's *Lilo and Stitch*. The point being – think ahead. Start to stockpile the embryonic ideas and scribblings that may become your future projects. It's best to start early when there is no pressure on you just having fun thinking of the "what ifs" that start all great stories.

Put your ideas into rotation by pitching them at studios and friends. And don't be discouraged. In the studio system, rejections come many times because executives just aren't in a position to pursue your idea at that moment. They may have something similar in development or too many "action concepts" and they really want comedy at the moment. But times they do change. Many great films were pitched continually to all the studios before an executive took a chance on them. George Lucas pitched *Star Wars* to every studio in Hollywood before one brave executive took a chance on the "science fiction cowboy movie." Sylvester Stallone pitched *Rocky* to tons of people all of which said a "boxing movie" would never sell. But as it became the highest grossing picture of that year and the winner of the Academy Award for best picture those naysayers were proven wrong. No one knows the right timing for an idea so keep them all in heavy rotation.

Don't be afraid of criticism. Getting people's comments on your idea is the best way to improve it. Sometimes a fresh eye is exactly what can make a lackluster idea into a great one. Take the logline of an idea (a short one- or

two-line paragraph of what the story is about) and pitch it around for feedback. Tell the barista at your local coffee shop. Pitch it to your babysitter. Even tell your friends and family! Ask them if it sounds like a story they would want to see and if not what would make it more interesting to them. You will be surprised at what the "layman" on the street will give you in feedback. Remember these people are your audience ultimately! If you are feeling intimidated to pitch your idea because, "it's too detailed to get it into a short pitch without a lot of set-up," that is a sign of an idea that is over-structured and even unclear to you its author. You need to streamline it. If you are finding it hard to pitch your idea because you're afraid you might "get it wrong" then maybe you are not confident in the idea yourself. The criticisms of the person on the street can be just as important to shaping your idea as a studio executive who has his own agendas.

Be Current

Whether you create animation with computer, pencil, clay or aluminum foil, it is important to your future to stay current in the newest technology. Every year the animation industry sees new technology advances, some proprietary and some "off the shelf", that become game-changers over night. It can be a struggle to be in the loop of the latest tech because it is constantly changing and improving but it is important to do it. As a director, it's not important that you can pick up the latest hardware or software yourself and make magic happen but you should be adept in your *understanding* of it. Know how it works and what it adds to your production. What can it do for the "look" of your project? What can it do to help things move faster? How can this software help to save time for my creative team, which will

Stuart Little 2 © 2002 Columbia Pictures Industries, Inc. All Rights Reserved. Courtesy of Columbia Pictures.

give them **more** time to reach my quality goals? By knowing the software, it also helps you to understand what it means to give a change order to a team member. When I first started as the Animation Supervisor on Sony's *Stuart Little 2*, I knew a lot about traditional animation but not so much about CG animation or the softwares used. I took a quick crash course in Autodesk's 3D software Maya and some of the rigging programs just to get an understanding of the basics. That helped me to understand what was involved for my animators when I gave them a note on a scene. I had a responsibility to the production to stay on schedule so I needed to know if a change I gave was a total redo for the animator or a quick tweak. That sort of information is crucial in making the right choices for the production.

There are many sources that can be tapped into for getting up-to-date information on the world of digital and computer generated animation. Probably the most popular is entertainment trade shows that showcase the latest in entertainment technologies. A few of the more popular are:

Siggraph – The largest international gathering for the techno-geek interested in research, technology and applications in computer graphics, animation and interactive techniques. This is the place to be to learn from the top CG animation studios and software companies in the world of computer animation and visual effects.

E3 (Electronic Entertainment Expo) – The world's premier trade show for console and computer-based gaming of all kinds. The future of interactive entertainment is here under one roof.

NAB Show (National Association of Broadcasters) – A multi-media trade show for mostly broadcasting. Besides being an international portal for buying and selling television content, they also showcase the latest technologies in broadcasting and digital production on the showroom floor.

CTN-Animation Expo – One of the newest and best of the trade shows because it is artist-driven and primarily about just one thing: animation. Software companies, hardware demos, as well as a plethora of interesting panels and workshops about the art of animation.

I have enjoyed attending many of these trade shows in the past but, for me, there is not enough time in my day to spend roaming the floors and showcases. So, I have learned to rely on the younger generation that seems to be on the cutting edge of the new technologies to give me consistent updates on the newest software and hardware. As a director, it's a good idea to make friends with a CG supervisor or technical director. They will be the guys in the know of the latest technologies and production software. There are also a ton of great websites that review the latest and greatest in technology.

Just as it's important for a director to take a step back to see the big picture of his or her story that they are telling, it's good to do the same in the industry as a whole. Take a step back from time to time and try to see the big picture of what paths new technology may be driving animation. New digital software may give way to new and unique styles of animation. New mobile media platforms are on the rise like never before. That means programming and storytelling possibilities we have never yet considered. Old movie and TV formats are becoming less of a standard and just two in a rising number of aspect ratios that your animation needs to fit into. Being proactive in understanding new technology and its possible uses will open the door for new possibilities in your career. Examine what is entertaining the audience as a whole and begin to move in those directions. How many of us "old dogs" now wish we would have moved towards the computer when those 3D animated films began to crop up? Try to be ahead of the curve not behind it.

The Product You are Selling is *You!*

My hat is off to artists who market themselves well. It is not one of my strong suits to go out and speak about myself or throw my banner in the air for all to see, but it is so very important in today's very competitive animation marketplace. These days it is not enough to do good work and hope that the right people will see it. Animation is not regulated to a handful of studios in Burbank, California like

If you don't have an agent (or even if you do), a website or blog is a great calling card for the director.

when I started in the business. No, animation is a world-wide game played by many players big and small. Your ability to market yourself well is the difference between a career of consistent longevity and sporadic employment. Fortunately, we also live in a time when it is fairly inexpensive and easy to make a big impact for yourself.

Marketing yourself is just another way of "advertising your portfolio." Getting the word out about who you are and what you can do so that the decision makers of our industry are thinking of you as often as possible. There is no better way to do that these days then the Internet. My brother, Tom Bancroft is a good example of someone that has utilized the Internet to present himself to the world. My brother is not a director but a character designer who has published two books on the subject (his last, *Character Mentor* published by Focal Press) and he depends on employers knowing his work for consistent freelance jobs. The books were just the first phase of marketing himself as an authority in the world of character design. From there he has started a blog, two websites (one for his book and the other his portfolio of work), a deviantART page and we share a popular Facebook fan page called "The Bancroft Brothers." When Tom completes a new job he has three to four places to post his samples online to let people see what he has been working on recently. The results have been explosive! Besides the fan base of young artists that look up to Tom he has garnered many art commissions and professional full-time jobs based on his self-created web presence. Tom does have to spend much of his own time in updating all of these websites, blogs and fan pages but it is time well spent that reaps great results. Outside the wonders of the Internet how else could an artist like Tom get job offers from countries around the world for pennies on the dollar? **Anyone that doesn't have at least a website that houses your portfolio of digital art and directing animation reels is crazy!** It is the cheapest and easiest way for a prospective employer to see your work. Check out www.deviantart.com for some great examples of demo reels. You can check out my humble work too if you search "Tony Bancroft website." It is simple yet effective to start the ball rolling on a discussion about who I am and points to the potential of what I can do.

My brother Tom Bancroft and I have a Facebook fan page called The Bancroft Brothers that has helped us connect with fans and create interest in our work and appearances.

Besides their own website, many young directors utilize the popular website YouTube (www.youtube.com) to create their own page of animation reels. It is easy to access all over the world but is not as secure if you are presenting things that have not released yet or are your own proprietary property. If you wish to have your reels on a more secure site than I suggest Vimeo (www.vimeo.com) which is a video hosting site that gives you the ability to make your page **password protected**. There are many more such sites popping up almost daily and most likely by the time you read this book there will be a plethora of more options for posting your work.

Also, don't underestimate the power of IMDb. For those that don't know, the Internet Movie Database (www.imdb.com) is the hugely popular website that has become the source for information on the entertainment industry. It literally lists every film and television show (at least in the US) with the entire credit list of cast and crew. It also creates individual pages for everyone in the entertainment business based on those credit lists. If you have a legitimate credit on a film, video or television show then there is a good chance you have your own IMDb page. Want to find out what films **Chris Wedge** directed compared to which he executive produced and the years they were released? Want to know which Ralph Bakshi animated film was the first on-screen starring role for Brad Pitt? How about what year did *The Lion King* first release compared to the second and third releases? It's all there. Producers, studio executives, agents and film financiers seek out IMDb as a first step **before** ever contacting you or your agent. It is crucial to make sure you are well represented on IMDb and that your page is accurate and up to date. **If your IMDb page doesn't look interesting then you don't either.**

Lastly, for a director it is good to consider getting an agent or entertainment attorney. These are professionals in the industry that have the top-level studio connections and can recommend you for future directing positions. That can be a big help in your career and take some of the pressure off you. The difference between an agent and an entertainment attorney can be somewhat subtle. The agent usually takes more money (usually 10 percent of everything you make) and may have more sway with the studios which can be helpful to you. But he does not negotiate contracts so you will still have to employ an entertainment attorney to review the final contract. The entertainment attorney is a specialized attorney that can help find jobs for you too (but may not have the kind of clout as the agent) and they will do all of the final contracts all at a cheaper rate (more like 5 percent). In my past, I have only used an entertainment attorney since I have a real problem with anyone taking money out of my hand for what is usually a one-time bit of work for them. At Disney, I had an attorney that represented all of the directors in the animation canon at the time. He was very expensive at **10 percent of everything** I made during the term of the five-year contract he negotiated. It was a very costly price to swallow but, in my mind, I justified it because I truly felt he negotiated a much higher salary rate then I would have on my own. He had that kind of control over the Disney executives! Since the negotiation only took him about two to three weeks of his time, it was really hard for me to write that 10 percent check to him week after week for **five years**! Since that time, I have been admittedly gun-shy about using an agent or attorney to find work. It is something you will have to weigh yourself to decide what is best for your finances and your career.

Make New Friends . . . But Keep the Old

The Beatles sang, "you get by with a little help from your friends" and as it is in life, in Hollywood it is even more true. In live action filmmaking they say success is based more on "who you know" than "what you can do." I like to think it's a combination of the two that lead to success in animation. It's important to create for yourself a reputation of doing consistently excellent work but having the right friends in the right places will only help. I have heard people talk about the "CalArts connection." That is, the students who went through California Institute of the Arts get each other jobs and always work together. Being an alumnus of CalArts myself, I would be lying if I said that I didn't see some truth in that rumor. But the full truth is that in the early days of our industry there was only one good school

It's good for the director to have more than one "friend pool."

that taught Disney quality animation and that was CalArts. So as the students went into jobs at Disney or created Pixar they looked back at the school that taught them for future employees. The industry sprouted from there to the point that most of the top directors, art directors and animators are CalArts alumni. As true as it is that in Hollywood your friends get you jobs the same is true in animation. Work on expanding your friend pool. Force yourself to get out of your small pool and swim in different circles from time to time. Go to festivals, academy screenings, conventions and talk to people. Let them know what you do and have done.

It occurred to me what a small industry we are in when, recently I was recommended for a job by no less than three friends that I didn't even know knew each other. And it was a job in China that was so far from what I thought my connections reached! Those positive relationships are so crucial for current and future work. The opposite is true too. In this small industry of animation, you never want to burn bridges. I once hired a guy with an impressive résumé and had worked at some of the best studios in the industry but never for more than a year. I discovered why after he came on to work with me full-time. He was a very talented artist but his attitude was negative and he loved to argue and fight with everyone. He became a cancer in the office and was fired before his six-month anniversary. The worst of it was that I discovered he had this reputation at every studio he had worked at. Every studio he worked at was the first and last time he was hired there. Because of his caustic personality he was making enemies instead of friends to the point that his pool of opportunities were shallowing. Eventually, this artist burned enough bridges that he was forced to leave the animation industry all together.

The old adage that says, "if you rub my back, I'll rub yours" is played out daily in the world of animation. Not that people are going around giving out free back rubs all the time. No, not literally! But if you want other artists to let you know when new jobs and opportunities come up then do the same for them. I have a good friend that lives this out continuously in his career. Through Facebook and email, he contacts artist friends to let them know of freelance jobs or full-time studio positions that he hears about. While some may keep the opportunities they hear about secret for their own selfish motivations, this guy sends out word like a beacon in the sky. Even if they are jobs he is applying for himself and he is creating his own competition! That friend has never **not** had work a day in his life because he has garnered such goodwill from helping others find work that they, in turn, have supported him in his times of need. Create a reputation for yourself of being a person that people want to work with not just because of your extreme talent, but because you are a trustworthy, giving and fun person to be around.

Continually Push Yourself for Excellence

It's easy to rest on your reputation. Your past successes can make you lazy or comfortable and that's all the competition needs to overcome you. Continue to grow and learn. As you age in this industry you might not be the "fresh young talent" that employers seem to always crave but you can be the "passionate and experienced talent" that always finds work.

Take a step back and assess what skills you are lacking and make plans to learn them. It is great to take a hard look at yourself throughout your career and ask yourself, "am I still valuable to employers?" If the answer gives you pause then look at what will make you more attractive to a studio, producer, or investors.

A great person has a good person behind him/her telling them where they could improve. Have a friend that will be an accountability partner to you. This could be your spouse, an assistant you trust or a friend from school who has been there from the beginning. Whoever it is, go to that person for advice about projects you should work on, what skills they think you are lacking, for their impression on your ideas, or to review your script. Friends like this are the truest kind of help in your career. I have several people like this in my life who are invaluable but none more so than my brother Tom. We both want the same thing in our careers even though we have gone about it in different ways. We just want to grow as artists and make cool things come to life. So we push each other. Like iron sharpens iron, we are there for each other. Sometimes it's as small as asking his advice on a drawing I am doing and sometimes it's something big like advice on a job transition.

Live Long and Prosper

My final advice is simple but may seem to contradict everything that has come before it:

Don't Work too Hard

It's so simple and yet so important that I saved it for last. I worked with a boss that expected me to work late every night and come in on my weekends even when we were not in production. To her long hours were the sign of true dedication to the all important company. Her pressure made all of the employees feel trapped at work and ultimately, want to quit. Your career – this life – is short. Enjoy the projects and people you work with. Take time off to be with your family. Don't miss out on your kid's plays and sporting events. That's the important stuff. Find balance between your time spent on the job and with your family. You may not become the next Cameron, Lucas or Spielberg taking this advice but you will be content.

At the end of the day, isn't contentment in life the truest form of success?

Strive to achieve the proper work-life balance.

interview: tim miller

The CEO and Co-Founder of Blur Studios, Tim Miller and his band of artists have been making innovative and groundbreaking strides in the animation world for over 16 years. A graduate of Virginia Commonwealth University, Tim began his career as a compositor and 3D artist until he got a job as a character animator at Sony Imageworks. After establishing his reputation as a multi-talented and versatile production artist and animator and ever the animation renegade who despises having a boss, Tim and his friend David Stinnet started Blur Studios together in 1995. It was in 2004 that Blur was nominated for its first Academy Award for *Gopher Broke*, a short film that Tim worked on as writer and creative director. Since then, Tim and his team at Blur have built a reputation doing short films, VFX work, credit sequences and cinematics for video games that put them in constant demand for client work in a variety of different animation platforms. Besides his job as Blur's creative director, where he often directs four or five different projects at a time and stays involved in every step of the pipeline, Tim is also currently developing a variety of feature projects to direct and produce through his company. I grabbed some time between client meetings with Tim at his Venice, CA studio.

Tony: Tim, how long have you had your own studio? What sorts of projects do you specialize in here at Blur?

Tim: Blur's been around for 16 years now, and we do a little of everything. The studio mandate was originally to take projects that were creatively interesting to us, rather than just making our decisions based on what was profitable, or had money, and I wanted the flexibility to at times choose a project that maybe didn't make any money, but I found creative interesting, and I knew that unless an artist was in charge of a company they would never make decisions like that, and so, I felt like I had to own the company so I could, for lack of a better explanation, make bad decisions financially, for the sake of the creativity.

Tony: So, it's really a creative-run studio?

Tim: It's a creative-run studio, yeah. I mean, at some point you have to make choices based on financial choices as well. I think the first mistake that anybody makes when they say, "I'm going to start my own company," is they think "Oh. Now I'm gonna get a chance to do whatever I want," but after you have one or two employees you realize that it's not about what you want, it's about what's good for everybody, and you have responsibility to people once you bring them on board to keep them safe and happy. Then in a larger studio, where you have people that have come to work for you, maybe from across the world, you really owe them something to not f*** it up, and abandon them somehow. And to answer the original question, Blur does a little bit of everything. We're known for our game cinematics that we do; the high-res, pre-rendered stuff that sort of tell the backstory of the games, or are involved in the marketing. But we do a little of everything else too. We did some shots on *Avatar*. We're doing a season of commercials for Goldfish. We do our own short films. Really anything that looks interesting. If I feel I can go and ask some of the artists, "Hey, would you like to work on this?" and they say, "Yes," then I'm willing to do it as a studio. There's a lot of projects we take that I may have no interest in, but I know one of the guys here may be interested in it.

Tony: In your studio, do you try to keep on your staff as much as possible, or do you tend to reduce and enlarge staff based on the projects?

Tim: No. We made a decision early-on to be an all-staff model. I don't want to expand and contract to take on certain projects: If it's too big we turn it down unless we have a chance to grow. We've done stuff before, like for Disney we did *Mickey's Twice Upon a Christmas*, and we took it knowing that we'd have to grow a little bit, but there was enough time that we felt like we could hire in a sane and artistically-driven manner, not just, you know, get a bunch of warm bodies in here, and hope it turns out well. We've had a couple of growth spurts like that, but, for the most part we find people that we like and then keep 'em here forever. We still have the first employee we hired. He's been here 15 years. Our executive producer's been here 13 years. Our senior concept guy's been here 12 years. And most of our supervisors have been here eight, or nine years at least. The one area where we have a little trouble keeping people, I think, is animation, because animators, by nature, are a faithless lot, and

maybe more itinerant than your average artistic workforce.

Tony: They're project nomads.

Tim: Exactly. It's weird. The lighters stay around forever. The riggers stay around forever. Animators, they get bored easily. I don't know what it is.

Tony: How'd you get into the animation industry? What was your start?

Tim: Almost 16 years. I think it'll be 16 years in March, yeah. I was a character animator at Imageworks before this, but Sony Imageworks was like 70 people back then, and before that I was a compositor, and I studied 2D animation, and illustration in school. I always liked drawing. I did it, like most animators, from when I was little. I always liked comic books. I loved animated films, and I thought, "Man, what could be better than to combine a love of storytelling with drawing and films?" and that kind of says animation, so I went into that. And early on I was very artsy, deep, you know, kind of existential s***, but then I got into the lighter stuff too and I decided to become an illustrator, which basically meant waiting a lot of tables, and working a lot of odd jobs, but I was doing OK, sort of, and I got an offer, back in 1990, something like that, to go and work at a company that made medical films, like, "Hey, you have a venereal disease. Sit down and watch this film while the doctor goes and takes care of another patient." I showed them my illustration portfolio and they said, "Do you think you can learn this computer thing?" This was back when they had a little 256-color paint system that could play back, I don't know, maybe 30 images in a row at like 12 frames-a-second, and I said, "Yeah, I can do that!" But as soon as I started working on it, as primitive as it was, I just said, "Holy s***! This is what I was waiting for." I mean, it combined my love of sci-fi, and all things futuristic, with art and everything else. I had this moment, when I was still doing freelance illustration, and I was doing this drawing. I got to this particular part in my process with oil pastels, where if I f***ed it up I'd have to start over, and, while sitting at my drawing desk I unconsciously reached over to hit the "save" button just like I did at work, and that's when I knew. I'm like, "This is crazy man. I can't save this s*** if I f*** it up?" So I said "I'm done with this, I'm all computers from here on out." And as the technology gets better and better . . . You can do anything. I mean, you can do anything you can imagine, and you can do it on your desktop computer at home. You used to hear all these excuses from people like, "Oh, you know, I could do better, but I don't have access to the equipment." S***, man, not anymore; no excuse anymore. But back then it was an excuse, but, if I showed any of my artists my original reels – Holy s***!

Tony: What do you like most about what you do?

Tim: Every part of a project has its moments, and all of them are good for different reasons. At the beginning when the job comes in, or a task, or a project, it's about the potential. You see this, and you go, "Holy s***. I can make that cool," and then when you're working on it, you get the story down, and you go, "Oh man. I can see this story in my head. It's gonna be great," and then you do the mocap [motion capture], or you're keyframing it, and you see these moments start to appear where, it's maybe a little different than you thought, and it makes it fresh all over again, and it's new, and then when the lighting starts to come together. That one's a big one, when you see the first pass of lighting, and you go, "Ooh. This is gonna look good." Every one of those phases has its pleasures, and every time you think it's just gonna keep looking better. I have to say, though, there's some level of disappointment at the end

where, A) It's finished, and B) You look at things, and you just go, "Man I wish that was just a little better. If I could've had two more shots, I could've done that."

Tony: Yeah, people from the outside, they don't see the pain. They don't see the arguments. They don't see all those things.

Tim: But they do see it when it's wrong and if it's really wrong, and early-on I kind of made that decision about the studio was that . . . I can't follow my work around, or the studio's work around, and make disclaimers. I can't say "Oh. The client f***ed us," or "That wasn't my fault," or whatever, so you've just got to fight every battle like it's the last one, and only give in when you have no choice. That's kind of the way I feel. And I don't think that I'm worthy of having a big reputation, but I do have a reputation in this business, and with people we work for, for being kind of a dick just for that reason.

Tony: But you produce quality work.

Tim: Yeah and I think that's why they put up with it. The problem is that people think that they're qualified to sit at the table and give you their ideas just because they write the checks, but that is not the case. Ultimately they can make the decisions, but all creative ideas are not equal. My basic opinion with a lot of these people is "You didn't go to art school for five years and I did, so shut the f*** up!" Sometimes in agency work, especially with commercials where you get a creative director who could have come up on the copywriter side of things . . . Look, I have immense respect for the written word, but if you're not a visual person as well, don't be giving me notes on the visuals.

Tony: What were some of the steps that you took to move up to directing animation for commercials, or shorts, or in general, directing a team?

From *A Gentleman's Duel*. © Blur Studio.

Tim: I would say that I always wanted to tell stories, but I never really thought, "Oh, I want to be a director," A) because that's incredibly cliché and B) because I was so in love with the process of doing it, that I didn't think I'd be interested in the process of directing. And then as you get more experience and as you move up, if you improve, if you're good at what you do, gradually more and more responsibility kind of accumulates to you, and then all of a sudden you're directing. For me, I always felt guilty about taking the title, because I feel like it's such a collaborative effort, and the industry, whether it's commercials, games, but especially movies, it

invests so much power in that director position that it seems to be an unfair accumulation in my mind. It's an important position, but there are so many people that contribute in so many ways to the ultimate project that I really wish you could spread it out.

Tony: Right. In animation, you and I both know that there's so many different artists that collaborate to make that project unique and special, and so many different voices that you need . . . A film can only be as good as the crew that's working on it.

Tim: That's true, and I'd have to say that if I felt like there was one skill that's paramount as a director, or a company owner, or a creative director, it would be **knowing** talent when you see it, and acquiring it, because you want to put it to work for your vision somehow.

Tony: That's a good point. I think that's one of the primary skill sets that I've heard multiple directors talk about: a director needs to know how to cast, and to know how to cast well you need to really understand and see what their skill sets are, how to use them, and how to push them.

Tim: Yup. And how to stay out of their way. It's funny because I'll go up and I'll give notes to the concept guys who, you know, on my best day I couldn't draw half as well as they can . . . But here I am giving them notes and telling them what to do, and I think balancing what I don't know, and just saying, "Hey, look. You know better than me, so here's what I need. Sort it out," is sometimes the way to go. They know it inside and out much better than I do, so I go big picture. That's the director's specialty . . .

Tony: How do you answer the common question, "What does a director in animation do? How do you direct cartoon characters?"

Tim: Well, if it's motion capture you're directing actors, and if it's keyframe you're directing actors, they just happen to be animators, and so I think you're the one that's deciding the performance. You may get a little bit of input from an animator, or you may get input from an actor. The nice thing about mocap is that it's a little more interactive in that you can try some different things really quickly versus having to be very sure of your decisions right off the bat and tell someone "OK spend two days blocking that out." That's a more weighty responsibility than telling an actor "Walk across the room this way. OK, that doesn't look good. Walk across the room that way," so it's a big difference. But the biggest single job, I think, is managing the whole process. You have to be the general leading the army. Obviously you can't fight the enemy by yourself, but you have to be able to talk intelligently with the producers about the budget and resources. You have to be able to talk intelligently with the writer, or, in many cases, talk to yourself about the writing, and the story, and then you have to be able to talk intelligently about the animation, and the lighting, and the music, and the sound design, and every aspect. I think some directors are focused in a few areas over here, and some directors are focused in a few areas over there, but all directors have to be reasonably good at everything, or at least so objective about their lack of skills in an area that they can leave that to someone else to fill. Being objective is another skill that a director needs to possess. I think it's important also to be open to ideas other than your own, and that's kind of a hard one, especially when you get really busy, because you just wanna say, "Just do what I f***ing said, why are you showing me this thing that I didn't ask for?" But sometimes that thing that you didn't ask for is cool. Often times these guys that are doing the production have more time to think about it than you do and they can try different things. I really value the person that says, "You know, I did what you told me to, but I had another idea; can I show you this?" Conversely, there are guys that don't show you your idea, the ones that say "You know, I tried your thing, but it didn't look good, so here's mine." I'm arrogant enough to believe that if you tried mine and it didn't look good then it probably wasn't the way I intended you to try, because I wouldn't tell you to do anything that looked bad. I may tell you something that's not the most optimal choice, but never bad. So show it to me, and I may agree with you that the other choice is better, but show me what I asked for first.

Tony: Are you "on the box," as they say, working on shots yourself these days, or are you more of a creative supervisor these days?

Tim: I stopped doing any animation, or anything else, because I come from the day of doing everything. In my projects, I modeled. I animated. I lit. I did everything. Then you go to a bigger studio, like at Sony, where I just animated, and when I would get ahead in my animation schedule I'd go to the producers and I'd go "Soooo, whaddya got?" and they'd go "Whaddya mean?" I'd say "Well, I'm ahead of schedule. What else can I do?" and they'd go, "Well model . . . the modelers are behind," and I'd go, "OK I'll take some modeling." "Really? You can model?" and I'm like, "Yeah. I can."

Tony: Yeah. They didn't expect that, I'm sure.

Tim: Yeah. It's really weird, They don't expect anybody to be ahead of schedule for that matter, you know? The pace at this movie studio, it just killed me. I was just bored s***less half the time. But just recently at Blur we were working on this project for Ron Howard, *Dark Tower*, and he was trying to get us to do more work and I said, "Dude. We are so f***in' tapped out. I did production work on this. I edited this thing here for the first time in a long time." I edit the reels, and I do a lot of editorial stuff: I was actually in there. I did some stuff in (3D Studio) Max to kind of work out some of the issues. I hadn't opened Max in probably six years . . . So to answer your question, I'll never be completely out of it. There's a quote from me from an earlier interview that one of the guys dug up the other day that said "If I ever have to stop animating, I will find another way to run the studio" back when we were like seven people or something. They had brought it up just to rub it in my face that I had "given up" animation.

Tony: "You're not an artist anymore!"

Tim: Yeah, they did it as like, "So, why'd you give it up man?" I'm like, "There's not enough time in the day," and again I think it comes back to the fact that you find that you have responsibilities to other people, and it's not what you want to do it's about what needs to be done for the greater good.

Tony: What are your day-to-day responsibilities when you're directing, let's say a commercial project?

Tim: I think it's a little different here than elsewhere because I'm such an in-house director. We have a few other directors but at any given time I'm usually directing at least three or four projects . . . and the other directors are rarely on more than one so I kind of rely on the supervisors to fill in for me a lot, whereas if I was just directing one project I would be focused on it. So, for instance, I don't go into animation dailies. The animation supervisor will sit me down and we'll talk about what needs to be done and then he'll go off and do it and then do a special review for me. I think that if you find animation supervisors that are in sync with you then you get a rhythm there that that works. For instance, we hired one guy and after a few reviews I'm like, "Dude, your default style is like 10 percent faster than what I like . . . You got a shot and you're trying to do three punches but you really only need to do two." My comments went from five phases of notes to three sentences. Upfront, I'm very involved with the storyboard process and our concept guys or the animatic. To me that's where I feel like I have the biggest impact, and if I don't get involved there I f*** it up because if you let the story process drag into the rest of production it wreaks havoc. So I really try and focus on that, but on any given day, it could be animation reviews to check progress. It could be a mocap session. It could be looking at renders, final renders on another sequence. I check every frame that goes out of this studio. "Pixel f***ing" is what the animators call it, but I feel like I have to because my name's on the door. But on any given day, our projects are so overlapping that it's kind of like I'm doing every stage of the process all the time . . . And sometimes, I'll say to one of the animators, "You know what? What if he raised his arm there?" and they'll go, "Dude. I showed you that last week, and you said, 'Take the arm down,'" and I just wanna go "You know what? You know how many shots I've looked at this week? I've looked at 400 shots this week, and I'm supposed to remember the note I gave you three weeks ago? F*** you. Just put the arm down!"

Tony: It's a lot to keep track of.

Tim: Yeah. I'm not infallible, so I just get used to saying, "Oh, I'm sorry. I'm an idiot."

Tony: What is the most difficult part of your job?

Tim: It's definitely the people management. I mean, it's something I enjoy, but giving criticism is always tough, whether it's deserved, or whether it's just part of the process. Sometimes you tell people to try something, and it just doesn't work, and you have to say, "Hey. I gave you bad direction. Change that," and that's uncomfortable. Sometimes it's "Hey. I gave you good direction, and you didn't do it, so change that." Sometimes it's "Hey. You suck," Then there's the worst moment of all, which is firing people. I used to do all the firing. Now I only do it every once in a while, but, far and away, that's the worst job anybody has in the studio. Well, you know what? I'll take that back. There's a guy that does it now. He was the first animator we hired and now he's in HR. But when he fires people at least he has the protection of saying "Look dude. I'm just the messenger." But when it's me, I not only ordered the ax man out there, but I'm holding the ax. This job is a blessing and a curse that sometimes you have this ability to make people feel great,

and sometimes you have the ability to make them feel terrible. But overall it's good because people, artists especially, want to improve and if your criticism is valid, and it helps the piece get better, then they're happier and better artists. But sometimes you just feel like you're just beating people up all day and those days can be tough.

Tony: What is the most important tool in your director's toolbox?

Tim: For me it's a sense of story. I can almost always come up with some bit of story from somewhere, whether it's a book, or a comic book, or a movie that supports any idea that I'm trying to sell, or convince people of. And I'd say that my second most important tool, the visual one, would be the Internet. It's just great to be able to say, "You know what? Let me give you an example of what I'm looking for" or, "Let me find a piece of reference for you that will help illustrate this idea that I have." Some directors I know, they love to sketch, and I was an illustrator so I used to do that too, but now, stuff's there, it's at your fingertips. Give me an hour, and I can give them all the reference they need to illustrate whatever concept I'm trying to do. And it's great because sometimes you say "Something looks wrong about the way the rain is bouncing off the shoulders in this shot. It just doesn't look natural," and I can go on the Web, and type in *rain bouncing off people* and video reference is there.

Tony: What do you start with in developing the story or gameplay for one of your projects?

Tim: Well, I think most of what we do, that's not a short film, comes from the building blocks that someone else has already laid down. Like if it's a game that has a backstory to some extent or another, so you're building off what somebody else has done. A lot of people pooh-pooh the stuff that's not original, and I love original stuff too, I've got tons of original ideas, but, man, there's so

From *A Gentleman's Duel*. © Blur Studio.

many books, and comic books, and ideas that other people have that I would love to be a part of. I'd love to help in some way and I have no problem whatsoever in taking other people's ideas and trying to add your own chapter to the story . . . Like for the cinematic that we did for this game DC Universe, they gave us this two-page backstory and there was this part written by comic book writer Geoff Johns: "The superheroes and the villains were so busy fighting amongst themselves that they didn't realize when Brainiac's invasion fleet arrived and began to take over the Earth" and I said "As a comic book fan, that's what I want to see. I'm a sucker for last stands. I wanna see that last battle where Lex defeats all of the heroes." And the client had

said, "We want something that's gonna really shock people," and so I said, "Nothing does that better than murder and seeing these icons destroyed: I wanna see that moment when Lex kills everybody," and so I pitched it to them in that form. And they said, "Yeah, we like it," so then I write up a script.

Tony: So, how soon do you get into animation? Are the boards locked by the client?

Tim: No. Like in DC's case they didn't even have a story. They just came to us and said "We like what you guys do . . ."

Tony: That's amazing that they give you such creative control.

Tim: Oh yeah. Our reputation in this industry means that almost everybody that comes in here says "Here's our idea, but we would really like you to give us some input . . ."

Tony: . . . and put that "Blur Spin" on it.

Tim: Yeah, "and work with us on it to make it better," which is kinda cool, sometimes to an *uncomfortable* degree. We had a Japanese client who just came in and said, "Well, you guys are great. We want you to do something for our game." And I'm like, "Well, I don't even know what your game is about. What is it?" and they go "You can change anything you want." They were really early in development and they wanted us to just come up with something so they could build a game around it. But then they had all these characters that were very visually distinct, and I would say, in my very linear Western mind, "So, why does this witch look like this, and that witch is forty-feet tall, and purple . . .," I'm not making this up, by the way, ". . . and this witch looks like a little girl," and they would go, "Well, there's no reason." I'm like, "Well, surely, there's a backstory, maybe they look that way because of how they were killed, or their powers, or . . ." And no. They had just designed them like that just because. So for me a situation like that is kinda difficult. I don't like being told "Well you can do anything" because I think "You're hiring me to do a job. It's not whatever I feel like doing, so give me some guidelines that I can work inside because 'Do anything' is too big a mandate."

Tony: So you've gotten into animation on a project before even though the storyboards are still in flux?

Tim: Oh yeah. Especially with commercials because they don't feel good unless they feel like they've exhausted every creative option that you could possibly put on the table. We did one for a client where the agency came in with these boards and I said "This is f***in' three minutes long. This is supposed to be a 60-second spot so you've just gotta knock some of this stuff out. Why waste time exploring this stuff that you know is gonna be cut?" and they'll reply "Well, let's just see how it goes . . ." but you look at it, and you go, "F***. That's not gonna work. I don't need to explore it. I know that won't work." So a situation like that is kinda tough, but most of the time we're handling everything from soup to nuts. I'd say about half the time they come in with a rough idea.

Tony: Like the Goldfish commercials. Something like that, I would think, is agency-driven.

Tim: Yeah, on something like that they do the scripts, and then we do the boards here.

Tony: Do your clients know that, when they come in here, that you're gonna wanna do the boards?

Tim: Not really. We have no sales whatsoever, so all of our customers are repeat customers or from word-of-mouth or they just heard about us somewhere and thought we were good. I'm pretty proud of that. And if we had a sales rep, that person would probably set expectations for how we work, or what to expect, but we don't have that, so when they call they're either talking to me, or they're talking to our executive producer, Al. It used to be me only, because I wanted to evaluate creatively before they went to the producers, but I just can't do it, so now Al does it.

Tony: That's amazing. I love that. How do you find a style for a project — say, one of the video game cinematics that come in?

Tim: Well, it varies, but with a lot of projects like that, usually the character design, and some of the world design has been established, to a degree, by the game client. But then there's a lot of other things that haven't been set in stone. For instance, the *Batman* thing that we just did, we decided that for the fight choreography we wanted to do really brutal, fast, *Bourne Identity*-style fighting, and that really wasn't how it was in the game. In the game it was limited by what the game could do, whereas we could kinda do anything, so we picked a style there.

Tony: What about the very realistic look that project had? Was that style choice from you guys?

Tim: Yeah, in that case the costume design of Batman was set by them and then we kind of interpret it. A lot of times we have to interpret stuff that maybe looks fine in the context of the game, but if we're going for more reality . . . We have to interpret some things. Some of the choices like color palette, or the tone, are our choice, but not so much the design, because that usually comes from the client, to a degree.

Tony: How important is the animatic to you when you're developing a project?

Tim: It's the roadmap for everything. Not the storyboard animatic; I find that moderately helpful. We do previs animatics and, lately, we've been shooting live action animatics. The animatic, to me, is really where you gotta make all your decisions there that you possibly can.

Tony: How do you "hand off" a scene to an animator?

Tim: Some people do it differently, but how we're doing it now is the animator comes in and the animation supervisor has already made his decisions on who's doing what, assignment-wise . . . And we bring 'em in one-by-one and tell them what I want out of the scene or the shot and tell them the character's personality . . . I f***ing hate it when guys don't do their part of the homework, like reading the script or looking at the reference. I think it's all there to be looked at before you sit down and I shouldn't be telling somebody how Batman acts, what his powers are . . . that's easy enough to find out on your own.

Tony: Right. He doesn't have heat vision.

Tim: Exactly. Sometimes you give them a pass, like on some of the more obscure ones, or if guys don't come from the US. you might say "OK, well, they don't have superheroes in France" but basically we bring them in one-by-one and say, "Here's what I want out of this scene – I want Batman to be powerful here, and strong, but not too fast."

Tony: Do you act it out a little bit?

Tim: Yeah. We have little handycams so the guys can go back and act it out, and if they want to change stuff – Like a guy came and said today "So, in the mocap he looks a little relaxed here. I'm gonna amp this up a little bit. Are you cool with that?" I'm like "Yeah, and if you wanna go shoot some reference and run it by me to show me exactly what you wanna do, that's probably a good idea, especially because this guy's a new supervisor." So, the animator will go back, and act it out and do it, but I have no problem with getting up, and acting stupid, and doing things in the middle of the studio.

Tony: Do you see the first pass by the animator, or do you leave that up to your supervisor?

Tim: No, I always see the first pass. In mocap what we call "first pass" is basically just slugging it in to the scenes, and getting it all in there. If something's not working, you'd best catch it right there if you can, because sometimes it looks OK on the mocap stage, but when you see it in the shot, it's a little different, and it's best to catch it right there. The director's gotta see every pass. Sometimes when it gets into second, and third passes it gets really chaotic because you're looking at a second pass from this guy, and a third pass from this guy, and this has facial, but this doesn't, and this has approved body animation because we needed to get shots to cloth, but the facial hasn't been in there yet so I can't make any comments on the body, because it's already gone to cloth, and I haven't seen the facial yet, and then you see the facial and you go, "F***. Well, it's not working. How bad is it and can I live with it, because if I can't then I gotta go redo the cloth too." When you get a stacked pipeline it's juggling all these parameters. To come back to that question earlier: What's the single hardest thing as a director? I wanna amend that, and say that it's letting something go that I know is not as good as it should be. And there's always that to a degree, but when you know something is really not right, and thankfully this hasn't happened more than maybe three or four times in Blur's 16 years, but when a client says, "You know, I really expected that shot to be better," or, "This facial animation doesn't look so good" . . . I dread that, and you just have to go "You know what? You're right. I'm sorry. I f***ed up, and I didn't fulfill my part of the bargain." That's really horrible.

Tony: Do you usually try and fix it at that point?

Tim: Yeah, I mean, all my producers understand when the client says, "This is not acceptable," – that means that it's gotta be fixed. But when *I* say, "This is not acceptable," then sometimes maybe there's room for debate. The guys sometimes get on me for being picky, but when I meet with clients, I show the work all the time, and so I know that I'm going to see that bad decision over and over again for the next two years when I show clients the work.

Tony: Is it difficult to keep a project fresh and fun in your mind when animation's such a long process?

Tim: No, but I can imagine that it might be if we were doing feature films. I think a lot of the animators, when they're doing what we do with shorter schedules, are desperately wishing for the day when we get our own feature, and they can

have these long schedules. But I guarantee six months in they're gonna be going, "F*** I wanna do a game cinematic again. Gimme a commercial, because this is killing me," and I might feel the same way . . .

Tony: Is it still your goal to do your own feature?

Tim: Oh, yeah. I'm very aggressively pursuing that. The difference is that we wanna do something that's very different, and edgy. More adult. But anything where the marketing guys don't go, "Oh, yeah. We marketed something just like that last summer and it was a huge success" is a problem. Everybody could love it in the room, and they love the creative aspect, but then they talk to the marketing guys, and the marketing guys go, "Mmmm. I don't know."

Tony: It's risky.

Tim: Yeah. Look, if I was a marketing guy I'd say, "Well, I'd much rather be trying to find a way to distinguish a unique thing in a marketplace where there's not a lot of uniqueness. That's an easier job for me than trying to sell the next Ashton Kutcher romantic comedy and distinguish it from the five others just like it. Boy meets girl. Girl doesn't like boy.

Tony: What do you look for when you're building your creative team? An art director, an editor, a storyboard artist, an animator . . .?

Tim: I look for someone, of course, who's talented and is great at their job, but you also look for people that are personable, because you could have all the talent in the world but if you're unpleasant to work with that's just not gonna fly. I spend more time with these people than my family, and I want to like them. I don't have to be friends with everyone, but you want to at least not dread their presence and so if I feel that way about them, chances are their team will feel that way about them, and I don't think that's gonna make for a happy team. I don't wanna work in a place where people don't enjoy coming to work every day. So talent and being personable are the two big things.

Tony: You've already talked about this a bit, but how much responsibility do you give to your creative department heads?

Tim: Yeah, I lean on those guys heavily, because I'm doing multiple projects. But it's all situational. For example, one of our directors came up from being an animator, and so he's obviously a little more involved in the animation side of it which gives a little less responsibility to the animation sups on his projects. One of our other directors was a lighting/compositing/modeling dude, and so he tends to be more involved there but he leans heavily on the animatic guy and the animation staff to do that end of the thing. I'm primarily story and animation, but I also did all that other stuff too, so I'm kind of in everybody's s***, but mostly up front in story stuff. I think that the simple answer is people get as much responsibility as they show they're capable of executing on. If a guy's really great, and they can do it, f***, I got plenty of other s*** to do, so I'm happy to let them do it.

Tony: Do you have direct contact with all of your staff when you're on a project that you're directing, or do you rely on department heads and supervisors to communicate to the crew below them?

Tim: Blur has an open environment, no cubicles, so I have direct contact with pretty much everybody in the studio. There are some guys that I literally talk to maybe two or three times a year, just because they're quiet, but I sit out on the floor with everybody else. People wander up to my desk all the time: "Oh, look. Tim doesn't appear to be doing anything important. I'm just gonna go tell him about my hopes and dreams and what I

wanna be when I grow up." That happens every day, but I have a lot of contact with them, and I think the other directors too. The real thing to be wary of is that you can't let your contact with the guys in the ranks supersede the supervisors. You can't let them come to you for feedback because it takes away from the sup's authority. I'm happy to answer questions any time to anybody, but if it's something that the supervisor should be answering first then I go, "You know, have you talked about this with your sup?"

Tony: You're the studio owner but also a director here. How do you combat the, "Us vs. Them," attitude that can arise on a production floor between creative management and a crew?

Tim: That doesn't really happen here. I mean, it used to be much worse. It was almost like I was beaten by producers as a child, because when we first started out my attitude with the producers was "Look. This is the budget and the schedule. You don't talk creative with the clients. If the clients want to give creative notes you get me, or another creative on the phone. You're not allowed to do this," I've loosened up a bit, but I think here it's always been the creatives driving the project. Producers have their own zone of power, but ultimately, if it's not looking good, the creatives are the ones that go, "We're gonna spend a few more days on that. I'm sorry we're out of budget, but it's not good. It's not right."

Tony: What are some of the things that you do for motivation purposes?

Tim: Well, you could do a lot of things, but I think the basic thing is really simple: If you're excited about a project, then it communicates itself to the crew, and they're excited about it. If you have an awareness of what people want to do and you choose people that are happy to be there, that want to be there, and then you kind of push things forward with your own enthusiasm, knowing that they're susceptible to it then it doesn't take much of a push. That's the biggest thing. Secondly, if it's truly an exciting project, you just need to communicate why, you know? "Holy s***! Did you see the monsters that we're gonna get to do? There's a giant snow crab in this thing! C'mon man. And it's gonna rip this thing apart. It's gonna be awesome!" Luckily, most of the jobs that we get are cool on some level. But sometimes you have to just say "Look. You're a professional, and you're getting paid, so shut up and do it." Or sometimes one of the guys wants to direct and so to motivate them to direct something that they're not thrilled about, you might say "Look. If you direct these commercials we're gonna use them to gear the crew up for this other stuff and we're gonna give you a little time afterwards to do development on your own stuff." I mean, on some level, it's manipulation, but I would say it's manipulation with the goal of making people happy, so then it really doesn't carry the negative overtones, you know? You're just trying to get them to do great work, and enjoy their job.

Tony: Now, we all know that budgets, and schedules are part of the life of the filmmaker. How do you look at them personally, friend, or foe?

Tim: Always a foe.

Tony: Always a foe?

Tim: Yeah. Always a foe. You never have enough budget to do what you really want to do, and if you did, you'd want to do something even more aggressive. I don't think there would ever be a story that couldn't benefit by having a little bit more money to tell it, so it's always a foe. Now, at the same time, I enjoy problem-solving so I look at the budget as sort of a puzzle to be solved. You know, here's the pieces in the box and I have to do something great. How do I do it? At some point, the budget could be so low that I just can't do it and it's just physically impossible to, as your client says, "Do something spectacular." "Well, your budget doesn't allow for spectacular." In that case, some people may go, "Oh, well, that's a cop out, because you could do something." Maybe they're right. I don't know. Maybe it's not impossible, but it's impossible with the time I have to devote to solving the problem . . .

Tony: And it's your experience that would tell you that it's impossible, because you've done enough of it to know what you can and can't do within certain budget restraints, and schedule requirements.

Tim: Yeah, and every once in a while somebody does do something that I would have thought was impossible, but he may have been sitting in his underwear in his room for three years to come up with that solution, and I don't have that time. So, budgets are always a foe, but never a hated foe; it's just one more s*** sandwich that you gotta eat on the way to doing something creative.

> budgets are always a foe, but never a hated foe; it's just one more s*** sandwich that you gotta eat in the way to doing something creative.

Tony: Do you have input into the budget, and schedule on a project?

Tim: Yeah, I used to be a lot involved in it, and now, not so much. Al will come over to me and say, "Look. The tightest I can get this is seven-fifty. The client's got seven. What do you wanna do?" and I'll go "OK Let's do it for seven," or, "You know what? I'm not crazy about that project, so f*** 'em." That's kind of my level of involvement in that sort of thing, and sometimes I look at the numbers, but creatively, especially if I'm going to direct the project, I say "OK, I got seven. What, what can we cut?" and then I'll go in and rewrite the script, or I'll say, "You know what? We can really get by with one creature here, instead of three," and I'll try and bring it back into that budget. I do think that I have a good sense of what's critical to a story, and what's superfluous, especially as it relates to budget. Like, "Look. I can't tell that story without this shot, or that moment, but I may be able to tell it without this shot over here, or that shot," and then I know whether or not it's important to the client.

Tony: Here at Blur, do meetings help you make the project, or do they distract from the creative process? What's your opinion?

Tim: I've never been a big fan of meetings, but they are necessary, to keeping people on track. I think one of the things you learn early on when you start a company is that there's how you like to work, and then there's how other people like to work, and they're not always the same thing. Part of your job as a manager is to suss out the different ways that people like to be managed. You might find that this guy wants a lot of hand holding and this guy wants to be left alone but if that guy needs hand holding to help him produce the best work, then it's my job to hold his hand. If this guy wants to be left alone, I'm happy to leave him alone. I think over time you tend to accumulate people who are like-minded. We don't have a lot of people that want to be hand-held here. Maybe you do it at first, but you hope that

From *A Gentleman's Duel.* © Blur Studio.

eventually they walk on their own or else you get 'em the f*** out. So I think meetings can help everybody stay on track in that regard. I think there's a lot of people that think meetings solve all problems. But I'm not one of them . . . Nothing can replace the artist who goes after the answers that he needs to solve his problems. Initiative. That is the basis for me, for everything. When I worked in other studios, if I don't have the answers then I'm going to go find somebody who does, and if they don't have the answers then I'm going to go talk to their boss. I think if everybody did that, to a degree, instead of just sitting back and waiting to be told what to do . . . So many times I would go over to an animator's desk and say "You know what? I really want that dragon's wings to flap a little faster," and the animator might go "Mmmmm, I can't . . ." I'm like, "What's the big f***in' deal man? Just flap the wings faster." And then I see him try to animate it and the rig is just so slow if he tries to move something he has to wait 15 seconds for the computer to refresh. So I'm like, "Holy s***. This rig is terrible. What's goin' on with this?" and the animator says "Yeah. The rig is really slow. That's why I've been slow with my changes." "Well, did you talk to anybody? Did you go over to the riggers, and go, 'What the f***?' Did you get in anybody's face?" and he's "Nah, you know, I don't wanna, you know . . ." and I'm like, "F***!," and by that time a week of time has passed, where he was sitting there suffering in silence.

Tony: And you hate that, right?

Tim: Oh. Man. I get up, I go over to the riggers and I go, "What the f*** is with this, man? You can't animate with this rig!" "Oh, let me take a look at that. Oh, here's the problem." If I was that guy I would be up in somebody's face going "This is not right. This is not what I need to do my job," and the guy that sits back and takes it, the patient,

nice guy, they're not the best production artists. I want the guys that solve problems. I want the people that go out and say "This could be better and I'm gonna make it so." Even now, when I dip my head back in production in my own studio, I find these little things that just make me wanna go, "What are you thinking? What do you mean you didn't capture facial reference video for this? How could you not?" It drives me berserk, because for every one of those I find I know there's 20 more that I'm not seeing.

Tony: Do you have interaction with producers, studio executives, or clients on a continual basis? Obviously you do with clients.

Tim: Yeah, nonstop.

Tony: Studio executives too when you work on bigger studio projects?

Tim: Yeah, and pitching films too.

Tony: What are those relationships like for you?

Tim: I think generally the people that we work with are working with us, because they respect us and our product. It's a whole different proposition when you're selling to someone who wants to buy the car that you're selling already. It's really a different conversation than if you're trying to convince somebody that you don't suck and so, for us, it's almost always pleasant. Every once in a while it's not, so we don't work with those people again.

Tony: From a director's standpoint, what is your definition of a perfect producer to have working by your side?

Tim: It's that person who's gonna support your vision that you've established, because a lot of times what you really want to say is, "That character needs some more time." You don't wanna have to go and talk about budget. I know we're done with our schedule. I know we're over budget on that, but the producer recognizes the fact that it really does need some more time, and they don't bother saying, "Well, we're over schedule." They just go, and find the time somewhere. They make it happen. That's what I really like in a producer.

Tony: How important is it for you to keep current on technology, like new software?

Tim: Oh, very important. I think it has a huge impact on the creative, and budget, and what you can do, so I'm always reading the tech magazines. I used to read 'em because I was a geek, and that's how me and my partner Dave became friends. He came into the department where I was and every night we were on the BBSs and the blogs. Back then there was no Internet, and finding plug-ins for the software and reading about the latest stuff coming out . . . I was obsessed with it, and so we'd go in every day and go, "Oh man, I downloaded this plug-in that does a ripple effect," and we would trade this stuff, and we became friends because of that. I love that stuff. Even if I'm not doing it anymore I can look at a tool and go, "Oh, you know what? Here's how that would fit in our pipeline," or, "Here's how that would work." But when I was a production artist it was like how I imagine a mechanic feels about adding a new set of wrenches to his box. I still get very excited about it, and you have to.

Tony: Where do you see the industry going in the future?

Tim: Well, I think, for us working on things like cinematics, I think it's gonna be over every year, because the real-time stuff keeps looking better and better. But in fact, we keep getting busier and busier. But what I think is that eventually computers are gonna get so fast and the tools are gonna get so powerful that it's all real-time. There is no rendering. You'll still have to create

things, of course, but the tools for that will keep getting better. It'll be less about knowing how to handle a particular renderer than it is about what makes good lighting. I think eventually the tech is gonna continue to fade into the background and then we'll be left with more of a purely creative element to storytelling. That's kind of where I see it going in the future. I don't see story ever going away. I see different kinds of stories able to be told, too. I've sat on this panel for gaming, and these guys are going "Well, we need to push gaming more toward storytelling and compelling characters" and I'm like "Yeah, maybe, but there's something great about just being able to run around and blow people up. I don't wanna know if I'm killing that guy because he killed my sister. I just wanna kill him!" It can be all of these things. I think that creating a compelling virtual environment that I can just roam around and find things, with no story to it at all would be compelling too. So I don't think that story will ever go away, but there'll be all these other things that you can do creatively as well. If you're just visual you'll be able to find a way to express that, and I think the tools that get in the way of the art is what's gonna go away.

Tony: Any last words for the young artists that want to direct someday?

Tim: I would say learn to do other things first. You're not gonna be a great director until you understand the plight of the other artist who you're called upon to direct. So you may not be able to learn every job of every artist that you may direct in your directing career, but you should know some of them, and know enough to understand what it is you ask of people. Empathy. Develop empathy.

INDEX